Insight Out

Insight Out

One Blind Woman's View of Her Life

Mary Hiland

Independently published

Editing, print layout, e-book conversion, and cover design
by DLD Books Editing and Self-Publishing Services

DLD Books

www.dldbooks.com

ISBN: 9781674098234

Dedication

Dedicated to the memory of all the strong women in my life
and to all those who carry their legacies forward

Table of Contents

Siblings, 1947: Dick Oliver, Mary Wilson, and Patty Wilson

Foreword

Tipping the aspirin into my hand, I accidentally let one fall into the sink. I tried to retrieve it, but it had already slipped down the drain.

Oh well, I thought. *I have this huge bottle. There are plenty more.*

But when that bottle is nearly empty, I won't be so casual about the loss of a pill here or there.

It's the same with anything we value. If we know we have plenty more where that came from, who cares if we lose some? Take money, for instance. It's easy to be generous when your wallet is full. It's tempting to spend freely when you have plenty of money.

But what about opportunities that have slipped down the drain, like making someone smile, doing someone a favor, showing affection, forgiving a transgression, asking for forgiveness, or sharing a story about your childhood with your grandchildren?

Indeed, what about our days in this life? Each time I let one slip down the drain, wasting it, I can't be sure there are plenty more. It's good to think of that when I make decisions about what to do or not do with each day as it comes and goes.

Now that all the people in my family who were older than I are gone, I find myself wishing I'd had the forethought to ask more questions about their lives before I came along. The world did not begin with me. I missed a whole lot of it. Not that I needed to know everything about everyone, but even though I heard stories from time to time, I still wonder why and how and when and where some important pieces of the story of my family turned out the way they did.

My descendants may not be at all interested in my history, but just in case they are, I'm not letting my story slip down the drain.

* * * * *

When you look at your family tree and see that you're the last living leaf on the top branch of the current generation, you might have questions that can never be answered. Old letters and records might give you dates and names, but there is no one left to tell true stories about what happened behind those facts on a page.

It's possible that the people I've met on my journey through life and my descendants might be curious about me, so in this book I'll tell them what most people don't know about me. I'll answer the questions they might be uncomfortable asking. Maybe they don't even know what they want to ask. Some of my answers could be touching, humorous, surprising, affirming, or just plain something they never thought of before.

My life has been naturally divided into chapters, so rather than telling my story chronologically, each chapter in this book focuses on a specific phase that describes who I am and how I lived my life as a person with first limited and then no vision.

Only the children of a blind parent know what it's like to have a blind mother, and most people don't know what it's like to be a mother who is blind. Only the people who share my love of dance can identify with the fulfillment that dancing brings to me. Only guide dog handlers can feel the joy and dedication that come with such a unique partnership. Only the people who have skied with me understand how important cross–country skiing is to me. Only the people who have ridden a tandem bike with me know what happiness I feel when I ride. Only the women I hike with know the reasons why I love to hike. Only other blind people who have lived as long as I have can tell the stories of the misguided attitudes of the seeing public. They know what it's like being defeated by insensitivity and then overcoming obstacles that we face every day.

Each chapter in this book addresses one of these facets of my life, so that by the end of the book, you will know how I came to be the person I am.

With this book, I hope to inspire individuals who are newly blinded or losing their vision and to educate the people in their lives. But most of all, it's my legacy to my family and friends. And that includes you.

Introduction

It was a lazy summer afternoon. I was trying to stay awake while listening to a friend read the local weekly newspaper to me. The crime report, the elections of school board officers, the latest study on whether or not to continue having fireworks on the 4th of July—all were like a lullaby. Then we got to an editorial column written by a woman who has multiple sclerosis. She said her disability is not the definition of her life.

I sat up and exclaimed, "Wait! Read that again. It's a great quote that I want to remember and adopt as my own."

You may have heard some version of this quote, but I think this is a good place to put it in this book. Blindness "is only part of who I am, not the definition of my life." Wow! How true this is for me.

I should use it as part of my signature after my email messages. Blindness is only part of who I am, not the definition of my life. Now if only the rest of the world would forget the stereotypical image of blindness and view those of us who have a vision impairment as people first.

As you might guess, I'm really big on "people first" language. You will never hear me refer to a group of people who are blind as "the blind," just as I refuse to say "the elderly" or "the homeless." We are people who have personalities, regrets, knowledge, sorrows, happiness, jobs, families, problems, joys, disabilities, and a host of other attributes unique to each of us.

Some of what you read in this book may surprise you, especially if you have never met a person who is blind. Somehow, I seem to always be the first blind person most sighted people have ever met. Am I the first for you? Well, welcome to my world. In this book, I'll talk about many aspects of my life that have relevance to my blindness, but sometimes, what I have to share has nothing to do with being blind, which illustrates that blindness is not the definition of my life.

This book is also for a person who is experiencing vision loss or who is close to someone who is. You can read all sorts of books about accepting blindness and the stages we go through as we lose vision, but in this book, you'll peek inside the life of a person who has experienced the whole journey, from poor vision to total blindness. I'll share with you the struggles of recognizing my limitations and the joys of overcoming them and everything in between.

I'm 73 as I begin to write this book, but the story begins when I was in the second grade. Clearly I've had plenty of time to adjust to blindness and make my life as close as possible to what I want it to be.

When people first meet me, especially those who have never met a blind person before, and they learn about my accomplishments, which are only everyday activities that most people, at least in this country, enjoy without a thought, they are impressed beyond belief. The first comment they make is something like, "You are so amazing," or "awesome" or "inspirational." Later in this book, you'll learn why I think these reactions are embarrassing and unwarranted. If I had become totally blind overnight and then proceeded with life as I have, I might agree with those people, but as I said, my blindness sneaked up on me and gradually changed the path of my life. It didn't ruin my life, just altered it to make me work a little harder to live it the way I wanted to.

I've been told that my sight has been replaced with insight. I'm not sure that's true, but let's go with it and see if it fits the title of this book.

Chapter One
The A–Word

"You are so amazing" is a comment I have never been able to accept. First, because it's not the way I think of myself, and second, because I'm still trying to come up with a clever but polite response.

Do they really want me to strut around thinking I'm amazing? What a burden, to have to live up to such a lofty description! God is amazing; childbirth is amazing; the Grand Canyon is amazing. But me? I'm a person who has been blessed with the tenacity required to live a normal life despite a disability. If you want to see amazing, watch *America's Got Talent* and hear a dog singing. I mean, he actually makes sounds that match notes and rhythms of a song as his person accompanies him on the piano. Now, that I will say is amazing. It's because he does something that dogs are not normally capable of doing.

I'm a person who does not have sight, but there are thousands, if not millions, of us who are blind but can perform most tasks that sighted people do. We just have to work a little harder.

I happened to be born to parents who were no doubt

devastated with my diagnosis of RP, retinitis pigmentosa, a progressive eye disease, but who did not allow it to ruin my life or theirs. They were determined to protect me from harm but not to protect me from living life. I wouldn't say that even they were amazing, but I have the deepest respect for their love for me and for each other, their work ethic, and their belief that I could do anything I set out to do, even with very limited vision. At the time of my diagnosis, I was a senior in high school, and my career goal was to be a professional dancer, perhaps in ballet or on a Broadway stage. RP smashed that dream, but it was not going to be the end of the world for me or for my family.

I was not declared legally blind until I was 18, but for the 10 previous years, my parents searched for the answer to the question, "What's wrong with Mary's eyes?" We visited doctor after doctor, every specialist from optometrist to ophthalmologist, to psychologist to specialists in lazy eye, since glasses for near–sightedness were of no help. The real question was, "How can we fix Mary's eyes?"

Meanwhile, I continued to thrive in school, play with friends, excel in dance, participate in church functions, ride my bike, roller skate, ice skate, play hopscotch, and a hundred other activities that fully sighted children enjoy. I had chores to do around the house: make my bed, rake the leaves, wash the dishes, dust the furniture, fold the laundry, and even iron the flat pieces such as sheets and handkerchiefs. (Yes, my mother and I ironed sheets back in those days.)

In other words, I was an average kid of the 1950s and '60s. Thus, I wasn't treated like a kid with a disability. I didn't know I was a kid with a disability. I didn't know I was "amazing."

I am not amazing, but I understand why sighted people,

especially people who have lived with sight all their lives and are now as old as I am, can find it hard to believe that I'm able to do what I do. They picture themselves trying to ride a bike, dance, cross-country ski, memorize a speech, use a computer, sing in the choir, keep house, cook, and take care of children, all without sight. Indeed, if they were to lose their sight overnight, it would be truly traumatic, but what they forget is that I've been living with progressive blindness for over 60 years, so I've had a lot of practice. Over my lifetime, I've learned to deal with blindness, not just cope with it. There's a difference.

The stereotypical blind person *copes* with blindness by depending on others to do almost everything for her. The blind person who *deals* with blindness learns how to manage her life as independently as possible, and sometimes she has to get a bit creative in her solutions, which I call workarounds. She must also keep her ear to the ground for tips from her blind friends and colleagues who are more advanced in living productive and satisfying lives.

It doesn't happen overnight, so it's not amazing. This process takes time and requires her to get outside her comfort zone, over and over again. Instead of calling me amazing, you might want to say I'm determined, persistent, or—as my parents often said—stubborn.

Chapter Two
Shall We Dance?

As I reflect on the happiest times in my life, I remember performing as a dancer. Let's pretend we're flipping through a scrapbook, and I'll tell you about the photos in my mind that pop out and beg to be described.

As we open the scrapbook, we see me as a little girl, maybe six or seven. I'm flanked by two other little girls my age, all in shiny black tap shoes and matching schoolgirl skirts and blouses. The song was "School Days," an old song even in the early 1950s. The primary steps were "step, shuffle, ball change, step, brush, brush," done repeatedly through the song, with some simple turns and a very proud bow at the end.

The picture was taken on the back porch of my Aunt Lynn's house; she was my mother's sister. Mother and Aunt Lynn had both taught dancing in their youth, but Aunt Lynn continued even through my high school years, although by then I had progressed to studying seriously with Jack Louiso, one of the most prominent teachers in Cincinnati.

Aunt Lynn taught dancing in her basement in an old house in Trenton, Ohio. Whenever my parents and I went to visit, Aunt Lynn always took me down to the basement for another half-hour dance lesson. It was our special time together and the beginning of my life–long love of dance and of Aunt Lynn. I'll talk more about Aunt Lynn in another chapter when we reminisce together about the characters in my family.

As I advanced through high school, my retinitis pigmentosa also advanced, but it hadn't yet reached the level of impairment.

Here's a photo I treasure, because it was the dance that made me feel in love. As the high school choir sang "Out of My Dreams and Into Your Arms," from the musical *Oklahoma*, I stepped out in front and interpreted that beautiful waltz with a ballet routine that Jack Louiso had choreographed for me. I wore a simple, full–skirted, turquoise prom dress that was coincidentally ballet length. As I twirled with perfectly executed piqué turns and pirouettes and held arabesque poses at the end of a series of turns, my heart was filled with the imagined joy of being in love. In this pose, you can see how my chin is tipped up toward my uplifted right hand, matching the extended left leg in a romantic arabesque.

My mother, who was beaming in the audience, reported to me afterwards that the woman sitting behind her said to her husband, "That girl is simply beautiful."

I was not a beautiful girl, but I was petite and graceful. Because I was feeling through the dance that I actually was in love, I felt beautiful. It may have been the only time in my life, other than my wedding day, that I looked beautiful.

Next we come to a photo of one of my favorite performances that was also the most fun. Toward the end of my studies with Jack Louiso, I was given many opportunities to do solos, but my favorite of all was dancing with Jack and his assistant teacher, Bob Miller, in a routine that Jack had choreographed for the two guys and me. The song was "Shall We Dance" from *The King and I*. We sang as we danced, and then they each in turn whirled me around the stage in a rollicking polka–style step. At one point, they lifted me as I kicked first one leg high into the air and then the other. During the dress rehearsal, I kicked so enthusiastically that my ballet slipper flew off into the audience. It would have been funny if that had happened during the real show, but I doubt that Jack would have found the humor in that. This was the memory that I cling to because it was the closest I would ever come to performing a Broadway–type number.

One memory that is not in this scrapbook is one that I wish I could forget, but it illustrates how my eye condition sneaked up on everybody.

During one of Jack's recitals, I had a very complicated tap dance solo, which I performed flawlessly. After my bows, I scampered off to the left toward the side curtain. A narrow opening allowed us to slip through to the back stage. But I could not find that slit in the curtain. I searched all over the place, feeling for a fold that would turn out to be my escape, but could not find it. Then, to my horror, I realized that I was in front of the curtain on the apron of the stage, and everyone in the audience could see me fumbling around with the curtain. In the silence of the auditorium, I froze in terror. I desperately needed to get behind that curtain and out of sight, but I had no idea how to get there. Jack, ever the poised performer, calmly walked over to take my hand as if leading me toward the dance floor and guided me around that front curtain and through the opening. To say that I was mortified would be an understatement. I could only imagine, with devastating embarrassment, what the audience was thinking, and my solos in Jack's shows were surely over.

At the end of the show, after the last of the applause died down, as Jack took his final bows for another fine recital, he walked directly into the dressing room and straight over to me. He folded his arms around me and held me tenderly as I wept into his shoulder. It was then that the reality of blindness cut through to my soul.

Remember when I said I was stubborn? Somewhere along the timeline of my life, I heard this truism: "Those who can, do. Those who can't, teach."

I still had enough vision to study dance, but there would be no more solos in Jack's shows. I accepted that, but in no way was I ready to give up dancing. Other kids my age had summer jobs and part–time work as car hops or store clerks, and I desperately wanted a job, too. Starting in junior high, I began to teach young children beginning tap dance lessons. My students were the younger siblings of my friends, and it was good practice for me. In high school, however, I followed in my Aunt Lynn's footsteps by teaching several classes and private students in my basement. My dad made a ballet barre out of some piping, and he found a large mirror to make it look like a dance studio. He even tiled the floor in a pattern that I chose, so that I could easily see where each child should stand. Although details were escaping my failing vision, I could still see large shapes, so I could pass as a pretty good teacher of beginning students.

I had enough students that the next step was to produce a recital. I realized that I couldn't do it alone, so I recruited help from my high school classmates. In exchange for their help with taking tickets, handling props and stage curtains, and performing spoken lines that I had written to tie the dance numbers into a story, the proceeds would go to the junior class. Even the boys got into the spirit and loved performing hilarious dances and songs that they wrote and choreographed themselves. This plan was so successful that we repeated it for the senior class the next year, and everybody had a ball. Not only that, but I received a small scholarship from the local women's club because of my creativity and initiative. I believe the exact words of the judging committee were "good business sense." In other words, I knew when I couldn't do something alone, when it was time to ask for help, and how to do it so it would be to everyone's benefit.

Following high school graduation and my move to Ohio State University, a hundred miles away, I needed a way to keep dancing and to keep teaching. I tried performing one more time at a talent show, held on a tiny stage in the football stadium, but I definitely could not see the edge of the stage in the dark, so I kept my traveling steps to a minimum and was very conservative with my turns. I was in over my head, but I wasn't ready to quit.

Six required credit hours in physical education struck dread into my inexperienced freshman heart, and at first I panicked. Then I discovered that five of them could be filled with more fun than I could ever have imagined. Two quarters of folk dancing, two quarters of modern dance, and one quarter of ballroom dancing—with football players, no less—changed my whole outlook on physical education. But then I still had one quarter left to fulfill the requirement. I took bowling, since I at least understood what I was supposed to do. My dad had taught me how to bowl when I could still see. The trouble was that I didn't do it very well. Back in those days, the adaptation of railings for blind bowlers hadn't been thought of, so mostly, I rolled gutter balls. But I tried, and for that, I got a C.

During my first quarter at Ohio State, I found that I missed teaching dancing. Although I had never been around blind children, I thought it would be a good experience for me as well as for them. I'm surprised that I, with absolutely no such teaching experience, was allowed to teach blind children. All I had to do was call the School for the Blind and ask. Those were different times.

We started with a weekly half hour of ballet in the gym, with six girls of age 10 or so. Their posture needed a lot of improvement, and their lack of awareness of their bodies in relation to the space they occupied was shocking to me. Most of them had been blind since birth, so I quickly learned that using such terms as "diamond shaped," let alone "over your head" or "out to the side," meant nothing to them. I began with teaching them first and second positions and then first and second position pliés. Hoping to be helpful, I told them that their legs would form a shape like a diamond. I found that it made more sense for them to feel my legs in first position plié, and then they got it. I learned as much from them as they did from me.

Next we moved to the basement for the tap lessons, where they were used to roller skating. Again, I was shocked. They actually let blind kids roller skate in the basement, where there were pillars that they could, and probably did, smash into. But there was no smashing into pillars or walls as I had expected. They moved around the room more comfortably than I did. Teaching tap was easier for me, because I could hear exactly what each student was doing when I asked her to show me the step individually.

They all loved the dance classes and looked forward to them each week. I did, too, even though it meant walking several blocks to the bus stop, riding the bus north on High Street, walking down a seemingly endless driveway to the School for the Blind, and then repeating the process with the addition of crossing High Street to catch the bus going south to the Ohio State campus. I felt full of purpose, and it allowed me to get off campus for a few hours.

But my philanthropic endeavors were short-lived. I had met a submarine sailor named Mike Hiland over Christmas break, and although our romance was primarily long distance, somehow the dance lessons for the blind kids faded from importance and eventually stopped. I'm still ashamed of myself for not sticking with them. Even so, about 20 years later, I was attending a work-related conference and ran into one of my students, now all grown up, and she told me how grateful she was for those dance lessons and how much fun they were.

I married that submarine sailor, and after getting a son and a daughter started on their way to activities outside our home, I grew restless, with a vague sense of boredom. One Sunday afternoon, while my husband was watching his favorite football team lose another game, I put on a record that I had used for teaching and began to practice some old dance routines. Magically, the melancholy dissipated, and I knew what I had to do next.

Soon thereafter, I joined a volunteer singing group called The Singing Moms, and a few of us who had studied dance in our youth formed a smaller group that performed once or twice during each show. Although performing at nursing homes could be depressing when we'd see half our audience asleep in their chairs, sometimes it could also be funny. I'll never forget the time we heard water pouring onto the floor in the middle of one of our songs. It turned out to be a man with dementia relieving himself right then and there. We had to struggle to keep from giggling. I was thrilled to be asked to do solos in the spring concerts, and the afterglow parties at our house brought the most fun and laughter of that era of my life.

Back to the photo album of my dancing career. Here's a picture of me wearing rolled-up jeans, a plaid shirt, and straw hat, elbowing my way through the Singing Moms, who were all dressed up in formal gowns. The pinnacle of those dance solos was an energetic, even athletic, routine to "I Ain't Down Yet," from the musical *The Unsinkable Molly Brown*. The character I portrayed through my dancing was a fierce and feisty young woman who wasn't going to let adversity defeat her. It was becoming my theme for life.

It might have been my intention to never let blindness defeat me. But when I began to fear misjudging the location of the edge of the stage or that I might kick somebody's grandma in the chin when I was doing one of my famous high kicks at a nursing home performance, I knew I had to hang up the dancing shoes. I continued to sing with the group and also with the church choir, but without being able to dance with abandon and with my whole heart, the way I did with "I Ain't Down Yet," the light in my heart was dimmed.

Then one evening, many years later, after my divorce and after the kids were out on their own, my next-door neighbor, Jan, wanted to invite a couple of her girlfriends over to learn to line dance. Because my family room had more space than hers, I offered my house for the lesson. We were all having such a good time that someone said, "Hey, let's pair up and do some swing dancing." You've heard of a runner's high? Well, you might say we were on a dancer's high.

After everyone left, my spirit slumped with that old feeling of loss. I did a little soul–searching and came to the conclusion that what was missing from my life was dance. I had hung up the ballet shoes, the toe shoes, and the tap shoes, and it was all I could do to keep from bumping into the lady next to me with the Electric Slide, so what could I do about this longing that seemed to be an impossible dream? The solution, of course, was to dance with a partner, to glide across the floor in a graceful waltz, to acquire an attitude in a steamy tango, to test my wits as well as my footwork in an East Coast Swing, and to wear myself out in a whirling Viennese waltz. In other words, I should sign up for ballroom dance lessons.

My daughter, Kara, looked online and found a studio called Dance Plus Ballroom, and I made an appointment for the very next Saturday morning. My teacher would be Mark Miller, and I warned him that I was totally blind. I didn't want to surprise him. I wanted him to have a chance to think about how he was going to teach me. Everything had to be explained in words. Later he told me that he was taught that every good teacher should be able to describe every move in words, and he did. Not only that, but he also divulged that he had just started teaching there, and I was his very first student. But that revelation came much later, after he was sure he had gained my confidence.

I had studied ballroom dancing many times over my life, including with my husband, so when we first began, I asked him not to teach me the box step. "I could teach *you* the box step," I said foolishly. Then he proceeded to teach me the box step— the *proper* way to perform it, which I had never been taught before.

Over the months, and many hundreds of dollars later, I felt confident enough to enter an event that wasn't exactly a contest, but outside judges observed us dancing and made comments on something like report cards. I received some encouraging remarks, but the best one of all had nothing to do with my talent as a dancer. Or maybe it did. After the dancing was over, we lined up for a buffet supper, and Mark accompanied me, offering me his arm, as any good guide for a blind person would. One of the judges was overheard to say, seeing how Mark guided me, "Oh, she really is blind." Until that moment, in Mark's arms and with his skillful lead, I had looked like any other person in the room. Unfortunately, after I retired and had to cut out expenses such as dance lessons, I had to hang up the ballroom shoes once again.

Now, here are two real photos to illustrate my life's passion. The first is of me at 14, in a ballet costume. The second is of me dancing with Mark Miller. To quote a song from *My Fair Lady*, "I could have danced, danced, danced all night."

Mary in a ballet costume, age 14

Mary dancing with her teacher, Mark Miller
Courtesy of Circle E Photos

Chapter Three
Sitting on the Sidelines

Following my divorce in 1991, from time to time I would engage in a fruitless effort to find a boyfriend, or at least a companion, on one of the dating sites, such as Match or eharmony.

Wanting to appear active and energetic, I would list all my athletic endeavors, such as cross-country skiing, cycling, jogging, dancing, and even ice skating. What I accomplished was to scare off any potential date. These activities, paired with intellectual interests such as reading, writing, and classical music, might as well have been condensed into these few words: "This woman is way too energetic and complicated and therefore much too hard to match."

The men that I was trying to find completely missed my intention of just trying to prove that even though I might have a vision impairment, I could be fun to be with. I especially emphasized the activities to dispel the stereotype that all I could do was sit around and read braille books or listen to the radio.

Perhaps if I had chosen a more moderate way to describe myself and had stopped trying so hard, I might have been more successful—or certainly less scary. While I would never call myself an athlete, I did have a history of needing to be active. I could have developed an interest in sports, like the rest of the people my age, no matter what age I was, but even the word "sports" was abhorrent to me.

Gym Class

When I was in the second grade, I was introduced to the most detestable requirement for a kid in public school.

To start with, we had to buy the ugliest dark–blue gym shoes a prissy little girl could imagine putting on her dainty feet. Then we had to actually wear them once a week. When Mrs. Schlichter announced that it was time for gym class, we rushed to the cloakroom, changed into our gym shoes, and then walked single file down a dark, dreary, endless hall in the basement, past the furnace room, where that creepy guy took care of the maintenance of the building, and into the big room that smelled of dust and sweat. Next, we were to grab a ball from a closet and start running around the room, bouncing it or throwing it at each other.

The little boys had a blast, free at last to do what little boys were meant to do, but I was mortified. One time, I kinda, sorta forgot to put on my gym shoes, and to my horror, I was sent back to the second–grade room to get them and return to the gym with them on my feet. The walk by myself was terrifying, but I managed to waste enough time to miss most of the class.

Dodgeball

Gym class was an unpleasant challenge for me. It wasn't that I was uncoordinated or weak or unable to understand the games. It was that I was beginning to lose my sight. I couldn't see the ball when it was coming toward my face, so I often got smashed in the nose or smacked on the side of my head. The very mention of the game dodgeball made me cringe with anxiety. Still does. Kids on the other team loved throwing the ball at me because I never dodged; I just let it hit me because I didn't see it coming. After three years of this humiliation, the teacher finally realized that I was not being stupid. I was simply not seeing the ball.

A recent article in *The Columbus Dispatch* brought forth a painful childhood memory. It involved a gym class game called Gaga, "a dodgeball–like game played in a low–walled enclosure called a 'pit,' where the object of the game is to swat a ball out of the air and hit another player with it below the waist, eliminating that player. Ten children play at a time at Edison, but the game can accommodate dozens. It's fast, but action stays low to the ground," says the article.

Oh, yeah? That's not the way I remember it. I can still feel the sting of the ball as it slammed into my face, and I can still hear the laughter of the kid who had hurled it at me, knowing I wouldn't be able to dodge it.

The article continued: "However, a national group of physical education experts denounces the game as dangerous. Schools have reported to the National Association for Sport and Physical Education that children have suffered head injuries and been bullied while playing. 'We call it the bully pit,' said Sheila Jones, physical education supervisor in Loudoun County schools in Virginia, a district of more than 66,000 students. 'At one school,' she said, 'the game has led to eight head injuries in a year. It's very physical. Kids get hit, fall backwards; they get hit in the face.'"

No kidding! I could have told them that. It's not only physical; it's stupid. How such a mean and dangerous game survived all these years and then developed into an even uglier game, I'll never know. If Gaga continues to be popular, it will be one more way that a child with less than perfect vision is going to be excluded.

Child's Play

At home, however, I played Four Square with my friend, Lynn, who lived next door. Only it was actually Two Square, which was probably boring for her. But for me, it was a fun and challenging game, one where I could easily keep track of the ball.

I also have fond memories of playing Wiffle ball with some kids in the neighborhood in the back yard of a kind and understanding mom. We played every night after supper, which happened to be the time of day when I could see the best. The mom was the pitcher, and she always warned me when the ball was about to be pitched toward me, and she always put me in the outfield—not really that far away, but far enough so that by the time the Wiffle ball got there, it was pretty harmless. I loved this game. I felt like a normal kid, and when my bat actually made contact with the ball, it was the most satisfying feeling in the world. As I said, I would never call myself an athlete, but I did enjoy the physical activity of interacting with other kids and achieving a goal.

Lynn and I would sometimes walk to the miniature golf place and play a round together. My vision was starting to get really blurry, so she would help by standing near the obstacles and then the hole to give me a little auditory help. I could never see where the ball landed after I smacked it, but even as a little girl, she understood how to help me.

High School Sports

In high school, as my vision deteriorated, my participation in gym class was limited to the units on gymnastics and square dancing, which for some reason included calisthenics. The teacher had put together a routine of arm circles, stretches, and kicks to music to make it more fun. At last I could get up off the sidelines and take center stage.

Because this activity did not involve a ball of any size, and it simulated a dance routine, I excelled and was often asked to stand in the front row, so the rest of the class could follow me. But my fame as the star of the gym class was short–lived, as the subsequent units, basketball, baseball, and volleyball, sent me back to the sidelines again.

The Flyerettes

The closest I came to participating in a sport was to join the drill team, the Flyerettes, which performed at our high school football and basketball games. The name Flyerettes came from the name of the football team, The Aviators.

I had no interest in the games, but it was fun to strut around in our uniforms, which by today's standards were downright dowdy. Our team colors were green and gold, so we wore yellow corduroy skirts that hit about mid–thigh over yellow, long–sleeved leotards, with long–sleeved, green wool sweaters on top. When the night air was frigid, we wore yellow tights to keep from freezing to death. And of course our white tennis shoes were topped with green pompoms.

The purpose of the drill team was to enhance the halftime shows. As long as I was within touching distance of the girl standing next to me in a straight line extending across the field, I did fine. Much of each routine involved putting our hands on each other's shoulders and kicking in unison, trying to keep our toes pointed, kicking as high as we could and at the same height as the next girl's toes. Since I couldn't see the next girl's toes, they all had to keep even with mine.

I was completely oblivious to what was going on with the game until the band played the fight song. That meant we were to run over and line up in front of them and do our kick line routine. When the band director and the drill team director got a little creative in their routines and started having us weave alternately between the lines of band members, life as a visually impaired drill team member got a lot more complicated. I tried to step through the moving line of band members by listening, but that didn't always work if they happened to have a rest in their music at that point and were just marching to the drumbeats. Here again, I depended on the kindness of my teammates. When it was my turn to go between two kids, the girl behind me would say something like, "Go" or "Wait, now go," to avoid a collision. I had some poor vision at that time, but my night vision was worse.

By this time, it was clear to me that I would not be able to fulfill my dreams of being a professional dancer in ballet or on Broadway. I knew I was talented, and I had the drive and the energy, but retinitis pigmentosa stopped me in my tracks.

As I mentioned earlier, I was not diagnosed until I was 18. For the previous 10 years, I'd been trotted around from one professional to another, trying to find out why I couldn't see very well. When I was declared legally blind, it was almost a relief. At last, I could stop holding out hope that the next doctor would unlock the answer.

From the time I began to study dance seriously at age 14, I'd had plans to make a career of it. My counselor at the Bureau of Services for the Visually Impaired (BSVI) and my parents had the daunting challenge of gently but firmly convincing me that being a professional dancer was not practical for me and that I should go to college instead and get a degree in something that would prepare me for a career in something else.

College Sports

Because all dreams of a career in dance were dashed, off I went to Ohio State University to pursue, albeit reluctantly, a degree in social work. While most of the classes held some interest for me, the dreaded physical education requirement raised its ugly head once again. However, as I described in Chapter Two, I was delighted to discover that in college, dancing was included in the physical education category. Suddenly, gym class was the highlight of my day.

Graduation, Marriage, and Two Kids Later

As a young wife, I found myself right back on the sidelines as my husband played softball with colleagues, including some of the women. There I was, sitting in the mostly empty bleachers, trying to look interested in the game and proud of my husband.

I played the same position for Little League games, and I was also in the audience for ballet recitals or on a cafeteria chair at baton competitions, with recorded marching music that went on for hours. I grew restless and longed for my own movement, preferably to music.

Gathering my previously undiscovered pluck, I formed an exercise class for women I called Dancercise, combining floor exercises with dance routines through the Y and a weight–loss program called The Diet Center. After all, I did have that experience of leading the calisthenics in gym class in the seventh grade. It wasn't exactly what I had in mind for performing, but much later, I would discover another way to be on stage with an altogether different talent.

In the meantime, I felt a longing for physical movement that was still missing in my life. It was time for me to accept my blindness and find ways to be active as a blind adult.

Chapter Four
If I Can Do This, I Can Do Anything

Cross-Country Skiing

In 1986, I discovered a sport—yes, a sport—that would change my life.

As soon as I learned to cross-country ski, the popular A-word ("amazing") made its undeserved appearance. In addition to claiming I was amazing, my sighted acquaintance would embellish his or her perceived praise with, "I can't ski, and I can see!" The truth is that seeing has nothing to do with whether or not you can ski. Now, running into a tree or flying off the side of a hill or sliding into a creek has everything to do with how poorly you see.

Another popular reaction was, "Cross-country skiing! That's way too much work." Believe it or not, that's one of the reasons why I love it.

I joined an organization called Ski for Light, a week-long event for visually impaired and mobility impaired people to ski together with fully sighted and able-bodied skiers. I was paired with a sighted guide who kept me from danger by talking to me as we skied.

My first year, I had to learn to keep my balance on those long, skinny sticks attached to my boots, but having studied dance for most of my life, that wasn't a problem for me. I did find out, however, that in the many years since my dancing days, my endurance had diminished considerably. And my arms! Oh, how my arms ached at the end of the day! I hadn't expected to have to use them so much with those ski poles. For the first three days, I stayed on the one–kilometer loop, just learning how to move efficiently—striding, double poling, climbing hills, and snowplowing—and, yes, getting up after a spectacular fall. On the fourth day, my guide decided it was time for me to ski the 5–K trail. After a hot bath and dinner, I wasn't sure I would ever walk again, but by the sixth day, I was in love with skiing and with Ski for Light.

In addition to the liberating feeling of gliding across the snow without holding onto anybody, Ski for Light provides much more than confidence and independence. Over 300 participants attend each year, including people who use wheelchairs. On the snow, they use specially built sleds that they propel with ski poles with almost no help from their guides. And on the dance floor in the evenings, they twirl their partners and have just as much fun as the skiers with two working legs. I must admit that when I first met these folks, I was tempted to use the A–word myself.

I loved the dancing more than any other part of the week. I used to say that I endured the skiing just so I could go to the hot tub and then dance the night away. In those early years, when I was at the peak of my physical fitness, I felt like the belle of the ball, dancing every dance until the band quit at 1:00 a.m.

Until I discovered Ski for Light, I had little contact with

other visually impaired people, and this turned out to be the right group to show me how to have fun. I became more involved by volunteering to be a guide trainer, one who teaches new guides how to guide blind folks on skis, how to assist around the hotel, and how to be at ease with people who can't see so well. In the afternoons, after skiing and before dinner, I led special-interest sessions on topics such as public speaking and the joys of tandem bike riding. I made scores of friends from all over the world, and in 1991, I was sent to Norway, all expenses paid, to participate in the Ridderrenn (pronounced rid-der-ren, with the emphasis on the first syllable), which was the model for the American version, Ski for Light.

I had only been attending Ski for Light for five years when I was chosen to be one of four, two blind skiers and two sighted guides, to represent the U.S. It was kept a secret until the banquet on the last night. I literally felt my jaw drop when they announced my name as one of the SFL representatives to the Ridderrenn, a 20-kilometer race held in Beitostølen, Norway.

Later that night, as I danced with one of the board members, I asked, "Why me? I'm not that good at skiing, certainly not fast enough to ski in the race."

"You're a good ambassador," he said.

Ever since then, I've tried to live up to that honor.

I want to tell you more about the Ridderrenn because it was an experience of a lifetime. But first, I want to paint a more detailed picture of Ski for Light by sharing with you letters and journal entries I wrote about this awesome and unique opportunity for people who are blind. It's just as awesome and unique for the guides, as you will see as I unfold my story.

I am using journal entries from a particular week, so the

emotions of my reminiscences will not lose their freshness. Time can often cause a memory to fade, but I believe that sharing with you the following journals and letters will enhance your understanding and enjoyment of the Ski for Light experience.

From January 25, 2013

(In this entry, I mention Pippen, my little Lab/Golden cross Seeing Eye® dog. I had also just had spine surgery, which certainly clipped my wings for a while.)

It's frigid out there, and I hear there's some snow, but I wouldn't know, because I'm housebound for a while. Each time I open the door to let Pippen out, I feel the cold on my cheeks and fantasize about skiing. Somewhere, there are people out there, basking in this wintry beauty, gliding across the snow and loving it. If I weren't recovering from recent spine surgery, today is the day I'd be traveling to participate in a cross-country skiing event called Ski for Light, or SFL.

I first got involved in 1986 and have missed only three of the annual events since then. Once you experience the joy of learning to ski and the kinship in sharing the sport with like-minded folks from all over the world, you're hooked for life. It's hard to describe in words what happens at SFL, but if I take you along while I imagine what I'd be doing over the next week, you might get a peek at the magic from my perspective.

Today, I would be traveling to Shanty Creek,

Michigan, in time for the first meeting of the guide trainers. At SFL, blind skiers are paired up with sighted guides to ski in machine–set tracks that wind through forests, climb and descend hills and valleys, run alongside creeks, and wander over prairies. The sighted guide warns the blind skier about turns in the tracks, changes in elevation, and any other information needed, like a track being washed out, a skier down ahead, or a low–hanging branch. A good one will also describe the scenery, and for new skiers, coach and instruct. And he does all this just with words as they ski side by side but without touching.

I remember with great appreciation how one guide exclaimed at the beauty of the snow as we skied past some blue spruce trees. "You can see the blue of the trees reflected on the snow underneath," he said. I had never heard of that before, and it never would have occurred to me, as a totally blind person, that that could happen.

Another asked me to stop while he gazed at a log with about a foot of snow on top, untouched, undisturbed even by tiny critters. I asked him to take a picture. It was a beautiful and serene image, and I had it framed and captioned, "Sight is a gift. Seeing is an art." I gave him a copy, and mine is part of a grouping of winter and fall photos that grace my living room wall, demonstrating my love of these seasons.

Most guides are experienced cross–country skiers, but few are experienced in guiding blind people on skis or even inside a building. That's why guide training is essential.

Before the new guides arrive on Saturday night for this week–long ski adventure, the guide training teams meet on Friday night to plan the training session for first- and second–year guides. Each team of one sighted skier and one blind skier will lead a group of five or six new guides through guiding techniques and reviews of skiing skills that they will be using during the week. Some brand–new guides are apprehensive about being responsible for the safety of a blind person on skis. Others are eager and excited about the challenge. All are there to share their love of skiing.

Tomorrow, the guide trainers will ski the 5 and 10K courses and make note of where there are good places on the trail to review uphill and downhill techniques with their new guides. They practice teaching these techniques to each other and remind each other of what has worked well with teaching a new blind skier. For instance, some blind skiers like to use the clock method for making a turn, as in, "The tracks are turning now to about 10:00," and some prefer more casual directions, as in "slight curve to the left."

On Sunday, the new guides will go out to the ski area with the guide trainer groups and practice guiding one another with blindfolds on. The blind guide trainer in the team skis with each new guide and evaluates his or her guiding skills. These evaluations are considered when the matching of guide/skier teams is determined and announced Sunday night.

I love arriving on Friday night, because at that time, the group is relatively small. The board members, guide trainers, and a few folks come early just to get in some extra skiing. By Sunday night, over 300 people will fill the dining room, and it's fun to reunite with old friends and drink a toast to the coming week, a week that will change all our lives in one way or another.

From January 27, 2013

"Would you like a wheelchair?" the ticket agent at the airline asks when I tell him I'll need assistance to the gate. *I don't think so*, I think sarcastically. *I'm going to be cross-country skiing for a week.* This might be the way I'd start this story if I were traveling to Michigan for the annual Ski for Light event, which I will not be attending this year. I always have stories of travel troubles, but today I'm just imagining the unfolding of the day.

People with disabilities from all over the world, mostly visually impaired, will be flying into a small town in Michigan, independently, for a week of experiences that will drastically affect their lives.

I remember vividly my first Ski for Light, which was held in Duluth, Minnesota.

For several years, I'd been hearing about this opportunity to learn to cross-country ski on the radio reading service. In 1986, I felt the time was right for me to take the risk on this adventure, and from the moment I stepped off the plane, I was enchanted. An

SFL volunteer met me at the gate and escorted me to the baggage claim. I was then shown a seat in a waiting area where other SFL participants were waiting for the chartered bus to take us all to the hotel in Duluth—where, I discovered, they really know the meaning of winter. Immediately, a kind woman—a sighted guide, it turned out, who was originally from Norway, named Brit, pronounced Breet—greeted me warmly and welcomed me to SFL. I could tell already that despite my fears and doubts, I was going to like this. SFL is a place where strangers embrace one another, treat blind people as equals, and spread the excitement and joy of winter sports.

Sunday, the first official day of the SFL week, is packed with activity, anticipation, and surprises. During the day, before most of the participants arrive, first- and second-year guides are out on the trails with their guide trainers, learning and reviewing how to guide a blind person on skis. They learn such terms as "track right," "step left," and "Sit!" That last word is the most important command of all, used only when it's necessary to avoid injury.

Later, as the buses arrive, full of happy and eager skiers, guides are there to assist in carrying bags, finding rooms, and orienting totally blind people in their hotel rooms and around the hotel. Meanwhile, guide trainers are huddling to make final recommendations for matching skiers with guides in preparation for the announcement that evening after dinner. Skiing skills are not the only criteria considered. Height, weight, and age, along with goals for the week, are part of the equation. One skier might want to ski 20K each day, while another one might want to be able to complete a 5K course by the end of the week. Although there are a race and a rally on the final day, goals are agreed upon by each skiing team, and if those goals aren't compatible, switches can be made.

The first night's dinner is noisy with exuberant greetings of old friends from previous SFL weeks, welcoming of new blind and sighted skiers, and rowdy Norwegian toasts for a great week. The idea for SFL originated in Norway, so there is usually a group of Norwegians who come all the way from Norway to share in the fun. Others come from as far away as Japan, France, Australia, Canada, and England.

The highlight of this day is the after–dinner ceremony. Each blind skier stands up in turn, introduces himself, and then the name of his guide is announced. This information is kept secret until this moment, so everybody, guides included, is in suspense. "Who will I guide?" "Who will be my guide?" "Oh, wow. I get to ski with him this year?" Thus begins a week–long relationship that will enrich and affirm their shared love of skiing.

From January 29, 2013

"Cross–country skiing? Oh, no, that's way too much work!" is the stock answer when I seek out possible skiing partners at home. I tried downhill skiing once, but that was enough. I'm not into terrorizing myself.

When I attended my first Ski for Light, in 1986, I discovered that trudging up a snow–covered hill and reaching the top was exhausting but exhilarating. When I zoomed down the other side and managed to still be on top of my skis, it was thrilling. When my skis found their rhythm as I strode across a meadow, the slapping sound of the skis, along with the rhythmic shussing sound, comforted my soul. Sometimes I would stop and just listen to the quiet. One year in Colorado, I marveled at how I could actually hear the snowflakes gently landing on my shoulders, like a whispered secret. The secret was the joy of cross–country skiing, and it was something to be shared.

Today at SFL, dozens of people, some of them for the first time, will share in that secret. Blind men and women who for many years haven't taken a step outside their homes without the aid of a cane, a dog, or a sighted human guide will bend their knees, plant their poles, and push off across the snow, independently, but with the calm assurance of a guide just beside them or just behind them, cueing and coaching, helping them to navigate through a crowd of skiers, stepping into their skis and preparing for a good run through the woods.

Some will be fearful, not sure they can balance, not sure they can get up if they fall, afraid they won't have the stamina to climb the hills, and even wonder why they've invested so much time and money in learning a sport that most people don't associate with people with disabilities. But at SFL, the motto is, "If I can do this, I can do anything."

Once we've tasted the Ski for Light experience, that motto keeps ringing throughout our lives. It's not just a sense of freedom of movement that we feel as we double–pole down a slight decline, a sense of accomplishment when we cross the finish line at the race on the last day, or the discovery of our own strengths, but a combination of all of these. After SFL is over and we've put away our skis, we find ourselves turning to other challenges with a new, positive attitude. Suddenly it becomes much more important to us to be more active, to develop more healthful diets, and to seek out other ways to stay fit. We become cyclists, runners, hikers, backpackers, sailors, rollerbladers, and leaders. We know that we can do just about anything, because "If we can do this, we can do anything."

On Monday night, after the first full day of skiing, the guides are invited to introduce themselves at the microphone at dinner. Over 100 people, whose careers are as varied as teachers, doctors, foresters, firemen, farmers, animal control officers, and any number of other occupations, one by one reveal that they keep coming back, year after year, at their own expense— not just for the skiing, but for the SFL community.

You see, that motto applies not to just the blind people, but also to the guides. What a challenge they are asked to meet! And how they love that challenge.

The guide introduction ceremony is very emotional for me. Where else on this earth will I find so many sighted people who get it? Here are people who understand that we are people first, that we are not helpless, that we have a sense of humor, that we are not amazing, not heroic, but just other winter lovers who want to get out in it and play. This is the one opportunity for this to happen with dignity and grace that doesn't happen anywhere else.

At my first Ski for Light, I heard there would be a dance on Monday night. Several times during the day, I asked various people if they were planning to go. I wanted someone to go with, just for the practical help of finding my way through the hotel to the dining room where the dance was to be held.

I couldn't find anyone who was going, so I gave myself a little pep talk, grabbed my cane, and headed toward the dining room alone. With careful listening and cautious movement, I found the dining room.

The next challenge was to find a place to sit. After standing at the door for a few minutes and realizing that nobody was going to rush up and ask if I needed help, I inched my way to the left, reasoning that there would most likely be a table near the door. With relief, I found a chair and sat down.

Not knowing if anyone was nearby, I gathered my courage and asked out loud to the air, "Is anyone sitting here?" No answer. Only at a place where there are a lot of blind people can you do something like that and not feel awkward.

Okay, then, I thought. *I will sit here for 15 minutes, and if nobody joins me or asks me to dance, I will leave, and it will be easy, because I'm right by the door.*

But within five minutes, I heard a man's voice addressing me. "Would you like to dance?" Marvin asked. We danced once or twice, and then he sat at the table with me for a few minutes until another fellow asked me to dance.

I will always be grateful to Marvin for that first dance at Ski for Light. I had almost given up and gone to my room, but I found myself dancing almost every dance that night. This is the story I like to tell to explain what it also means when we say, "If I can do this, I can do anything."

I felt pretty gutsy walking into a dance alone as a totally blind person, but it was Ski for Light that gave me the courage to do so.

From January 31, 2013

If this year's Ski for Light event is like most of those in previous years, tonight's après–ski entertainment will be a talent show. Don't groan. It's one of the many happy surprises we uncover during this magical week.

Who does that beautiful soprano voice belong to? When I met her out on the trail yesterday, she seemed so shy and quiet, and now here's this big sound that so confidently fills the room.

Who's that playing Chopin on the piano? Seriously? You mean that tall man who introduced himself as an attorney? Can attorneys have such an emotional and tender side?

The truth is that when we offer an opportunity for folks to let their hidden talents shine, we open another avenue for enriching our lives. Because we don't go around bragging about this talent or that, our acquaintances know us only by what is evident in a casual conversational exchange. When the empty stage is presented, it's an invitation to share a gift.

Sometimes, in life's other settings, the stage is already cluttered with the same people who have starred there before, week after week or year after year. We often take the path of least resistance, that is, what we know, and ask the same old person, time after time, to MC a program, chair a committee, be the spokesperson, lead the singing, or otherwise occupy the spotlight.

Sometimes we need to step back and invite someone unknown to take the stage. The result can be startling. In other words, it can be a "Who knew?" moment. To all the new Ski for Light performers tonight, I say, "Break a leg." But not really. You'll need it for skiing tomorrow.

From February 2, 2013

"I don't want to race. I just want to learn to ski," I recall telling my guide that first year I went to Ski for

Light. Just managing to stay upright on those long, skinny sticks on those frozen trails was enough of a challenge for me. Yet, on race day, the last day of SFL, there I was, wearing a racing bib, shivering with the cold and the excitement as I waited my turn to push off and begin the 5K rally.

In the SFL rally, we ski five kilometers, trying to match our time from the day before. We are not allowed to look at a watch, and the winner is not determined by who skis the fastest but who comes in closest to their predicted time. So it's possible for the slowest skier to win the race if he crosses the finish line closer to his predicted time than anyone else in the rally.

At the beginning of the week, I had never even seen a pair of skis before, and it took me four days before I could progress from the 1K loop. I was glad that the 5K rally was not a race, because all I wanted to accomplish was to do the distance. Still, as I approached the finish line, I could hear the cheers, the ringing of cowbells, and the encouragement of the announcer on the loudspeaker. I couldn't believe they were still out there, cheering me in. I might have been the last one to cross the finish line that day, so in later years, when I really was racing the 10K race, I would hurriedly grab some water, put on a warm jacket, and stand at the finish line to cheer in the new skiers.

There's nothing quite so emotional as the moment you and your guide give it all you've got to shave off a few seconds, then slow to a stop and receive a hug from the volunteers at the finish line, who loop a medal around your neck. Everyone gets one. It doesn't mean you won the race, but it does mean that you did your best, overcame your fears, met your challenges, and proved that "If you can do this, you can do anything."

After the race, everyone goes back to the hotel to pack for the journey home the next day and to get ready for the awards banquet, all except for a few of us who stay and ski the course just for the joy of skiing. The pressure is off, and the trails are virtually empty, so we can relax and just have fun. It's a bittersweet time for me, because I know I won't be skiing again until the next SFL, and I won't be seeing these wonderful friends for another year.

The race was yesterday, and although I wasn't part of it, my heart was there. I pictured the start of the day, with the display of flags from all the countries represented. I heard the national anthem of each country being played and a few voices raised in pride. I heard the muffled applause from mittened hands and saw the frosty puffs of air escaping from smiling lips. I smelled the wax being applied to skis with an iron. I felt the good cheer as skiers and guides high–fived one another as they stepped into line for the start of the race. I heard each team's name announced as each in turn was given the signal to start. Even before the last team took off, some of the teams were returning from a fast run of the 10K course, no doubt led by a Norwegian. I tasted the hot chocolate as we cheered in the MIP skiers, those using specially designed skis for people who are "mobility impaired participants." Talk about inspiration! I wonder if they, too, get tired of being called amazing. "If they can do this, they can do anything."

From January 23, 2015

It's now two years later.

I had just completed the application for Ski for Light, 2015, to be held in Granby, Colorado.

My finger was resting on the Submit button, just lightly, ready to press, but hesitating for one more minute to be absolutely sure. It was going to cost a lot of money. I wasn't sure my back pain would allow me to ski. What if I wasn't able to get up quickly when I fell? What if the altitude gave me a headache? What if the airfare was ridiculously high? What if I didn't have the energy to ski anymore, since I had not been skiing in three years? Then I did it. I hit Submit. I was committed.

Last week, as I glided alongside my guide on the perfectly groomed trails of Snow Mountain Ranch, under a brilliant sun in a perfectly blue sky, I was keenly aware that for the first time in years, I could think to myself, *I'm happy*. In fact, I kept remarking to my guide, Betty, that I was so happy. It truly was a Rocky Mountain high. One night after dinner, our entertainment was provided by Jim Salestrom, a well-known folk singer in the area, and the song he sang that clutched my heart and brought tears to my eyes was "Rocky Mountain High." That's what Ski for Light is all about.

My third SFL was in 1989 in Bozeman, Montana. One of the first–time guides, Betty, was assigned to be my guide. We loved skiing together and found that we had a lot in common, and we chatted gaily as we climbed hills and skied across the meadows. My confidence in Betty's guiding ability was boosted by knowing that she was a physical education teacher of children with disabilities, and she even taught them to cross–country ski.

Over the past 26 years, we've kept in touch, seen each other at subsequent SFL weeks, and hiked together at the last several hiking events [which I will talk about in Chapter Six of this book]. When they announced the guide matches at the first meal together last Sunday night, we stood in amazement that here we were, 26 years later, skiing together again. Who knew? Who could ever have predicted that we would still be at it at our age, and loving it? I was so glad I pressed that Submit button. Did my back hurt? Yes, but I pushed through the pain. Did I fall? Of course, but I amazed myself by being able to pop right back up. Did I run out of energy? I had enough to ski 50 kilometers in six days. Did I dance the night away like I used to? Sadly, I'm afraid those days are over.

I have other stories to tell about this year's wonderful SFL, but I think you get the idea that I discovered that elusive state, happiness, which is still warming my soul.

Sometimes an SFL event will open doors and offer opportunities never before presented to a visually impaired individual. Cross-country skiing had not necessarily been on my bucket list, but it soon became the highlight of my year, almost every year since 1986. But because of my love of dogs and my fascination with the Iditarod, driving a team of dogs on a sled, even for a few miles, moved to the top of my bucket list, especially when I got to see the opening ceremony in Anchorage the year that SFL was held there.

Not enough snow had fallen for sleds to be pulled through the streets for the ceremonial start, so trucks brought in snow and dumped it onto the path that the sleds would travel out of town and into the woods, where there was plenty of snow. It tickled me to see snow being brought in instead of ploughed away. My guide that year, a man named John R., lived in Anchorage and knew the answers to the hundreds of questions I had. I longed to be on one of those sleds, although I would never say I would want to actually experience that brutal race. Here's what I wrote about my experience on a dog sled several years later in Colorado.

"Glacier, gee!" the musher called to the lead dog, a compact Alaskan Husky at the head of the lead line on my dog sled.

Yes, finally, I got to stand on the runners of a dog sled, behind a team of yelping, jumping, excited dogs, poised to lean into their harnesses and take me for a thrilling ride. It's been on my bucket list for years, and I had hoped to fulfill that dream on my birthday, earlier this month, but I was very sick with a cold, and the weather was terrible for traveling. It looked like I was going to have to put my dream ride off for another year. But then, at Ski for Light, held in Colorado this year, dogsled–riding was offered as an extra activity, not part of the SFL event. For $35, we could stand behind the musher, on the rails, or sit in the basket of a dog sled, and ride for 10 minutes. Ten minutes doesn't sound like a long time, but when you're standing on the rails, clinging to the bar in front of you for fear of getting thrown off the sled, it's enough.

As we prepared to line up for the ride, I kept being asked if I wanted to sit or stand. I guess they doubted my ability, given my age. But I kept insisting that I had wanted to stand for years. I wanted to feel the motion of the sled beneath my feet, to feel the strength and the pull of the dogs ahead of me.

My musher's name was Tim, and I told him I was totally blind, so I would appreciate any verbal description he had time to tell me.

He warned me, as he did every participant, that once the brake was released, we would start off with a jerk, and we were to hold on tight. It was just as he said. One minute, we were standing calmly, but in anticipation, and the next, we were off with a jerk and gliding down the trail.

I must admit that I squealed like a teenager on an amusement ride, but I quickly composed myself for the trip through the woods. Only it wasn't exactly a smooth glide. The sled jerked from side to side, and when we took curves, we leaned so far that it seemed the sled might tip over, but it didn't.

Because our sled was a bit heavy with me standing behind the musher and another woman sitting in the basket, when we went uphill, Tim would hop off and run with the dogs. I had read about this practice in books about the Iditarod. In fact, reading these books, plus witnessing the ceremonial start of the Iditarod in Anchorage one year at SFL, had whetted my appetite for experiencing a taste of it myself. As I clutched that bar in front of me for dear life, as we jerkily swayed from side to side, I got that taste I had been longing for, and it was awesome! It was one of the highlights of my week at SFL.

What made this experience complete was the opportunity to pet some of these sweet and endearing dogs after our run. I didn't get to pet Glacier, but I did get to say hello to Rickie, Rosie, and Nancy as they sprawled in the snow for a brief rest. As a dog lover who missed her dear Seeing Eye dog, Dora, it was just what I needed to keep the SFL Rocky Mountain high.

Now I'd like to tell you a little about what it's like to be a guide trainer—that is, the visually impaired part of a guide training team.

After I had attended several SFL events, I was invited to be a guide trainer, and of course I was delighted to help. I had done some other jobs, such as training the hotel staff, telling them things like, "Don't open the draperies if the occupant of the room left them closed when she left," and, "If you find a nightgown hung on the bathroom doorknob, don't put it where you think it should go. The occupant will never find it if you've moved it." I'd also helped train the transportation volunteers, telling them, "Offer your elbow for the blind person to hold onto. Don't grab her arm and try to steer her."

But training new guides was going to be much more fun. I could teach them techniques that I prefer that might be a little different from the way former guides had guided me. I could emphasize the difference between telling me to stop and telling me to sit. "Stop" means come to a stop, but it's not urgent. "Sit" means it *is* urgent, and the quickest and safest way to do that is to put your behind right down into the snow, right now! And the guide must say it authoritatively and without hesitation.

Guide training takes place two days before all the skiers and experienced guides arrive on Sunday. On the Saturday before, the guide trainers practice and review guiding techniques, so there is no confusion when the new and second-year guides arrive that evening. Saturday evening, the new guides get oriented to the hotel and learn what to expect during the week. The visually impaired and the sighted member of the guide–training team share in this presentation. In fact, all the various training teams, the committees, and the board of directors are made up of equal numbers of blind and sighted participants.

On Sunday, during the day, the trainers take small groups out on the trails and demonstrate the best ways to teach new skiers, called VIPs (visually impaired participants), and make suggestions for coaching returning VIPs on improving their skiing skills.

Each guide trainer team has four or five new people in their group. Each new guide takes a turn at guiding the visually impaired trainer, which can be fun if they're getting it but a little scary if they haven't been paying attention. It's my least favorite part of this activity. You have to get to know your guide before you can trust him or her.

I had one that seemed not to know her right from her left, and after I figured that out, it was scary as heck to start down a hill and hear her call out, "The tracks are turning to the right," when she really meant to the left, and the next thing I knew, I had skied off the track and into a snowbank. It could have been worse. It could have been a tree, and then she would have needed to have the presence of mind to yell, "Sit!"

Every time we approached a hill, I'd have a little conversation with her. "Do you really mean right? Or do you mean left?" Since she skied in the tracks to my left, we resolved the issue by saying "my way" or "your way." Communication, and I mean precise communication, is crucial when it comes to guiding a blind person on skis.

I had several guide–training partners over the years, but my favorite was also my favorite guide, John K. John had a fabulous sense of humor, and he loved to put people at ease by making them laugh.

Our favorite part of our training routine was to teach a new skier how to get up from a fall. Several techniques can be used, depending on how badly the skis and poles got tangled up as a result of the fall. Mostly, it involves getting your center of gravity to a place where you can get your feet under you and stand up. It's best not to try to lift the skier yourself, not only for your own safety, but also so that the skier learns to do it on her own. When John and I got to that place in the demonstration, he would first "instruct" me to fall down. Then in a loud, stern voice, he'd say, "Get up." It always brought a laugh. Well, maybe you had to be there.

Now here's what I wrote about one of the years that John and I were teamed up—not only as trainers, but also partners for skiing that week.

Once again, I have returned from a magical week of cross-country skiing in Colorado. Prior to the trip, when I told my local granddaughters that I would be skiing the next week, the 16-year-old asked if I would be snowboarding. Well, I might be a pretty hip grandma, but that's a little too wild even for me. In fact, I tried downhill skiing once and successfully got to the bottom of the bunny hill, still vertical and still breathing, but that was enough terror to last me a lifetime.

Cross-country skiing is work, which is the reason a lot of people don't like it, but I love the feeling of gliding over the trails, pushing myself to get to the top of a rise, and then hearing my skis sing as I accelerate going down the other side. No, that's a lie. Going downhill still scares me, but when I have a competent guide by my side, encouraging me with affirmations that I'm doing fine and keeping me informed about how much curve there is to come and how much farther it is to the bottom, and when we've come to the flat, and then when we are starting up again, it's actually fun.

I've been to SFL almost every year since 1986, and I've had some pretty terrific guides. John, pictured with me at the end of this chapter, is the one who makes me laugh the most. When I'm just about to run out of gas toward the top of a hill, John tells me jokes and sings silly songs to keep me going, although sometimes it's hard to laugh and ski at the same time. John also has a talent for making sure I'm still in the tracks and prepared for turns while describing some interesting sights along the way. On one trail, he told me about two trees that had separate trunks, then grew together, and then apart again. It would have been a great photo op, but I'm afraid all we have is a picture of two happy skiers.

One of the funniest photos would have been the two of us laughing our heads off after we had shared a drink of water. We had just climbed a very long and steep hill and were standing at the top, breathing in the fresh, clean air and gazing up at a beautiful blue sky with white, puffy clouds that a child might have drawn in a picture of blue sky over perfect white snow. I had been celebrating my belief in God, because how could you not believe, standing in a scene like this? I remember feeling like I could just reach up and touch God himself.

After we had caught our breath, John offered me his water bottle. It was the kind that has the little opening at the top that you pull up and then squirt the water into your mouth without touching it. I tipped it up, squeezed, and the next thing I knew, icy water was all over my face and down my front. John had unscrewed the top, thinking he was being helpful.

Again, I guess you had to be there, but we thought it was hilarious. That's what happens when you have a Rocky Mountain high.

John and I were guide trainers together for nine years, teaching new guides how to guide blind skiers. Over the years, we have developed a vocabulary that makes our skiing together smooth and efficient. If the curve in the tracks is a gradual one, he'll say, "Long right." If the tracks turn sharply to the left, he'll say, "Sharp left, starting now." When he says, "Half track right," I know to sidestep once, and I'll be back in the tracks. It saves a lot of words, so there's more time to ski.

This year's skiing was a little more challenging than in other years because of strong winds and blowing snow, not to mention altitude issues and the old sciatica returning. But sharing stories over dinner with another 100 visually impaired skiers and 100 guides makes us forget about the huffing and puffing up the hills. We greet old friends, make new ones, and share in the glow of overcoming the challenges we'd met that day. As the SFL motto goes, "If I can do this, I can do anything." But I'm not quite ready for the snowboard.

The Ridderrenn

Earlier in this chapter, I promised you I'd tell you more about the Ridderrenn. It's a week of cross–country skiing for visually impaired and mobility impaired people who come from all over the world to participate once a year. Sound familiar? That's because the Ridderrenn was started in Norway, many years before two Norwegian men brought the idea to the United States in 1975 and called it Race for Light. Many changes have taken place over the years, but the primary purpose has always been to give people with visual and physical disabilities the opportunity to ski.

Each year, Ski for Light has sent four participants, two skiers and two guides, to the Ridderrenn as official representatives of the United States, although other Ski for Lighters are welcome to go along at their own expense. As I said earlier, I was totally taken by surprise in 1991 when I was chosen to go. I was not only shocked, but a little confused and not entirely happy. I liked the Norwegian people I had met, but I had no burning desire to go to Norway, and I knew that almost anyone else in that room would have loved to be in my place. In addition, I worried about how my husband would take my being gone for two weeks without him, what my boss would say, and how I was going to get a passport on such short notice, to say nothing about how I was going to get in good enough shape to ski for 20 kilometers, 10 of which were up one side of a mountain and down the other.

Surprisingly, my boss was happy for me and allowed me to take the two weeks off—using all my vacation, of course. I borrowed a NordicTrack ski machine and worked out on it every day on my lunch break in the storeroom. With the help of a co-worker, I jumped through all the hoops necessary to get a passport. Unfortunately, my husband was very upset with me for wanting to go to Norway on my own. I knew that would be a problem, but I was not going to let his insecurity spoil this once-in–a–lifetime honor.

By the time I arrived in Oslo, I was exhausted, not having slept a single second on the flight, but thrilled to be there. How could I ever have not wanted to go? From the moment we stepped onto Norwegian soil, we were treated like royalty. Young Norwegian military men were assigned to drive us up the mountain to Beitostølen to the hotel and back and forth to the ski area. They maintained the pristine tracks, sometimes having to move snow onto the trails where the wind had blown it away or the sun had melted it. They showed us how to shoot specially designed guns that used sounds to help us locate the targets for the biathlon.

By the way, I was a terrible shot, so I took no prizes in that event. In fact, I didn't win any of the races that week, but it didn't matter to me at all. Two memories are much more important to share.

My guide's name was Liv (pronounced like "leave"). She was one of the Americans who came with us, but she was from Norway. One afternoon, she brought the whole U.S. contingent, about 10 of us, to her parents' home for cake and coffee.

To prepare for this visit, Liv taught me some Norwegian phrases as we skied along on the flats. The tracks were so beautifully groomed that Liv didn't have to do much guiding, so we had time to work on my Norwegian. I learned such basics as "please" and "thank you," but also "It's nice to meet you," and "Yes, please, I'd love some cake." As we filed into their home and shook hands, Liv's mother was very impressed that I had learned to greet them in Norwegian. They spoke almost no English, but with the help of Liv and another woman from Norway, Bjorg, who was also part of our group, we had a lovely visit.

During our Norwegian lessons, Liv also taught me some very important phrases that I would need in the evenings, when there was dancing every night. "Will you dance with me?" was easy to learn and fun to understand. "You are a very good dancer" in Norwegian always brought a smile to my partner's face.

It was on the dance floor that I learned one of the most fascinating lessons of the week. A man who spoke no English and had only one arm asked me to dance. Because it was his right arm that was missing, I was intrigued as to how we would hold a dance position and how he would lead. Having studied ballroom dance, I knew that most of the leading is done with the man's right hand on the woman's back. The left hand does some of the leading as well, but in this case, his left pinky finger did it all. At first, I was concerned about how to approach the dance position. Should I put my left hand on his shoulder, even though he wouldn't be using a right arm? He was used to this look of confusion and very calmly took my left hand and placed it on his right shoulder. Of course. How silly of me to not think of that. Then with my right hand in his left, he led me around the dance floor like a pro. I was awed at how he could indicate that I should turn to the right or left just with the movement of that one finger.

Another dance ended with laughter and a bit of anxiety. This man spoke no English and was totally blind. Liv had interpreted for me that he wanted to dance with me, so she led us both to the dance floor. She said to me in English and in Norwegian to him that she would come back for us when the song was over.

The song ended, but no Liv showed up. So we danced again. No Liv.

We danced a third time, and then it was time to say thank you and go back. But without Liv, we had no idea how to find our respective groups of friends.

Together, we set out into the tables and chairs, bumping into them and bumping into people, asking them if they knew where the Americans were. Nobody knew. We wandered what seemed like all over the place until one of his friends observed our plight and led us back to where the Americans were sitting. There was Liv, deeply engrossed in conversation. She had completely forgotten us, but we'd had quite the adventure finding her. Again, "If we could do this..."

Naturally, I wanted to return to Norway because it was the quintessential SFL experience, with the additional fun of sightseeing tours and being in a snow–covered wonderland of a country. Still, I was just as eager to return to Ski for Light again and again.

Skiing in Ohio

It turns out that skiing in foreign lands and in many different states in the U.S. is easier than skiing at home.

After you arrive at the event destination, your worries are over. Your guide is chosen for you. You are shown to your room and given an orientation tour of the hotel or lodge. Transportation to the ski site is already arranged. Your meals are prepared and served to you. Lessons in cross–country ski techniques are available for free. New friends are ripe for the picking. Old friends are back for more hugs. And the choice is yours whether you want to ski for recreation or for competition.

Without joining an organization created for people who are blind or mobility impaired, the story is quite different. Many snowy mornings at home in Ohio, I have longed to be out on skis, enjoying the bracing winter air, the joy of gliding across the meadow or through the woods, and, if I'm lucky, feeling the treasure of winter sun on my face. But first, I have to find a friend who likes to ski, who is free during the day, and who isn't afraid to guide a totally blind person.

I've been very fortunate to have friends from my cycling club who have taken me to a nearby golf course, and while I'm grateful for that, it's not the same as skiing full out with the confidence I feel on well-groomed tracks set over gentle terrain alongside a Ski for Light guide. Perhaps the bigger problem is that if we have enough snow to ski on, we also have icy conditions on the roads, and no one can get to me.

Thirty years ago, I helped plan an Ohio version of Ski for Light, and it's still being held at Punderson State Park each January. Counting skiers and guides, about 30 people with varying interests in skiing attend, so we changed the name to The Winter Sports Retreat. Most years, the snow has been plentiful, but for some of the retreats, the main outdoor activity was taking walks in the woods. And for some, the main attraction has been playing cards.

It's not exactly what we had in mind, but those who really do want to ski, like me, get to do so as much as we want. We even skied at night until the rangers saw us and put a stop to that. We were clearly having way too much fun.

What Is the Light in Ski for Light

As high as we were on Race Day at SFL, with the national anthems ceremony, the thrill of crossing the finish line after skiing our hearts out, the leisurely skiing afterwards, the awards banquet, the dance, and the parties, we were just as low on the following day, Sunday. The first bus back to the airport often left at 5:00 a.m., which meant schlepping ski bags and luggage around in the middle of the night and saying sad goodbyes over a quick cup of coffee in the subdued morning melancholy.

Then came the arduous trip home, which involved a bus ride and up to three flights and two layovers, plus dealing with unenlightened airport personnel.

The difference between the SFL world and the real world was evident the moment we entered the airport. People in the real world don't speak to each other in an elevator. People in the real world don't offer assistance to a blind person in an unfamiliar restroom. They stand and stare. People in the real world assume you can't do stairs or an escalator. People in the real world cannot imagine the respect, the laughter, and the kinship we shared as an SFL family.

After my first SFL, I went back to work the very next day. By noon, I had to go home, sick. Not only was I exhausted, but I was sick at heart. It was the classic "back to the real world" syndrome. Each year after that, I included the Monday after SFL as part of my vacation days. I needed to decompress.

Three years later, I was able to put into words, in the form of a poem, what I felt at SFL. Here it is.

What Is the Light in Ski for Light

Ski for Light is a state of mind,
A slice of time out of the context of life,
A transcendental world of timeless relationships
That begin and end in the space of a week,
Yet last for a lifetime of Ski for Light weeks,
Where everyone accepts me as I am,
And everyone expects to be my friend,
To help me find my strengths,
To help me say "I can,"
To mirror my smile and extended hand,
To share my zeal for life and all that it can offer,
To taste the sweetness of trying and doing,
To sip from the common cup of conquered fear,
And toast the glory of freedom,
To celebrate my triumphs,
To teach me how to laugh again,
To heal my wounds of frustration and doubt,
To strengthen my sense of self,
To light the flame of independence,
And fan that flame each time I think of Ski for Light,
And like the flame of the Olympic torch,
That keeps alight throughout the year,
So I bring it with me when I return,
And proffer it to someone new,
Someone like you
Who needs to ski for light.

Mary cross–country skiing

John K. And Mary at Ski for Light, 2007

Chapter Five
It Takes Two to Tandem

When you have spent time with cross–country skiers for a week or so, you soon get the bug to get involved with other sports throughout the year, or at least to strive to be more active and engage in a more healthful lifestyle. It happened to me. As I flew back from Minnesota that first year, I vowed to find other activities that would keep me fit and be fun as well.

I had been walking every day with my Seeing Eye® dog, Mindy, which I enjoyed immensely, but it didn't feel recreational enough for me. My husband and I had bought an old clunker of a tandem bike with two speeds, pump and pump harder, which we used to tootle around the neighborhood, maybe to go get an ice cream cone or to drop in on friends. Later, we bought a custom–made tandem with 18 gears, built for short people. We considered ourselves hot stuff when we rode seven miles over to the airport and back, and then we rewarded ourselves with a milkshake when we got home.

My husband considered biking a way to spend time together occasionally, but for me, it quickly became a new passion. And just as with skiing, I wanted to share my enthusiasm for cycling with other blind folks.

Drawing from friends I knew from the Columbus chapter of ACB, the American Council of the Blind, I formed a group of people who wanted to rekindle their love of bike–riding from when they were kids. They would learn to be stokers, the term used for the person on the back of a tandem. I recruited serious cyclists from local bike clubs to bring their tandems, provide transportation, and captain the bikes on Saturday mornings during the summers for three or four years. It was a lot of work, but the benefit for me was that I met some great cycling enthusiasts and like–minded people who became my very good friends.

It started with Tricia, one of the captains I had recruited for the first ACB ride. It rained that morning, so I cancelled the ride. But then it cleared up by noon, and Tricia asked if I wanted to ride with her anyway that afternoon.

She invited me to join her bike club, where I developed into a fairly strong stoker. Several of the members took turns being my captain, and it turned out to be a good way to get to know them as individuals. Soon I was able to ride 50 to 60 miles in a day.

For three years in a row, I rode my tandem in the Great Ohio Bicycle Adventure, GOBA, each year with a different captain. It was a week–long event, starting in a small town in Ohio and making a circular route through many little towns on back roads. We'd ride about 50 miles each day, with the last day's route taking us back to the start. One of those years, I had a different captain each day, which was a real feat of orchestration. At the annual banquet at Christmastime, I received a special award. It wasn't for "most improved" or "most miles ridden" or "oldest member." It was "Most Promiscuous Stoker," which was the best joke of the evening. I had all my captains sign it, and I have it proudly displayed in my office.

Two years in a row, I rode in El Tour de Tucson, 111 miles in a day around the perimeter of Tucson, with my dear friend Eve. It was a fundraiser for leukemia. The first year, it took us about nine hours, and when we finally stopped, I felt like I needed to be peeled off the bike. The second year, we shaved off about a half hour—not because we rode any faster, but because we were a little wiser and knew where the porta potties with shorter lines were.

After two years, we'd had enough of fundraising, but we loved the adventure, the challenge, and the camaraderie of hundreds of riders working toward a common goal, to wipe out this awful disease and do the distance.

In other years, a woman named Ann and I rode in a ride called the Marietta River Rendezvous, an 80-mile ride over rolling hills, and some steep ones as well, to Marietta, Ohio, and then back again over those hills the next day.

I was in my 50s in those days, at the peak of my physical fitness, so the sticker on the back of my bike that read "Girl Power" was a good one for Ann and me. I was working full time at the radio reading service in Columbus, so all my riding had to wait for the weekends.

I told the pastor at my church that I was a rainy day Christian, because on sunny Sunday mornings, I'd be worshiping from the back seat of a tandem bike instead of at church. And to tell you the truth, I did appreciate the glory of God's creation as we heard the cheerful songs and the territorial cries of various birds, felt the early morning sun on our faces, smelled the nostalgic fragrance of wood–burning stoves, and imagined people sitting by a fire in their pajamas drinking coffee and reading the Sunday paper as we pedaled by.

One captain, Glenn, summarized the whole experience this way. When we were riding with a group one Sunday afternoon, and our destination was an ice cream shop in a little town about 20 miles away, one of our group asked, "How far till we get there?" And Glenn answered, "What do you mean? We *are* there." His point was that the joy was in the journey itself, not the destination. He also enjoyed describing the colors of a sunset as they changed with the passing of the early evening.

My captain on my first GOBA, Tricia, seemed to enjoy pointing out scenes that you might not notice from a car. One such vivid photo in my mind featured a cow standing in the middle of a creek to cool off and Amish overalls hanging from a clothesline. One day, she spotted a snake making its way quickly across the road, and I could hear it thrashing through the leaves on our side of the road.

Being on these GOBA rides convinced me that the best way to see Ohio is from a bike. On an especially pretty day after a stretch of gloomy ones, I liked hearing the different ways people celebrated life. Children splashed in a backyard pool. Teenagers roared up and down hills on their ATVs. Couples paddled down creeks in their canoes. Little girls squealed as their daddies pushed them on swings. Grandparents sat on their front porches with big smiles on their faces. Little kids always waved, and we always rang our bells as we flew by.

Informal rides with the bike club always had a destination of a food stop, usually lunch, but sometimes breakfast. We liked to say, "We ride to eat."

One of my favorite rides included a stop at a farm market, where the owner, the brother of one of our members, cooked sausages on a grill and served us hot and tender corn on the cob. We finished off our delightful break with slices of sweet, juicy watermelon, fresh from the garden. Afterwards, we would buy produce from their roadside store and stuff our goodies in panniers or backpacks.

We would often ride to festivals, passing the lines of cars waiting to get into a parking lot. We'd tie our bikes up together and secure them to a tree, and off we'd trudge to get ice cream, corn, pumpkin chili, or warm, gooey cinnamon rolls. I also loved the organized rides that drew riders from all over Columbus, not just our club. These rides would be longer and more challenging, often with food stops along the way, with bananas, cookies, and other quick snacks to give us a little extra energy for the next big hill. A few times, I rode with one club that would end their rides with pizza and spaghetti, so it was a social time as well as a workout.

An annual ride in Ohio that was a sort of rite of passage was TOSRV, Tour of the Scioto River Valley, a two-day event starting in Columbus and ending in Portsmouth, a 105-mile journey, usually in the rain, on the Saturday before Mother's Day. Riders would sleep in tents, on the gymnasium floor, or, for some lucky people who booked a room a year in advance, in a motel. Then on Sunday morning, usually in the rain with the addition of strong headwinds, they'd ride back to Columbus.

Thousands of cyclists thought this was great fun, and I must admit that I decided to give it a try one year, but only for the first day, and only if it wasn't raining. No way was I going to sleep on a gym floor after riding 105 miles and then get up and do it all over again the next day.

My captain's name was Glenn. He and I began our ride about 25 miles outside of Columbus, so as to cut off some of the distance for me. When we started out, the sky was overcast, but it wasn't raining. And then it was.

"Now this looks more like TOSRV," Glenn said, with his dry sense of humor.

I was not amused. In minutes, we were soaked. I had no rain gear with me, but Glenn, being the kind soul he is, gave me his rain jacket to wear, while he wore the rain pants.

At the next stop, 25 miles down the road, I asked, "Are you having fun? Do you want to finish?"

I was willing, but I really didn't want to go another inch. Luckily, we had a friend with a car with a wife driving SAG (support and gear), and we got a ride back to Columbus. In fact, we got invited to have a hot dinner with them at their house. Nothing ever tasted so good, and never had I been so happy to end a day of cycling.

I could go on for pages with descriptions of memories, but I'd rather share with you some letters and journals that will give you a better flavor of the joys of cycling, all written at various times for a variety of reasons, such as advertising for captains, a constant quest. But I'll start with an article written by Mike Needs, a reporter from the *Akron Beacon Journal.*

Monday, June 23, 2003

Okay, I admit, my knees were shaking. I was gripping the handlebars so hard, my right hand went numb. Cotton mouth describes perfectly the feeling in my mouth.

What made me so anxious? Well, Monday night I captained a tandem bike for the first time. Fortunately, I had a great partner in Mary Hiland, my stoker, the person who rides in back.

Oh, by the way, Mary is totally blind.

I need not have worried so much; it turned out to be an exhilarating experience.

When Mary heard about the Ohio Odyssey, our 20–day bicycle adventure around the state, she sent an e-mail and asked whether I wanted to ride with her and some of her bike–club friends. She said it would be a learning experience I would not soon forget. She was right.

Still, after riding more than 40 hot miles during the day and then writing my daily stories for the *Akron Beacon Journal*, I was tired and cranky. Okay, I'll go so far as to say I thought about canceling. After all, climbing aboard a bike with a person I didn't know in unfamiliar riding territory—that didn't sound too appealing to me.

But a commitment is a commitment, so photographer Dennis Gordon and I drove out to Hoover Reservoir, where we met up with Mary and her friends.

I quickly learned the three rules of tandem riding with a blind person: communication, communication, communication. I'm told that tandem riding with a sighted person requires a high degree of teamwork.

With a blind person, every move, every turn, every stop, everything must be forewarned and described in detail.

Just getting started was a challenge. After taking a spin around the parking lot by myself to get a feel for the tandem, I pulled up next to Mary and told her to hop on. Well, not really. At this point I was near hyperventilation with anxiety.

You see, when you pilot a tandem with a blind person, you accept total responsibility for the safety of both people.

Talk about guts. Mary didn't know me from Adam, yet she was willing to put all her trust in me. As she described it, "If I don't trust, I don't ride." And Mary loves to ride.

So, on command, I gave a great push off with my left foot and we went about 10 feet before stumbling to a stop. That was not promising. We backed up the bike and received more instructions from the friends. This time I really pushed off, and so did Mary. And so did one of the friends running alongside in back, just like dads do with their kids. This time we rolled.

For the first few miles, I barked out everything I was doing, even the obvious. "I'm pedaling, Mary, I'm pedaling. I'm still pedaling." That was unnecessary. However, loud, clear announcements were essential at every turn and every stop. With the turns, Mary needed to know which way to lean. With the stops, she needed to know when to step off.

Soon, the bike–riding part became natural, almost

easy. At that point I started to describe the surroundings, seeing things in exquisite detail—the better for sharing with Mary.

At one point I described the sky as clear and deep blue. Then, like many sighted people around the blind, I thought I goofed. How would Mary know blue? No problem, she said. Now 58, Mary started losing her sight at age 8, giving her memories from childhood. "Blue is my favorite color," she said.

After a while, even the necessary announcements became automatic. I started to relax, and we began talking about her job—she manages 250 volunteers for the Columbus organization that reads for the blind— and other parts of our lives. Mary has done GOBA, the Great Ohio Bicycle Adventure, three times—including once with a different captain each of the seven days. She's been riding for 10 years.

She asked me a lot of questions about my job and admitted she had an ulterior motive for asking me on the ride. People needed to know that bike riding is not only possible for blind people, but it's great exercise and a lot of fun, she said. The only problem is that more sighted people are needed for piloting. Maybe I could spread the word, she suggested coyly. Don't worry, Mary, I understood from the start why you wanted to do this, I replied.

Then, something magical happened. We were riding down a shady lane that suddenly opened up into bright sunshine. "Ah," said Mary, "I love to feel the warmth of the sun." Then, a bit later, she said, "Can you smell that? It's almost like someone is burning something in the fireplace. I love to ride in the fall, when people use their fireplaces." That's when I fully relaxed. I stopped worrying about the terrible burden of responsibility.

This was turning out to be like most bike rides on a pleasant summer evening down a tranquil country road. This was fun. Mary was enjoying herself. And so was I.

Perhaps I should have sent the following little tutorial on tandem cycling to Mike before we met for our ride.

How To Ride a Tandem
Without Killing Your Partner

If you're considering buying a tandem bike or captaining for a blind stoker, here are some tips from an experienced blind cyclist.

First, let me get the terminology out of the way. The captain is the person on the front of a tandem bike, or a bicycle built for two. The person riding on the back is called the stoker. The captain steers the bike, and the stoker, well, stokes. There's not much to do from the back except pedal and be charming company for the captain. I know of some stokers who have installed the gear-shifting on the back, but this really only works well if the stoker can see what's up ahead, or the captain has really good communication skills. I prefer to let the captain shift the gears, because he can see, and I cannot, but I do like to be warned of a gear–shift, so I can let up on the pressure on the pedals.

Riding a tandem bike has been compared to driving a limo, especially if you've only ridden a single-person bike. It takes a little more upper body strength and awareness of the time it takes to stop, start, and turn.

The most important skill you can bring to your tandem partner is good communication. Even before you get on the bike, talk to your stoker about which side of the bike you like to mount from, which foot you put down when you stop, and which way you like to let each other know you're ready to pedal.

Some people like to say, "One, two, three, go," but I find that unnecessary and awkward. Typically, after we're in position to start, my captain asks, "Ready?" and if I'm ready, I just say, "Ready." And off we go. New captains, who are insecure in their ability to handle this job, often start by pushing off with a foot on the ground, much like you did when you were a kid on your first bike. This is actually a very inefficient way to start. Agree on which pedal you want in the up position for starting, and then push down on it, and immediately get your other foot in the pedal and PUSH. Doing that thing with the foot on the ground slows you down and can cause you to tip over.

If you're captaining for a visually impaired stoker, you'll need to announce when you're getting ready to turn, and which way. If your stoker leans the wrong way, you could wind up in the ditch. Let her know if you need to slow down and when you're going to stop.

Say "Slowing" and "Stopping," just as you do when you ride with a group. Say "Shifting" when you need to shift gears. You don't need to say if you're shifting up or down.

Some stokers like to do the signaling for a turn. I like to, for two reasons. First, it makes me feel like I'm contributing something to the team effort besides stoking. More important, that allows the captain to keep both hands on the handlebars.

Some captains prefer for their stokers to stay seated when they stop, while others, especially those who are not much bigger than their stokers, prefer to have their stokers put a foot down as well.

After you've become comfortable with the tandem, you can enhance your blind stoker's enjoyment of the ride by describing what you see along the way. After all, when you go for a bike ride, unless you're a "hammer–head," a big part of the experience is enjoying the scenery. Even if there's not much to describe, you can always say, especially in Ohio, "Corn fields on the left and soybeans on the right." I like it when my captain tells me if there are kids waving, so I can ring my bell and wave to them.

Tandem cycling is a great way to ride with someone who has a different skill level from yours. Neither one can lag behind or drop the other. It's also a terrific way to share the joy of riding with a visually impaired person, who otherwise would never be able to ride.

Now here's a report of my first River Rendezvous for our club's newsletter. My captain was Tom, the man I was dating at the time. Tom was not a cyclist when we met through a personal ad in a magazine called *Columbus Monthly*, but because he liked me and wanted to score points with me, he agreed to learn to captain my tandem. Our adventures were not always happy ones—that is, on the bike—as you will see here in my article for our club newsletter.

Marietta River Rendezvous Review

November 23, 2003

Tom arrived at my house promptly at 5:15 a.m. on Saturday, May 31, ready to tackle his first attempt at carrying a tandem, my brand new Cream Puff, on a bike rack. With a little trepidation, we set off for Duncan Falls. I probably asked him every five minutes or so if the bike was okay. We left Duncan Falls in a light drizzle at about 8:10. Soon we broke out the rain gear, which was pretty thoroughly soaked by lunch time. We also had two flats, both at the same time, about a mile shy of the lunch stop. Tom was wringing his hands in anxiety, trying to gather enough courage to attempt to change the rear flat, when thankfully, someone showed up in a van and SAG'd us in. Fortunately, Chuck Harris was there with his rolling bike shop, and after about an hour, we were on our way again, fortified with peanut butter sandwiches and homemade cookies.

Who said this was a fairly flat ride? Tom certainly got experience in shifting gears and grinding our way up the "flat" roads. Then he had the thrill of controlling the bike as we tore down the other sides with the rain stinging his face. Aside from the constant rain, it was a beautiful ride, with wonderful rolling hills, and three or four of them to make you really work off the cookies, and the scenery and ambiance were magnificent. I kept wishing that other club members were there to share this GOBA–like experience.

Because it was still raining as we rolled into Marietta, we had not planned to stick around for the strawberries and ice cream. But just then, the rain stopped, so there we were with our faces in the ice cream bowls. We stayed at the Lafayette, where Tom had his first experience with horsing a tandem into a teeny elevator. Dinner at The Levee House café, where we watched the barges and other river traffic parade before us, was followed by a very pleasant cruise on the Muskingum and Ohio Rivers.

Miraculously, the rain held off for the evening. But it was back the next morning as we set off for the return trip. We only got about seven or eight miles out of town, however, before the rear tire blew. Again, we had the wringing of hands and beads of perspiration starting to pop out, when we were blessed again with the arrival of a van full of guys who knew what they were doing, and in about 20 minutes, the tube was changed. But wait. They suddenly discovered that the tire itself had some serious damage, so off we went in their van to the lunch stop again. Someday, I want to ride into that lunch stop on my bike and not in a van.

The good thing about this trip was that one of those guys, Frank, works at the same place a lot of our club members do and might start coming on our rides. We waited for two hours, staving off boredom with more peanut butter sandwiches and more homemade cookies, waiting for good old Chuck. Then we learned that Chuck's van had broken down, and he wouldn't be coming to the lunch stop at all. So, onto the SAG wagon we piled, along with two other flat-tire victims. But the drive back to Duncan Falls was actually pretty interesting, as our driver was a Marietta newspaper reporter who knew all the gossip of the county and the history of the area.

I learned a lot of lessons on this trip. One is that there really is a good reason for not riding in the rain. That's the greater possibility—no, probability—of flat tires. The second is that you don't need to carry any food on this ride. The third is that rain gear, even Gore-Tex, only puts off your getting wet. And finally, don't believe anybody when they tell you the route is flat.

Now here's an excerpt from our thank-you letter to all our financial donors in 1997, when my dear friend Eve and I rode in El Tour de Tucson.

TUCSON TWOSOME RIDES AGAIN

My most recent adventure was a 111-mile perimeter ride around the city of Tucson. My captain was Eve Holland. This was the second year Eve and I were part of the Leukemia Society's Team in Training. Together, we trained in the heat and humidity of summer and the cold and rain in the fall so that we could raise money for leukemia patients by participating in one of the most revered rides in the country. Not only did we meet our fund–raising goal of $2,700 each, but we also had a terrific time in Tucson.

We arrived in Tucson two days before the ride, so we could do some sightseeing and shopping. First on our agenda was to hike about five miles in the Sabino Canyon, where breathtaking vistas presented themselves each time we crested a boulder–strewn hill.

It was a challenge for Eve to guide me through the narrow paths, where I could trip over loose rocks, bang my knee into a hip–high boulder, or stumble into the ever-present cacti that lined the so–called path. But just as our teamwork served us well on the bike, our teamwork on the trails was a sight in itself to behold.

One of our teammates who walked behind me was amazed at how efficiently Eve got me through some really tough spots. Eve would say, "Oh, boy," wondering how she was going to verbalize where I should place my feet to avoid catastrophe, but we succeeded and were victorious every time. With a water bottle in one hand and Eve's shirttail in the other, I followed her as we squeezed our way up and down hills, between prickly pear cacti and palo verde trees, around giant anthills, and over boulders and jagged rocks.

On the second day, we toured the Sonora Desert Museum, where smooth, paved pathways led us through delightful displays of desert wildlife. We witnessed a fascinating drama of what we guessed was a mating dance of prairie dogs. We woke up sleeping mountain lions, and I held in my hands the complete skulls of coyotes and other animals of the Wild West. One of our teammates had to touch every cactus she could, just to see if they really hurt. I did that last year, so I kept my hands to myself this time.

Of course we had margaritas every night as part of our training for the big ride on Saturday.

Although we had eaten a huge breakfast at 5:30 Saturday morning, after about 50 miles or so, we as much as inhaled the peanut butter and jelly sandwiches Eve had packed for us. She's had lots of practice making PB&J's for CFC (Columbus Fall Challenge), TOSRV (Tour of the Scioto River Valley), and other such rides, so these were serious sandwiches, made with thick, heavy bread and loaded with strawberry jam. There were bananas, oranges, and oatmeal cookies available at all the rest stops, but there was nothing like a PB&J to get us back on our way.

The weather was spectacular, in the low 80s, sunny, and clear. The sky was the deep blue that you rarely see in the Midwest, and there wasn't a cloud to be seen for miles. The mountains surrounding the city of Tucson looked like giant, burnt chocolate drop cookies with their crusty, jagged peaks poking into the sky. All around us were happy cyclists on every imaginable type of bike, including one that the rider used his arms to propel, as his legs lay limply in front of him. No pity for this guy. He stayed ahead of us for the whole way, even on Tangerine Hill, which lasted for 12 tedious uphill miles.

Back in Ohio, Eve was used to saying, "Corn on the right and soybeans on the left" as we pedaled over the country roads, but on this ride it was "Cacti on the left and cacti on the right."

We saw another visually impaired stoker with his female captain. We knew he was visually impaired, because why else would the man relinquish control of the bike? We chatted with them as we ground up the hills and flew down the other side, reveling in the reward that only a tandem on the downhills can enjoy.

We had a friendly rivalry with the only other female tandem team. We rode faster than they did, but they stopped less often, so whenever we were standing in line at the porta potties, and we'd see them whiz by, we'd have to jump on our bike and try to catch them. The last time we saw them, we were pulling ahead of them, and we didn't stop for the rest of the way in fear that if we stopped to rest our weary buns, it would be just like the story of the hare and the tortoise.

Later, after we returned to Ohio, Eve looked it up on the internet and found that we did finish about 45 minutes sooner than they did.

The route was the same as last year's, but somehow it seemed like they'd put more hills in it, and the hills seemed longer and steeper. Could it be that we could have used a little more training? Or was it the margaritas that slowed us down? It was a long day, and I had decided that 111 miles was too long to be fun and that I wouldn't sign up to do it again the following year. But then I'd think of the struggle that people with leukemia face every day of their uncertain lives. I know it sounds corny, but thinking of the reason, the real reason, gave me the inspiration and the motivation to keep on stoking until the finish. I love to ride for a cause, but I also love riding just because.

Fifteen massage therapists greeted us at the finish with their tables lined up on the small patch of grass in front of one of the downtown hotels. Talk about heaven! Those folks were saints as they kneaded sweaty, dusty muscles and stretched our tense and aching backs. We hopped off those tables—no kidding—refreshed and ready to ride again. But fortunately, we just had a few blocks to pedal to our hotel for a hot shower and a celebratory dinner.

The next morning, we strolled around the downtown area, soaking up the sunshine and breathing the wonderful desert air as if to store it and carry it home with us. We did bring back souvenirs, like cactus jelly and turquoise jewelry. But the best one was the medal they presented to us at the finish and what it stands for.

I am so thankful to have my cycling friends, especially those who are willing to captain for me. Being out in the fresh air, getting a good physical workout, listening to the joyful noises of the birds, smelling the distinct fragrances of the countryside, and feeling the sun on my face are all part of the joys of cycling. I truly enjoy riding with a group, because it's fun to catch up on what's been happening in their lives while getting some great exercise. Riding a tandem is not just a necessity for me, but also a great way to get to know people. I recommend it for couples. It takes real teamwork, especially for me. Ideally, my captain will warn me if we need to stop, slow down, turn right or left, or bear down for a steep incline.

I had one female captain who liked for both of us to stand when going up a steep hill. She taught me how to do that and not be worried when the bike swayed from side to side. Most captains prefer for one or the other of us to stand, but not both of us at the same time. It takes timing and courage.

It's important to let me know which way we're turning, so I can lean to help the bike through the turn. Once I scared a new captain half to death when I demonstrated how the stoker can actually turn the bike by leaning. I like for my captain to tell me when we're starting an incline, so I know that the reason it's harder to pedal is not just that my captain has quit pedaling. I'd like to have a dollar for every time someone standing in their yard and watching us pass by yelled, "She's not pedaling!" They always think they're so clever. Believe me, you can tell if your tandem partner isn't pedaling.

I have one captain who likes to tell me that we're getting ready to go up a hill so I'll start working harder and he can rest. Not really. He likes to tell people that, but he's actually one of the strongest captains I have.

Joining a bike club is one of the best ways to make friends

and to stay in shape. I am so thankful for mine.

For several months following back surgery and then again after a series of injections for sciatica, I had to let my tandem gather dust in the garage. Gradually, starting in the spring of 2016, my truest cycling friend, Tricia, took me on some short rides to get "back in the saddle again." Here's my account of a ride that is fitting for the end of this chapter.

Three Girls and Two Bikes

Sunshine in March is like getting a present when it's not even your birthday. Here in Ohio, we get one of those bonus days every once in a while, between days that are cold, windy, and gray. Last Wednesday was one of those gifts of a warm and sunny day. For me, there is no better way to celebrate a sunny day than to ride my tandem bike.

My biking buddy Tricia was my captain, and our friend Jan joined us at my house on her single bike. We rode from my driveway to a restaurant in New Albany, a distance of almost exactly 10 miles. I had asked Tricia to create a route that was no more than 20 miles, since this was my first ride of the season, and she did it. When we pulled into my driveway three hours later, we had 20.33 miles on the odometer. Not bad, since I'd wondered if my hips and back could hold up for that distance. Of course, we had about an hour's break for lunch before we headed back.

It was such a pleasant ride, full of girl talk. Because we weren't riding with our regular cycling friends, we pedaled in a leisurely manner. There were no boys to try to keep up with. I say boys and girls, because when we're on bikes, we're young again. Only instead of talking about our kids and upcoming parties, our conversations include sharing information about retirement and Medicare.

It was relaxing to feel the sun on our faces, get some good exercise, and share what has been on our minds and in our hearts. Talk about girlfriend therapy. We hope to make this a regular outing once a week. My goal is to increase the miles each week, so I can get back to being able to ride with the guys. But in the meantime, I'm so grateful to Tricia for being responsible for getting me back on the bike and to my doctor for finally finding the right injection to make my hips and back behave. Of course, to help make this a successful ride, I had to take a steaming hot bath afterwards, followed by an ice pack on my back, but you do what you have to do to keep doing what you love to do.

Lest you think that I started riding a bike after I became an adult, I need to add one more story. I got my first two-wheeled bike when I was about 10, but I was only allowed to ride it around the block and only on the sidewalk. My vision had begun to decline, and back then, kids in the city were expected to ride on sidewalks. Even when I spent the summers with my cousins at Grandma's, down in the country, we rode our bikes only in the yard. Because it was a rather small yard around a very small house, to get in any distance at all, we had to ride around and around the house. Leading from the back porch to the outhouse in back, planks had been laid to keep from having to walk in mud when it rained, but we were skillful enough to squeeze through the spaces between the planks in order not to have to stop or turn around and go the other way.

One afternoon, Carolyn, who was three years older than I, got us started singing "100 Bottles of Beer on the Wall" as we rode around and around. Our plan was to keep riding until the end of the song. If you recall, this is a very long song, because each verse is a subtraction of one bottle. Sing with me. "One hundred bottles of beer on the wall, 100 bottles of beer. Take one down and pass it around, and now there are 99 bottles of beer on the wall."

I'm not sure what happens when you get down to one bottle of beer, because just as I was rounding the back of the house and getting ready to squirrel between the planks, and we were almost down to one bottle of beer, my tire caught the edge of one of the planks, and down I went. I wasn't hurt, and seeing that I wasn't injured, Carolyn joined me in uproarious laughter and singing the rest of that verse.

But then Grandma came out and declared the song was over. Whether it was because she was worried about our getting hurt or because she was sick of hearing the song, I'm not sure, but it kept us entertained for a very long time. Maybe on one of our longer rides these days, I should suggest we sing that song sometime when we're on a long, boring stretch of road. Oh, wait. There are no boring stretches of road. We talk, laugh, comment on the view, and think about how many more miles till we get to lunch. Some people eat to live, and some live to eat. We live to ride and ride to eat.

Mary, ready to ride

Chapter Six
Take a Hike

On a beautiful fall day, when the air is crisp and cool, when the leaves have fallen and lie strewn around the forest floor in a splendor of color, when a whiff of fireplace smoke tickles my nose and my nostalgic imagination, and the toe of my boot kicks a buckeye in the path, I know it's the right time to take a hike.

When I was a little girl and my dad was occupied with skeet shooting at his sportsmen's club, my mother and I would take long walks through the woods and around the lake. We'd gather cattails, especially beautiful leaves, and bittersweet to make a fall bouquet. We'd try to identify the bird calls and squint to watch a squirrel scampering up a tree, its cheeks no doubt bulging with acorns. Pheasant feathers and buckeyes were the precious treasures I'd bring home from our Sunday afternoon adventure, but the memories of the feelings from those outings are the real treasures.

As an adult, I can hardly wait for fall weather to brighten my spirits. Although I still enjoy cycling on the warmer days, I look forward to hiking, because I don't hike in the summer. I can't stand bugs and sweat, so I have to wait at least until October.

I was fortunate enough to have two or three friends who would take me to a place to hike now and then, and I went with a group from The Columbus Outdoor Pursuits on a few organized hikes. One of my favorites is an annual event on New Year's Day in an area in Ohio called the Hocking Hills. It's the quintessential way to spend New Year's Day. Here's an account of one of those extraordinary days.

> We could see our breath in little puffs of freezing air as we spoke, climbing out of the car and feeling that little catch in our throats when our lungs weren't quite ready for the shock of unwarmed air. We were glad we had worn our boots. In the city, the streets had been cleared, but out here in the Hocking Hills, the snow lay undisturbed except for the animal tracks. The sky was a solid gray, but in the east, there was a promise of winter sun, creeping into the icy air and painting the barren branches with glittering icicles.

> Soon, other cars would crunch over the gravel, and more happy hikers would emerge, blowing out their own little puffs of frozen air from smiling lips that called out joyful greetings to other winter–lovers who had forsaken their warm beds and comfy couches. I opened the back door of the car, and my Seeing Eye® dog, Sherry, bounded out with gleeful expectation. She snorted and sniffed the air, sniffed the excitement that would be hers today. It was New Year's Day, and we were out here to celebrate with a seven–mile hike and

a picnic in the meadow, perfect for the first of January.

When 8:00 a.m. arrived, and it appeared that we were all there, we began our trek down the snowy path, two by two, two by three, with Sherry in the lead, of course. Guide dogs always like to be first. We stepped over snowy roots and icy rocks, climbed over fallen tree trunks, and ducked under brittle branches, heavy with snow and ice. We stopped to listen to a groaning tree as it swayed slightly in the breeze and the cry of a hawk as it split the sky.

Now we were warming up, pausing to take a swig from our half-frozen water bottles or to munch on a granola bar, kept chewable in a warm inside pocket. The path wandered up hill and down and occasionally along a creek. We slipped as we struggled to keep off our knees going up and just slid on our backsides on the steep descent.

A recent flood had washed away a bridge over the creek, but a good-sized log had been placed there for a crossing. All the other hikers stepped up onto the log and tromped along to the other side, but Sherry and I held back. This was not going to work for a blind hiker and a guide dog, not without help. But one of the guys came to our rescue. He cheerfully and easily scooped my 70-pound Sherry up in his arms, threw her over his shoulder, and carried her across. I followed by holding onto his backpack. Sherry was embarrassed to be carried, but I was afraid of getting her feet frostbitten in the half-frozen creek. And as dogs do when they know a joke has been played on them, she jumped around and acted like that was the most fun she had ever had. But the most fun was yet to come.

By noon, we had come to a clearing for our picnic lunch. Most of us had brought sandwiches, but one well-equipped hiker had brought a camp stove and offered everyone hot soup or hot chocolate. Life seemed pretty perfect, sitting in the winter sun, sipping a hot drink with new friends. A stand of trees stood about 50 yards away, and except for that, there was nothing around us, so I unbuckled Sherry's harness, and she was off like a shot into the woods— free at last to do a little exploring of her own and make a pit stop while nobody was looking. In a few minutes, just as I was beginning to worry, she came racing back to me. She might as well have said, "This was the best time I've ever had!" But she was ready for our trek back along the path.

The sun had warmed the snow just a little, enough so that as Sherry's paws penetrated the top layer of snow, it stuck to the hair between her toes, making hard little snowballs that might have looked cute on a toy, but for a real dog, they were painful and made it hard to walk. Seeing her limping, my friend and I stopped to dig out those icy little balls of snow, and again, she was back to her joyful self.

Back at the cars, we shouted out, "Happy New Year!" We kicked the snow off our boots, climbed into our cars, and sighed with the pleasure of one of the happiest New Year's Days ever, even for Sherry, who was sound asleep in minutes.

Hiking with one friend was pleasant and good exercise, but I discovered that hiking with a group of friends was even more fun.

A Unique Hiking Group

At a ski event in January of 1999, my guide, Julie, and I found that we had much in common and became close friends. She had described to me a ski trip she had taken with a friend in New England, where they skied from inn to inn. Staff members of the inns would carry their luggage for them, so it would already be in their room when they arrived at the next destination.

I fell in love with the idea and made a decision to see if it would be possible to hike from inn to inn on the Appalachian Trail. Well, if I was going to dream, I might as well dream big.

The next step was to find a hiking partner—because, once again, I would not be able to hike on my own. Walking around town on sidewalks with my guide dog is one thing, but hiking on the Appalachian Trail alone was not happening for me. Since I was no longer married and did not have a significant other or even a friend who loved walking as much as I did, I wrote to Julie, and the idea of a group of women hikers took shape.

Every year since then, we have come together to hike—many times in the New England area, but also in Tennessee, Pennsylvania, Minnesota, New York, Canada, and even in Ohio. Oh, you don't think we have mountains in Ohio? You're right, but we do have challenging and beautiful trails, hills, valleys, rivers, lakes, Appalachian towns, and Amish country.

Each year, surprises of one sort or another have provided stories and laughs at future hikes, starting with the first year in Vermont.

While we were expecting to hike from one inn to the next, with our luggage being schlepped for us, as the brochure had advertised, the innkeepers greeted us with blank stares. They had never heard of such a thing. We guessed that some marketing writer had forgotten to check with the inns to see if they really did this.

So we took a day hike, packed up our belongings, and drove to the next inn, which was much more pleasant, anyway. Sadly, we had to move the next day, too, but we stayed two nights in the one that turned out to be the best.

To add to the hilarity of the first inn, when I climbed into bed that night, I found a small box hidden under my pillow. Thinking it might have been a surprise from the man I had been dating, I opened it, and to my consternation, unwrapped a set of handcuffs. My story at breakfast the next morning brought peals of giggles. What could this mean?

The mystery was solved when I took them to the innkeeper, and then the joke was on him. "Oh, my gosh," he sputtered out in his charming New England accent, between gales of laughter. "I'm so sorry. A bride and groom were originally to have that room, and a friend had asked for the handcuffs to be hidden under the pillow. But I forgot that I had switched them to a different room. I didn't mean for you to be the one to discover them." I was the one who was surprised instead of the happy couple.

During dinner the first night, we discussed where we would hike the next day and for how long. My thought was to hike on the Appalachian Trail for about 15 miles. Since none of us knew what a pie–in–the–sky dream that was, we all agreed. None of us knew how challenging the Appalachian Trail really is, how slowly we would progress, and how we had overestimated our strength. Possibly 12 sighted women would be able to manage 15 miles in a day, even with stopping for water and bathroom breaks, but when half the group needed to be warned of rocks and roots, fallen tree trunks over the trail, and the dangers of narrow paths with a drop–off to the right or the left, it was no wonder that by the end of the day, we had only hiked three miles, and that was counting the way back to the cars. We were all tired, but also disappointed in ourselves. That night, we planned a more realistic hike that wasn't quite so tedious for the next day.

Many of the women returned year after year, but a few have had to drop out because of illness or other obligations. One has retired from guiding at age 80, and sadly, three have passed away. As I write this book in 2019, I am the only one of the original group who is still trudging along after 19 years.

Now that I've given you a little bit of our history, I want to share with you a speech I wrote for Toastmasters. I won several contests with this speech and have presented it to many groups, including the banquet for the national convention of the American Council of the Blind. When you see the word "bawk," imagine the sound that a chicken makes, because our annual events are known as the Hen Hike. Of course you would enjoy the speech much more if you could hear it, but reading it will give you a pretty good picture of who we are and why the Hens are so important to me.

Banquet Speech for ACB, July 13, 2013

There is something in the autumn that is native to my
    blood,
Touch of manner, hint of mood,
And my heart is like a rhyme,
With the yellow and the purple and the crimson
    keeping time.
The scarlet of the maples can shake me
Like a cry of bugles going by,
And my lonely spirit thrills to see the frosty asters
Like a smoke upon the hills.
There is something in October that sets the gypsy
    blood astir.
We must rise and follow her,
When from every hill of flame,
She calls and calls each vagabond by name.

    That's a poem by Bliss Carmen, written in 1894.
    Yes, there's something in October that draws me

to a hiking trip with 11 of my favorite women friends.

"Twelve women?" you say. "Oh, I can just hear it now. Yackety yack. Cackle, cackle, cackle."

Well, you wouldn't be too far off. During our first gathering, we decided we needed a name for our group, and by the end of the week, we had agreed on The Hen Hike. Some of the women balked at the idea, but they soon let their sense of humor take over, and they eventually bought into the idea, calling the oldest member of our group the mother hen, and the place where we stayed at night the roost, plus coming up with such rules as, "No roosters allowed."

Sorry, guys, but there are some pretty practical reasons why we don't invite men on the hike. I'll bet you can think of one or two. For instance, when one of us has to go to the bathroom—and this happens frequently, given that we are middle-aged and older women—one of us will spot the perfect grove of trees that allows for just the right amount of privacy, and we declare it the tinkleorium.

We don't need a lot of privacy. After all, we're used to going to the restroom in groups. You know how it is when you're out with women. One will say, "Excuse me, I'm going to the ladies'," and immediately, another one will pipe up and say, "Oh, I'll go with you."

You might be wondering what it looks like to have 12 women hiking together when half of them can't see. Picture this. Each morning, when we get ready for our hike, at the crack of 9:30 or 10:00, we pair up. Each visually impaired hiker, or VIP chick, as I like to say, holds onto a loop or a strap of the backpack of a sighted partner, the guide chick, and off we go, two by two, down the trail. When the terrain is level and the path is narrow, some of us have a rather unique way of using a hiking stick. The guide chick holds onto one end of the stick, while the VIP chick holds onto the other end, walking slightly behind, thus forming a sort of elongated guide dog effect.

Because we hike in pairs, we have a lot of time for girl talk between instructions that sound like this: "There are a bunch of roots to step over. Watch out for this big rock on your left. There's a tree up ahead that's fallen over the trail, so we're going to have to either climb over it or crawl under it, and whatever you do, don't lean to the right, because there's a big drop–off."

Being a blind hiker takes a lot of trust, but being the sighted guide of a blind hiker takes a lot of courage. Just like at Ski for Light, it's all about trust and courage.

On the first day of our very first hike together, we came to a little stream over which had been laid a steel beam. This was our bridge. No railing. Not wide enough for two hens to cross together. So we had to face sideways, with heels extending over one edge and toes over the other edge, and ever so cautiously and slowly, inch by inch, we scootched sideways to the other side, repeating to ourselves the Ski for Light motto: "If I can do this, I can do anything." When the last two hens crossed safely, we all cheered and had a group hug.

Ever since that day, we've enjoyed hiking up and

down steep hills, over muddy trails with rocks and roots to negotiate. Sometimes we hike on leafy forest roads where we can stride out and put on some miles. Sometimes we hike on the Appalachian Trail. You should see us when we come to little streams where there is no bridge, not even a steel beam. We just have to hop from one wobbly rock to the next to get to the other side. On rainy days, we hike through antique stores and gift shops. Sometimes we have to hike to the nearest liquor store to replenish our supply of wine and cheese.

When Julie and I started talking about forming this hiking group, I had just read a wonderful book called *A Walk in the Woods*, by Bill Bryson. It's a hilarious story about two ill-prepared guys who decide they're going to hike the entire Appalachian Trail.

I was inspired. I, too, wanted to hike—not the whole thing, but part of the Appalachian Trail. So I said, "Julie, would you be interested in going on a hiking trip with me?" To my amazement, she said, "Yes!" Sometimes you just have to ask. Then she said, "That's a great idea, Mary, and what would you think of inviting a couple other gals to go with us?"

So we did, and they in turn invited a couple more women friends, and the next thing we knew, there were 12 of us. We had to stop inviting people after 12, because you can't get 12 women to agree on anything, much less on what to have for dinner that night.

At dinner the first night, we're all full of travel stories, because we've all flown the coop. That means we've had to deal with airport personnel all day, and as you know, that can require a lot of patience and a good sense of humor.

You all have your favorite travel stories, but here's one of mine. It comes from Anna, one of our VIP chicks. This was back in the days when you actually talked to a real person when you made a flight reservation. She told the guy that she was visually impaired and would need sighted assistance when she made her connections in Philadelphia.

"Got it," he said. 'Is there anything else I can help you with? Connect you to Avis, Hertz?"

When she got to Philadelphia, she descended the steps from the plane and was greeted by not just one, but two assistants—one for each elbow, it turned out, to escort her across the tarmac and up the 17 steps into the airport. How did she know there were exactly seventeen steps? Because they counted out loud as she took each step! "1, 2, 3, 4," all the way to 17. She was so amused by the time she reached the top that she said rather sarcastically, "You count very well." To her surprise, they took it as a compliment. They said, "Thank you. Now wait here while we go get a wheelchair."

What if you wanted to start something like a Hen Hike? Of course you'd want to get a group of like-minded people. There are three considerations for planning such an event. First, this group would need to laugh easily and be able to laugh at themselves. Our ages range from 40–something to 70–something, with most of us over 50. When Marie, our 40–something–year–old, came for the first time, I was horrified at breakfast on the first morning as the conversation migrated to a discussion of Medicare. *Oh, no,* I thought, *Marie will never be back. Who wants to hang out with a bunch of women talking about Medicare!* But I think that Marie enjoyed not wearing make–up the whole week, not fussing with her hair, and not having to hold her stomach in the whole time.

The second thing you need for a Hen Hike is the perfect roost—that is, a bed and breakfast, or at the very least, a quaint old inn. These chicks don't camp. Nope. We like our fresh clean sheets on four-poster beds in 19th-century homes with gourmet meals served to us by very nice people with New England accents. The innkeepers try not to sound alarmed when we make a reservation for 12 women, half of whom are blind. You can almost hear them gulp with panic when they think of the narrow, steep, winding staircases in their charming old houses, with antiques sitting around that could be knocked over and broken. The servers are always nervous at first, but after a couple of meals, they realize that we're just like any other group of women—happy, noisy, talkative, and full of fun.

The third thing you need for a Hen Hike is to let the child in you come out. Have you ever been outside when a gaggle of geese flies over, you can hear them honking, and it sounds like they're having a conversation? One gloriously sunny afternoon, we were walking on a forest road when a gaggle of geese flew very low overhead, and we could hear them flapping and honking, and you might think they sounded a lot like us. We, as mature, intelligent, dignified women, could do but one thing. We clasped hands. Two of us got out in front. The others formed a V behind, and down the road we ran, beneath the geese, going, "He honk, he honk, he honk."

I mentioned forest roads, but most of the hiking we do is either uphill or downhill. One day, when we climbed a particularly steep hill, we stopped at the top not only to rest, but also to give the guide chicks a chance to enjoy the view. Down on the trail below, they spotted an older man walking with a younger woman.

Let me tell you, there was a lot of discussion about that among the hens. "Bawk bawk bawk bawk. Why do some older men think they have to have a younger woman? Bawk bawk bawk bawk. And what does she see in him, anyway?"

We found out the next day—from his wife, no less—that the younger woman was their daughter. It turned out that they were staying at the same inn we were, and the next morning, one of our VIP chicks, Barbara, got a little turned around on her way to breakfast. The man and his wife were also going to the dining room at the same time, so he offered his elbow to her.

Boy, did we ever tease Barbara as she strolled into the dining room on the arm of the elderly gentleman. And did he ever puff up when he announced to the whole dining room that he was our token rooster. We all had a good laugh about that, including his wife.

We asked her to take our picture with him as we got ready for the hike that day. As we turned to wave goodbye, we knew there was a look of wistfulness on her face. It's an expression they always have when they wish they could be with us, because we're fun, no matter what happens.

One year one of our new hikers, Cindy, turned her ankle, fell down, and actually broke her leg. Since we were way out in the boonies, none of our cell phones worked, so two of our fastest walkers ran back down the trail to the road to get help. A couple of the gals stayed with Cindy to try to make her as comfortable as possible while the rest of us picked our way very carefully and solemnly back down the trail to the road.

No sooner had we got to the road than here came the paramedics. We pointed up the hill to where Cindy and the others were waiting, and they jumped off the truck, unloaded the ATV, and rumbled up the trail as far as they could. Then they yanked off the stretcher and ran the rest of the way. Gently and carefully, they lifted Cindy onto the stretcher, then onto the ATV, and finally into the ambulance, and off they went to the hospital.

I don't envy Cindy her broken leg, not at all, but darn. All six of those paramedics were big, strapping, gorgeous guys. Some women get all the attention. And whatever happened to no men on the hike!

We always carry food in our packs so we can have

lunch somewhere on the trail. Even though we've had a scrumptious breakfast of maybe crisp bacon, fluffy homemade waffles, fresh blueberries, and rich Vermont maple syrup, by noon, we're starving, and a peanut butter and jelly sandwich really hits the spot. We always pick a pretty place, like a spring, where we can hear the water trickling over the moss–covered rocks, deep in the woods, sitting on a log, where we can breathe in the fragrance of fresh pine needles, or maybe on an escarpment overlooking a spectacular view, puffy white clouds in the sky, a mountain range in the distance, a river down below.

Do you ever get to a place in your life when you are so happy that you just feel like bursting into song? We feel like that when we're sitting on a hill with a beautiful view, and of course we feel like singing, "The hills are alive, bawk bawk bawk...." But none of us is Julie Andrews, so we content ourselves with Girl Scout songs. Nothing is sweeter than hearing 12 women in their 50s and 60s harmonizing to "Make New Friends" and "bawk bawk bawk."

We're not always singing and making noise. Once a day, we pause by a peaceful stream for five minutes of absolute quiet. This is a very hard thing for 12 women to do. "Bawk bawk bawk bawk!" "Shhh." "Bawk bawk." "Shh." We might pray, or meditate, or think about... absolutely nothing. Just soak in the serenity of our surroundings. During one such pause, Carol, one of our VIP chicks, was inspired to recite a poem she had memorized half a century before. We stood in awe of the beauty of the words and of the moment.

Here was a poem from 1894, but it could have been written for us, for that very day.

Later that night, as we sipped our last glass of wine for the last time that year, I, being the ham in the group, announced that I, too, had a poem to recite, one that I had written in honor of the Hens. I'll close tonight with my ahem, poem.

Well, I come from the Midwest to be with my friends,
Eleven other women, and we call ourselves the hens.
We cackle and we crow as two by two we go
Down the Appalachian Trail through the leaves and the
　　snow.
We marvel at the colors. We're awed at the sights.
Keep to the left, there's a drop off to the right.
Step over those roots. Climb over that log.
Touch the pretty moss. Listen to the frog.
And when we have to tinkle, we just pull down our
　　drawers.
Even our bottoms love the great outdoors.
It's time for lunch, so pull up a rock.
Loosen your boots and air out your socks.
Peanut butter sammies never tasted so good
When you're skippin' over rivers and hiking through
　　the woods.
Switch your partners now, get going again.
Catch up on the news from yet another Hen.
Waddle down that path now two by two,
Till you get to the roost and take off your shoes.

Jump in the tub. Lie on the bed.

Get up again for wine and some sort of spread.

Now waddle into dinner. Eat all you like.

You know you'll burn it off on tomorrow's hike.

We don't count calories. We don't watch fat.

It's just us chickens, and we like it like that.

It's the great Hen Hike. Can't wait to get bawk!

Who Are These Women Who Hike?

You might wonder what makes the Hen Hike so exclusive and why we know women who are just waiting for the day when they will get invited.

It's an invitation–only event so we can keep our numbers down and simplify the logistics of organizing it.

For the past several years, there have been 12 of us, but as of this year, we are limiting our number to 10. You'd be surprised at what a difference that can make, and I'm not sure why, but let's just say it's easier and not as complicated.

One reason is that we need to drive to trailheads, and having 12 of us means we need three cars, unless one of our drivers has a minivan or SUV. If she has flown to the venue, that means she has to rent a larger vehicle. If we only have 10, then we only need two cars. Of course, we all chip in on the cost of the rentals, gas, wine, and snacks.

One of us makes the arrangements with an inn or bed and breakfast, and while at first it was Julie or I who took the lead, in recent years, others in the group have taken on that role. Twice in 19 years we've stayed at one place two years in a row, but we like the variety and excitement of staying someplace that's new to us and hiking on unfamiliar trails. We love learning about where other people call home, listening to their accents, and literally walking through the pages of history. It's also fun to buy gifts where the locals shop. One of our ladies commented one year how different the trees look on the East Coast from where she lives in Minnesota. Who knew that even trees would be a fascinating part of the experience?

Julie and I started by inviting only women friends from Ski for Light, and through the years, the majority have either been guides or VIPs at SFL or have participated in a regional SFL event. That way, we could be certain that they were physically ready to hike and were up to new adventures. Because we always needed an even number of guides and VIPs, some years, we've had to invite friends to fill a spot for either a guide or a visually impaired hiker. Even though they may never have been to SFL or a regional, we welcome them and often entice them to come to the next SFL event. We already know that SFL women are strong and energetic gals, and they've already earned my seal of approval; the new hikers we recruit need to have the same traits. But two of the most important qualities are loving to laugh and enjoying a small community of women.

A Typical Day on a Hen Hike

Because we don't camp, mostly because I don't camp, we start our day with a beautiful breakfast prepared and served to us at a quaint old inn or a lovely B&B. There's no frying bacon or burning toast over an open fire at a Hen Hike. We may have bacon, and many of us do, because we don't cook it at home, and often we delight in fluffy hot waffles drenched in locally made maple syrup, accompanied by fresh fruit, yogurt, granola, or all of the above.

I recall with great fondness one morning when our server went around the table asking if we'd like to have Eggs Benedict or maple pecan waffles, and Carol said with exaggerated false boredom, "Oh, I don't know. I have that every morning." The woman who would dare to mumble, "I don't eat breakfast" would be kicked off the trail in a heartbeat.

Most of us do love our morning coffee. One of my favorite inns, the Winter Clove Inn in New York, was one that we visited twice. The twelve rocking chairs lined up across its huge front porch provided the perfect setting for an early morning treasure of having some quiet time. Whoever came downstairs first would pour a cup of coffee and get to sit out there by herself for a few minutes, listening to the call of a hawk or the coo of a mourning dove, or pet the family dog as she wandered up on the porch to see who you were. I was an early riser, so I often reveled in the peace and quiet of the morning, but I was just as glad to greet the next early riser. One by one, they would all appear, coffee cup in hand, until the porch was full of happy gabbing, until the innkeeper would come out and tell us that breakfast was on the table.

I think this morning ritual is what I miss most when I have to go home. Nobody serves me crisp bacon and piping hot pancakes, drizzled with real butter and blueberry syrup. Nobody clears my table and washes my dishes, packs my lunch, and prepares a three–course dinner every night.

After breakfast, we pick up our packed lunch bags, which usually contain a sandwich, a piece of fruit, and a cookie or brownie. Then we disperse to our rooms to pull on hiking pants, boots, and as many layers as we need for the morning. We stuff our lunches into our backpacks, along with water bottles, tissues, lip balm, rain gear, and a sit–upon. A sit–upon, you may recall from making them in Girl Scouts, is a square of cloth or newspaper, covered in plastic and sewn around the edges. They are used to "sit upon" when the ground is wet.

We always carry rain gear even if it doesn't look like rain, because in the mountains, even low ones, the weather can suddenly change. I also carry gloves of differing thicknesses for the same reason, and hats, too. However, most years, although we gather in late October, we are often hiking in short sleeves by the afternoon, even in New England. Sometimes we have to adjust clothing by mid–morning, especially if we're climbing and we build up body heat.

Lunch is around noon or whenever we find an inviting spot, like a waterfall, an overlook, or just a good–sized log by a path in the woods.

One item we carry in our packs but hardly ever use is a cell phone. One year, we could get no cell phone reception at the inn where we were staying, so as soon as we got to the top of a hill, several of us took them out to check for messages or check in with our offices or just to say hello to husbands and children.

But our focus is on the beauty of our surroundings, the joy of movement in the fall air, and the stories told by our hiking partners. We paraphrase a worn–out saying: "What's said on the trail stays on the trail." After lunch, we switch partners, so we have new stories to hear, news to share, and plans or dreams to test out on a sympathetic ear.

By 4:00, we are back in our rooms for showers, a quick nap, and perhaps to reorganize our backpacks for the next day's hike.

For me, that often includes making a few notes in my journal. I always keep a journal when I go on a trip, because somehow the days seem to run together, and I want to have a record of each day's special memories.

Happy Hour is at 5:30. Most of us enjoy a glass of wine and some sort of salty snack or some cheese and cut–up veggies. While we munch and sip, we take turns telling the whole group what we've been up to since the last time we met. We might have shared these stories with our hiking partners, but the guides wouldn't get a chance to share them with the other guides, and the same with the VIP chicks.

Each person is to take only five minutes, but some of our women take such extravagant vacations or have such exciting adventures, and we ask so many questions, that before we know it, it's time for dinner. If we have a lot of high adventurers, it might take all week to get through all the stories. For instance, one of our gals guided one of our VIP chicks down the Grand Canyon and back up. At one time, I might have thought that would be such fun, but now, it makes me a little queasy just imagining it. Two of our visually impaired women have gone parasailing, and several of our guides have volunteered in third–world countries.

Most years, it has rained at least one morning, and that's when we have our "book club." Because we have so many of our own stories to tell, we don't discuss a certain book that we've all read, like most book clubs. What we do is take turns sharing the titles of three books we've especially enjoyed and would recommend. Again, I put a limit on the number of books we could each talk about, because as it happens, we are all avid readers, and we could go on for hours. If it hasn't rained all week, we might use the last evening's dinnertime to have the book club around the table, because nobody wants to leave it out of the week's fun.

One of us takes notes and then sends the list out to everyone a few days after we get home. It's my go-to reading list each year, and some of the women who couldn't make it one year ask me to forward them the book list. They also want me to send them my journal. Here are some excerpts to give you an idea of what the Hen Hike is all about.

> Putney Inn near Brattleboro, Vermont, 2002
> Dear friends,
>
> I just returned from one of the most healing vacations of my life. Before I left for Vermont, for the fourth annual Hen Hike, I was extremely stressed and tense. For about a month, I had been rushing through my day's work, then dashing around in the evenings, trying to get everything done in time—all the arrangements made, all the loose ends tied up, and the errands run—and I was exhausted. But ahead of me was the promise of clean mountain air, brilliant October sunshine, and the love and friendship of 11 other women. That promise was kept and surpassed.
>
> The Putney Inn, where we stayed, is in Putney, a tiny Vermont town about 10 miles from Brattleboro. It is not a particularly touristy town, but leaf peepers are everywhere at this time of year. The leaves didn't present much of a show this year, because of the drought, but on Thursday, the colors were striking against the background of snow.

On Monday, we hiked up Mount Wantastiquet, which is on the New Hampshire side of the Connecticut River at about 1200 feet, and had lunch on a rock overlooking the valley, where you could see the rolling hills and treetops and the Connecticut River glinting in the sun. After lunch, we descended to the valley and walked along the river road to add another two miles for those of us who wanted to really stretch out and get in some miles. Climbing the mountain was tedious, as there were many rocks and roots to negotiate, but we all enjoyed the challenge.

That evening, we met in Bjorg and Julie's room for our wine and snacks to celebrate our day, as we did every day. Dinner each day was a spectacular event, everything from winter squash soup to maple mousse, with exquisitely prepared vegetables, seafood, breads, and pastas in between. After dinner each night, we would waddle into the lounge, where we would play games like Taboo and Scattergories. Bedtime was about 9:30. Believe me, we were all ready.

On Tuesday, we climbed up the 350 or so wooden steps that scale the highest natural ski jump in the Western Hemisphere. It was fun to experience the steepness of the hillside that is used as a ski jump. On this hike, after the steps adventure, we wound our way through some woods. Two of our group, Linda and Susan, somehow lost the rest of us, so we had to send out two scouts to find them. While we waited, we found a golden pool of sunshine and entertained ourselves by singing rounds—you know, like "Tell Me

Why," "On My Garden Wall," and "Make New Friends," all the old Girl Scout favorites. What a pretty sound we made in two- and three-part harmony. Only in a group of women would you do that and not feel silly. After lunch on a log, we walked through a golf course and some wooded lands and wound up at Sandi P.'s house in Brattleboro. Then we walked through the town, appreciating the old houses along the way, back to where our cars were parked at the ski jump.

On Wednesday, it was rainy and snowing, so in the morning, we gathered in Carolee's room for our annual book club and exchange. We all brought books or tapes we were willing to share and also our writing equipment to write down book titles we each recommended. It took a good hour and a half, but we all came home with "must read" lists.

We walked into town and decided to walk through the campus of Landmark College, a school for students with dyslexia. (That's what they called it in those days.) A young woman happened to be coming out of the Physical Education building and asked about our group. Being an observant person, she could see that half of us were blind. She was fascinated with the idea of a Hen Hike. She told us that she teaches there, a course called Aesthetic Experience, and was delighted to show us around, particularly the gym, where she proudly showed us the climbing wall. We weren't allowed to climb on it, but it was very interesting to learn all about it, as many of us had never seen one before. She said she was on her way out to get some lunch, but this was "way more fun" than lunch, so she spent about an hour with us. She was very eager to learn about Ski for Light, and she seemed genuinely interested in becoming a guide.

On Thursday, Debbie, a friend of Sandi's, led the hike. To get to the trailhead, we drove up an old dirt road, high up into the foothills of the Green Mountains. We set out on a trail dedicated to the life of a young man named Jamie Latham, who was a dear friend of Debbie's family. He had died in a boating accident at age 23. The trail took us to the highest point in the county, an absolutely gorgeous path through the woods, where the sound of a vehicle was never heard. At the top, we found ourselves at a newly renovated lean-to, built by the loving hands of volunteers in memory of Jamie, and we had our lunch on the wooden steps, soaking up that glorious sun. With our faces tilted upward toward the warmth, Carol recited a beautiful poem about Indian summer, and again I was keenly aware of the gift of female companionship.

Reluctantly, we tore ourselves away from this beautiful spot and started the descent, which curiously included more ups than downs, I'm sure of it. At last, we reached an old dirt road that eventually led us back to civilization. On this day, it took us so long to get back to our cars that we missed our beloved cocktail hour, but it was worth every step. It was a poem of a day.

Twice this week, we were approached by curious observers (one was a newspaper reporter and the other a member of a Lions Club) wanting to know more about our "program." I bristled at our holiday together being called a program. It is not a program. I feel so strongly about that that I was glad that Julie stepped up and answered their questions, much more tactfully than I would have. I guess people just can't imagine that 12 women can go hiking together, play games together, eat together, laugh and sing together, with half of them being blind, without its being a program. It's unfortunate that we can't invite all our friends to join us—but then, if we did, it would become a program.

Hilltop Acres, Jewett, New York, 2010
Monday

Walked five miles today, mostly on easy trails, but there were places where we had to step down such steep embankments that we had to sit on a rock and then scoot down. One of our guides, Joanne, who had hip surgery two years ago, had a great fear of falling, so she had a lot of problems with these down–stepping challenges. Bjorg was my morning partner, so she would give me a hand down, then help Joanne, and then help Joanne's partner.

We had lunch at a picnic area at the site of where a huge hotel once stood back in the 1800s. We've visited this site twice before, but it's always awesome to look over the escarpment and see the Hudson River 1600 feet straight down. It was a clear day, so Bjorg could see way over to the Green Mountains. Lunch was very pleasant, sitting in the sunshine.

I had to stand for a while and let my hiking pants dry in the sun, as I had sat down on a rock by accident, just losing my balance a little, but there was a puddle on the rock. But if I don't come home wet and dirty, how will I know I had a good time? The pants were dry by the time we started back. Instead of climbing back up that hill with those steep inclines, we walked on the road, which was much easier.

Hancock Inn, Massachusetts, 2003

This was the year that Bjorg taught us the word "escarpment." Bjorg was an avid hiker as well as a skier, having been born in Norway. If you can imagine a New York accent with a Norwegian lilt to her speech, that was Bjorg. She was always pointing out different species of moss or harmless snakes. I didn't care much about learning about moss or snakes, but I loved learning new words. Those of us who are city dwellers had never had the opportunity to ever hear or use the word escarpment, let alone see one or have lunch near the edge, but not so close that it was dangerous. The guides described the view, which was breathtaking. They could see for miles, and straight below us was a river, the name of which I've forgotten, but I remember that there was a little house way down there as well.

Today's hike was about six miles of a mixture of fairly easy walking on flat rocks, some pretty steep declines, some very steep declines that might have been easier to just sit down and slide down, but we side–stepped (like in skiing) and tried to avoid the big puddles in the middle of the trails. I still smile when I remember how Carolee, who had a wonderfully dry sense of humor, would say, "Let's take the old lady trail," which meant stepping off to the side of the trail and walking through the weeds.

We picked our way across little streams by stepping from one rock to another. The trails were pretty wet, because there has been a lot of rain, and since the Catskills are not true mountains, as I learned yesterday, but piles of rock and sediment, the drainage isn't very good.

We had lunch on an arrangement of rocks overlooking a drop–off, and the sun was out for most of that time. The rest of the day, it was mostly overcast and a little cooler, with highs in the low 50s but with no wind.

It was supposed to be a horse trail, but I think it would be rather difficult for a horse to navigate some of the narrow spots and that one very steep slope that was at about a 45–degree angle.

The last mile was on the road, which was a relief from negotiating the rocks and roots and hills, but it's hard on the feet walking in hiking boots on pavement. I was one tired puppy at the end. Mary N. had accidentally left her hiking stick about a mile from the start of the trail. She and Bjorg ran back to look for it, but it was gone.

One point of interest was a structure built so that people with disabilities could mount a horse. Ironically, it was a mile from the road. I don't know how they expected a wheelchair to get to that point. Probably another good intention with not much thought.

At breakfast this morning, I mentioned a possible hiking trip in the Grand Canyon, and my tablemates thought it would be doable with a lot of advance planning. I walked with Mary N. this morning, and we had a good, intimate talk about dealing with some very personal things I'm struggling with. She has life coach training, so it was like a therapy session as we walked. This afternoon, I walked with Bjorg.

There was no time for even a short lie–down, as we didn't get back until after 5:00. After a quick shower, I checked my work messages, and there were five to return, which I did immediately after dinner. Dinner was a salad, then eggplant parmesan and pierogies that were heavy but delicious, and then apple pie for dessert.

Wednesday

Another gorgeous fall day. The sun peeked in and out, but there was very little wind, and the trail was not too technical, just up and up forever. We had to negotiate some pretty serious puddles, and we got a good workout climbing for about three miles, but we never found the pond that the map promised. We were planning to have lunch there, but when it got to be after 1:00 and there was still no pond, we found some rocks and a log and had our lunch.

Carole recited two poems about fall, one being the

famous one by Robert Frost about the road not taken. She has such a talent for remembering just the right poems for the right moment. It brought tears to my eyes, because we were in a quiet spot in the woods, surrounded by trees that looked like someone had come along and dabbed gold, yellow, red, and orange paint all around. It was one of those priceless moments.

The day's highlight, though, was meeting a couple on horseback as we began the trail. They were riding two Paso Fino horses, which are very rare. They do not trot. They are a walking horse, and they can walk very fast, but they don't trot or gallop. I was intrigued. I might be able to ride such a horse. What was so fascinating was that the man and woman were eager to educate us about their horses, because they raise them and sell them. They had pieces of carrots at the ready to offer for us to feed their horses, which several of us eagerly did. The horse that I fed was so dear. She was the friendliest horse I have ever seen. She nuzzled my arm and licked my hand after I had given her the piece of carrot. It was just like in the movie I had watched with my granddaughters a few weeks ago.

After lunch and the beautiful poems, the walk back down the hill was considerably easier and took far less time, except that we got separated into two groups. Betty and I and Mary K. and Sandy M. got way ahead of everybody else, and we waited awhile, but then we thought maybe they had stopped to rest farther up the hill, so we finally continued. I had walked up the hill with Sandy M. and down with Betty. Betty and I did a lot of reminiscing about past Ski for Lights, and we did a little sharing of religious beliefs and thoughts about faith.

When we finally got to Sandy's car, we waited another fifteen minutes or so after the next pair showed up and told us that the rest were on their way. Joanne had fallen twice, but she was okay. After having had a hip replacement, she was very worried about falling. If nothing else, she has learned on this trip that she can still fall and not be injured. She had a couple of scrapes, but she'll be all right.

Halina, the innkeeper and cook (who was from Poland), came to our table after dessert and asked us about our cause of blindness. She is so amazed at how happy we are. She had expected us to be sad and bitter. Those of us who have lived with blindness could be annoyed at such ignorance, because when you think about it, why would we all be on a vacation together if we were miserable? Then we explained that we had been living with blindness for many years and that it isn't something we think of as a tragedy. We have such wonderful sighted friends in the Hen Hike who also know that it isn't a tragedy. They help us without making us feel like we are a burden or a bother. What amazes me is how lucky I am to have found such a unique group of sighted women friends.

Wayside Inn in Bethlehem, New Hampshire, 2013

This was the first time my friend Eve came with me, and it

was so much easier to have someone to travel with, to say nothing of being more fun. The Wayside Inn had two parts, a bed and breakfast building and a row of rooms across the parking lot that lined a little rushing river. It was slightly inconvenient to have to walk across the parking lot to our meals, but having the river to listen to right outside our back door made up for it. Here are a few snippets of that year's journal.

Expression of the day: "Just powder your pits and go on," said Sue, in her English accent, when somebody mentioned that they were getting sweaty as we climbed Mt. Willard. It was a three–mile round trip, but after an hour of climbing, and after some guy who was coming down said we weren't quite halfway up, yet, we rested for a while and then decided to turn around and go back down. No use in climbing another hour with nothing to experience up there, only to have to come back down. The thing is, it was much more difficult to descend than to climb, or so we thought. It turned out not to be that bad, and we sort of wished we had gone the rest of the way, but I had no regrets.

After we had our lunch outside the visitors' center, we walked the trail around the lake, about a mile, plus a side trail up to a lookout, which meant more climbing and descending and stepping from one wobbly rock to another to cross several little streams. I had to tease Eve about this being her first Hen Hike, when, on the first day, she and Lil fell into a stream and actually sat down in the water. Eve regained her confidence as she got first Mary K. this morning and then me, this afternoon, over those streams without anybody getting wet. I almost fell backward one time, but she yanked on me to keep me from it. We met a Bassett Hound this morning at the inn and two dogs on the trail.

Bjorg pointed out a larch tree, which is like an evergreen or a pine, but the leaves turn yellow, are very soft, and then fall off, like deciduous trees. Eve showed me a log that had fungus on it, which she thought was pretty.

The lake was so still and clear that the trees reflected in them looked more beautiful in the water than in the air. When we hiked to the lookout this afternoon, what we saw was Mt. Washington nearby, and it appeared to have snow on top.

After dinner, we adjourned to the parlor and just talked for a while. On the way from the airport, we got on the subject of reminiscing about when it was that we had our favorite sandwich. Eve and I talked about the hamburger we had on our first Tuscon ride. That prompted us to ask the group, and it was interesting to note that every single person's story had to do with an athletic event: a bike ride, a ski event, or a hiking trip.

We drove to a park in town called Bretzfelder Memorial. The trails were gently up and down, and there were plenty of rocks and roots, but nothing as rugged as yesterday's trail. There were streams to cross, but they all had little bridges. One reminded me of the bridge on my blue willow plates, curved up and over the stream. There were several trails to choose from. One had descriptions of different kinds of wildlife, like salamanders and tadpoles, and another had descriptions of 11 different kinds of trees.

We now know that a sugar maple has U-shaped cutouts in the leaves, while the red maples have V-shaped ones. We learned the difference between lichen and moss and which one was symbiotic, the lichen, and which one fed itself, moss. I was invited to touch the moss, but I declined. I've seen moss before.

We also got to see where beavers had chewed off bark and where they had actually chewed the trunk of a tree until it fell over, so they could build their lodge. We learned that beavers have a transparent eyelid, and that they can close their mouths and still chew something under water. They're pretty amazing creatures.

In fact, as we took these science lessons, we were in awe at how nature is so amazing. I mean, we've all heard this stuff before, but seeing it in real life as grownups is a much more meaningful experience. Since we were in the midst of learning about trees and enjoying the fallen leaves, I asked Carol to recite "A Vagabond Song," by Bliss Carmen.

We drove back to the inn and had our sack lunches over in the main part of the inn. Cathy, the innkeeper, graciously made pots of tea for us. Bjorg had brought Dove chocolates for all of us, and we enjoyed reading the little sayings on the insides of the wrappers. We made a plan for the afternoon, returned to our rooms to freshen up, and drove off again. We went to Rock's Estate, a Christmas tree farm, and walked maybe about two miles altogether.

Some of the trees had been claimed and tagged, and some had even been decorated. There were crumbled old foundations of buildings long gone and the frame of an old playhouse, built for the children of the family that lived there in 1820. It was about the size of my living room, certainly bigger than most modern day playhouses.

We got to see and actually climb up on a stile, something I had read about but had never seen before in real life. Three or four steps led up to a platform that crossed a stone wall, and then there were steps going down on the other side. (This is what I meant when I said we literally walked through history.)

They also had snowmen built out of short sections of logs stacked on end on top of each other, complete with fleece hats and scarves.

At the top of a hill, we were delighted to find a raised line drawing on a concrete block. It depicted the view of the mountains you could see in the distance, Washington, Jefferson, Monroe, Madison, and many others. It was as if somebody had made that drawing for us. Some of the mountains were shrouded in clouds today, as it was a cloudy day and even rained on us this morning a little, but we all had rain gear.

The walking today was easy, but still very pleasant. We met a wonderfully joyful Black Lab named Nellie, who wore a cowbell and was super happy to see us. Her mom said they walk through this tree farm often. Nellie thinks she owns the place.

On one of our first hikes, we discovered that most recreational hikers and their dogs on trails are pleasant people who don't mind stopping to chat. Naturally the dog–lovers in our group always had to stop and pet the dogs on the trails, but of course, we always asked permission if the dogs had not come up to us first. "Oh, here are more people to talk to," the dogs seemed to say.

One Golden Retriever tugged at my heartstrings because he was carrying in his mouth a stick that was about five feet long. His human companion, a friendly older gentleman, told us proudly, "We walk this trail every day, and every day he picks up that stick and carries it the whole way, like it's his job." We didn't hike that same trail again, so we never got to see him again, but we saw plenty of other dogs as they happily accompanied their people.

We find that hikers are not only friendly and helpful, but they also usually have a great sense of humor. One man, on seeing a line of twelve women walking toward him on the trail, said, "Oh, boy, there goes my nice, peaceful walk." But he was smiling as we passed by, and we had our nice, peaceful walk, too.

As I mentioned in my funny little poem, we often stop by an especially peaceful spot, usually a quiet stream or deep in a forest, where all we can hear is the distant call of a bird or the soft landing of a leaf. Once we get everybody to stop yakking and realize that we are in the perfect spot for five minutes of silence, it can be the most refreshing part of the day.

A recent newspaper story I read talked about "forest bathing," and I believe they could have been thinking of the Hen Hike when they dreamed up that phrase. At the end of one of our Hen Hike weeks, one of my Hen friends said to me, "Mary, you look so relaxed. Last Sunday, your face was pinched and you looked unhappy, and now you look so refreshed." That's exactly how I felt. And this is the reason the Hen Hike is more than a vacation from the stresses of work and life in general. It's a retreat, where the biggest decision I have to make is whether or not to have dessert. Female companionship, especially with physically and mentally active women, is the best antidote for almost any troubles you might have. In other words, as my grandmother would say, "It's good for what ails you." It certainly is for me.

Chapter Seven
Public Speaking, Another Passion

It's been said that most people would rather have a root canal than stand up and speak before an audience. Not true for me or for thousands of Toastmasters around the world.

I hinted earlier in this book that although I could never dance on stage again, I would find other ways to perform. In my 30s and 40s, I sang and danced with a group called The Singing Moms, later known as The Entertainers, but when it was time for me to move on to another stage in life, pun intended, I discovered Toastmasters International quite by accident.

I was hosting a Mary Kay party, and one of the ladies I had invited, who happens to be blind, said that she'd had a busy day that day because earlier she had competed in a Toastmasters contest. We asked her what her speech was about, and then we insisted on hearing it, right then and there. "Speech! Speech!" we all sang out.

With her new face on, she stood up and delivered her speech as if we were a crowd of thousands. She presented it well, but all the time I was listening, I was also thinking, *I could do that. I want to do that.* Here would be a way to be on stage again: to entertain, to educate, to give my audience something to think about, and to feed the ham in me.

Joining a Toastmasters Club

I looked for a Toastmasters Club in my area, but there were none. The only solution I could think of was to start one myself. After all, I was used to starting groups: The Hen Hike, The Red Hat Society, La Leche League, and even 4–H, all in Gahanna, where I lived. Why not a Toastmasters club? How hard could it be?

I put an ad in the local paper, asking for anyone interested in a Gahanna Toastmasters Club to call me. The first call was from a man named Alan Meisterman, who offered to help me get the club started. He was already a member of a Toastmasters Club, but he offered to coach me and to organize a demonstration meeting at the Gahanna library.

I remember thinking that his offer was kind, but did I really need his help? I accepted, and was I ever glad I did. There is much more to a Toastmasters Club meeting than people taking turns getting up and saying whatever is on their minds.

Meanwhile, I visited a club in a nearby suburb of Columbus and was intrigued. It wasn't anything like what I'd expected. It was much more formal and scripted than I had imagined. Each person in the club had a role to perform as the agenda for the evening unfolded.

The Roles in a Typical Toastmasters Meeting

The pivotal role is that of "Toastmaster" for the evening. (Note: From here on, when I refer to the role "Toastmaster," I will use the quotation marks to differentiate it from a member of the Toastmasters Club.) The "Toastmaster," or the MC, not only introduces other speakers, but he or she is also expected to tell short stories or add some information between speakers to make a smooth segue between speakers. He or she may set the agenda in any order he or she wishes.

When I was the "Toastmaster" in our club, I would often introduce the Jokesmith first, because laughing helps to get everybody relaxed. Even though we love speaking, we can still be a little nervous.

In our club, the next speaker usually gave the Thought for the Day or the Inspirational Moment, which could be a poem or a spiritual story that was only a couple of minutes long. I suppose in some clubs, it could be a prayer: "Dear God, please don't let me make a fool of myself." Just kidding.

The next speaker, who could realistically fit well as the first speaker, gives the Word for the Day. In the role of Wordsmith, the speaker presents a word that each subsequent speaker should try to use while they have the floor. It should be a word that is not in everyday use, but also should not be so obscure that it's hard to think of a way to use it. The point is to strengthen our vocabularies.

In our club, we then launched into the meat of the meeting, the speeches that the members composed, using manuals that suggested various skills to concentrate on with each speech. For example, the first speech that a new member gives is called The Ice Breaker. This speech should be the easiest and the best one to start with because the speaker gives a four- to six-minute talk about himself or herself. I say easy, because most people like to tell about themselves, but the challenge is not to ramble. It's an opportunity to have the experience of standing up in front of an audience and talking for at least four minutes and no more than six. This time limit is one of the most important lessons we learn as Toastmasters. It has served me well many times when I've been asked to give a presentation at other venues.

The next part of the meeting is devoted to extemporaneous speaking, with very short speeches called Table Topics. In other clubs I've visited, the Table Topics have appeared elsewhere in the agenda, but I like the way we did it because it gave the Evaluators some time to prepare their speeches for the last part of the meeting.

The last section of the meeting is devoted to giving evaluations of each speech, making suggestions for improvement, and most importantly, giving encouragement so that the speaker will enjoy the art of public speaking and will grow in his or her skills as a good communicator.

Overcoming Stumbling Blocks

Early on as a Toastmaster, I could see some obstacles for a person who is blind. But these obstacles had to become merely challenges if I were to succeed at this new endeavor. For instance, it is extremely important to make eye contact with members of the audience, something I hadn't been able to do since I was very young. I had to learn how to make it appear that my eyes were focused on a particular spot, and consequently I became pretty good at faking the eye contact. I think it helped that I could see for real when I was young. Learning to turn my head, and sometimes my whole body, without looking like an oscillating fan is an art described in one of our Toastmaster manuals. I became pretty proficient at it, despite not being able to see a thing when I looked straight at it.

You have to approach the lectern with confidence, shake hands with the "Toastmaster," and after your speech return to your seat with poise and dignity. If the room is set up with tables and chairs in a "U" shape, with a table lectern placed at the bottom of the "U," a blind person would have very little difficulty navigating to and from the lectern. But our meetings were held in a very large room, with chairs arranged theater–style and the lectern placed out in front. I was constantly working on a better method of making my way to and from the lectern independently.

If I tried to use my guide dog, she would instinctively go around the lectern instead of taking me to it. And then there was the probability that she would upstage me with her cuteness. If I tried to use my white cane, I had the dilemma of what to do with it once I got there.

Sometimes I would just ask for someone to take me to the lectern, using the sighted guide technique, which was just as awkward as the other two methods and made me feel even more conspicuous. To make matters worse, the audience would be distracted by watching me move to the lectern and forget that Toastmaster etiquette calls for applauding each time a Toastmaster approaches the lectern or returns to her seat. That silence always infuriated me, and sometimes, when I'd had a hard day and wasn't in the mood to ignore such rudeness, I'd say, "You're supposed to clap"—although I tried to smile when I said it. It wasn't exactly an endearing way to open my speech, but I wasn't necessarily the model blind person who always keeps her cool.

Another pitfall for me was when a new "Toastmaster" would forget that he or she was not to leave the lectern until after shaking hands with the next speaker. So, when I did reach the lectern, I'd sometimes stick out my hand to shake, and there would be no one there. Fortunately, I never scolded the new, neglectful "Toastmaster" like I did with the rude audience, but I always found a way to point it out when it happened when I was the General Evaluator. This role entails remarking on the positive skills demonstrated by each speaker and the points that need improvement.

You can use notes, although you should never read your speech. Glancing at notes is perfectly acceptable, but surreptitiously glancing at my notes was not a possibility for me, so I memorized most of my speeches. If I had a lot of material to cover that included facts, I'd braille just a few words of each sentence and rely on my memory to finish the thought. This worked well for speeches given at our club meetings, but for contests, I always memorized.

My method was a little out of the norm, but it worked for me. I would start with memorizing the last paragraph and memorize to the end. When I felt I had that down pat, I'd back up and start one paragraph earlier and memorize to the end. Paragraph by paragraph, I worked my way up to the beginning, and by that time, the rest of the speech had been practiced so much that it was like running down a slide. Sure, there were times when my mind went completely blank, but that didn't happen until late in my Toastmasters career, which is part of the reason I moved on to other endeavors.

However, when I gave speeches for other organizations, I used either braille notes or a very old piece of technology called the Braille and Speak. Using earbuds, I could listen to abbreviated notes much the same as I did with the braille notes, half listening and half using my memorized thoughts. The trouble with using technology, whether very old or brand new, is the possibility of a technical error, so I pray that my good old Braille and Speak lasts as long as I do.

You may use PowerPoint technology or physical props. I never mastered or even tried to master PowerPoint, so for one speech I gave that would have been enhanced by a PowerPoint presentation, I simply used handouts, which worked just fine. After all, isn't that what presenters used for decades? For one speech, I used the old–fashioned flip chart and enlisted the help of a fellow Toastmaster to write on each page. I jokingly called her my Vanna White, as in *Wheel of Fortune.*

I never used props, except for the speech in which I tried to teach my audience how to use the word "me." I had made large diagrams on poster boards, illustrating how the word "I" should never be used as the object of a sentence or a prepositional phrase. I probably bored most of them to tears, but it happens to be a grammatical error that I'm passionate about. And speaking of grammar, one of the roles for each meeting is Grammarian. I loved being the Grammarian, because grammar was my favorite subject in school, but they always groaned when it was announced that I would be the Grammarian for the evening.

You should not cling to the lectern for dear life but move around the performing area and use gestures to keep your audience's attention. I hadn't been able to see facial expressions or gestures in many years, so I had to learn how to gesture effectively. I'll never forget my icebreaker speech. I stood behind the lectern and held onto it with both hands, partly to have something to do with my hands and partly to keep from swaying, which is a bad habit new speakers have without realizing it. My Evaluator was extremely kind. He said that eventually I would feel comfortable enough to let go of the lectern and even move around a little. It was much better than saying, "You looked like you were scared stiff."

As I developed as a pretty good speaker and started entering contests, I knew I had to come up with some way of moving around the lectern without losing my position in relationship to the audience. I didn't want to wind up trying to make eye contact with the back wall. I said I never used props, but that's not exactly true. Whenever I competed, I brought with me a small throw rug that I placed directly in front of the lectern. Then I would begin my speech standing on the rug, which I could feel through my shoes. I would step to the right or the left, making one point to one side of the audience and then the next point to the other side, and then some points squarely in the middle of the rug. I always kept contact with that rug, either with one foot or the other, and just to make sure I was in the center, I'd ever so casually touch the lectern, just to make sure it was still where it was supposed to be. I choreographed my movements to go with certain phrases, and I'm pleased to say I never got lost on the stage.

Speaking of contests, I don't want to brag, but I did win several on the club level and the next three levels, the area, the division, and the district, which is the last stop before you compete on the international level. I never made it that far. Twice, I competed on the district level, winning third place with a speech about the Hen Hike, and second place with a motivational speech about pursuing your passions. Both times I did well, and my Toastmaster friends claimed I'd been robbed. Sure, it would have been nice to make it to first place, but just getting up the nerve to compete and then to place was a victory for me. Unlike my sighted competitors, I had to orchestrate how I was going to get on and off the stage and how I was going to keep from getting too close to the edge of the stage, besides planning how to charm my audience and the judges.

For me, part of the fun in becoming a Toastmaster was overcoming these obstacles and eventually becoming a successful public speaker.

Beyond Toastmasters

When I said "becoming a successful speaker," I didn't mean to say that I was successful financially. I have never been paid for speaking, but I've been fed well at lunches and dinners at various clubs and organization. When I say "successful," I mean that my speeches have been well received and I've had fun performing them.

I spend a lot of time preparing and practicing, and I try to learn from mistakes. For instance, when it became risky for me to perform a speech completely from memory, I began to use notes. I realized that as long as I kept the speech moving along and maintained the rapt attention of my audience, it was successful, even without the impressive talent of being able to perform without notes.

I felt my speech was successful when members of the audience came up to me afterwards with praise and compliments. Sometimes a person wanted to tell me about his or her experience, whether or not it was relevant to my presentation, but I listened and tried to be interested and agreeable. That way, they left feeling good about themselves and about what they had heard that day.

The best compliment I ever received came from the father of a middle–school student. I had just given a keynote speech to a group of honors students and their parents. He came up to me and said, "You know, I've been to many of these events, and this is the best speech I have ever heard." That was better than pay, as far as I was concerned.

I have spoken on behalf of the radio reading service in Columbus on numerous occasions, including before the House and Senate Financial Committees for the State of Ohio, in addition to many Lions Clubs, Kiwanis, Sertoma, and Rotary clubs. Each time, I felt I had done well because I had practiced the heck out of that speech. I would go back to one of the recording studios where the phone couldn't reach me and nobody knew where I was and practice until I was satisfied.

Whenever I'm selling the idea of joining a Toastmasters Club, I remind my audience, whether it's a group or a friend, that there are many times in life when your job or your position in an organization requires you to be a good speaker. In addition, the other skills taught in Toastmasters enhance the success of your presentation.

When I was the Director of Volunteers for the radio reading service, I hosted a volunteer recognition party each spring, and I basked in the role of the master of ceremonies, the equivalent of a "Toastmaster." I introduced guest speakers, such as the president of the board of trustees, and said something nice and/or funny as I called each of the hundred or so volunteers up to receive a token gift. I was on a high for the whole evening, and it took me hours to come down, because judging by the compliments at the end, I knew I had done well.

I belong to an organization for women over 50 called The Transition Network, and I'm often called upon to speak in front of the group. Because of my Toastmasters training, I'm never nervous, and I always have a good time. I feel sorry for the person who hates having to stand up and speak in front of people. They're missing out on a way to build their self-confidence, as well as a way to sharpen their skills in organization and time management and nurture a relationship with other members of the group.

When I was promoting my first book, *The Bumpy Road to Assisted Living: A Daughter's Memoir*, I did book signings and readings for church groups, seniors' clubs, and women's organizations. I felt that I held their attention by using many of the skills I had practiced at Toastmasters meetings. I opened with an attention-getting question. I used humor and vocal variety, two essential components of a good speech. I kept on topic, because I used notes. And I made sure I kept within the time limits given to me by the organizer. I solved the obstacle of not being able to read parts of my book, as you do at book signings, by asking friends who were good readers to read certain parts for me. Now there's real vocal variety.

A few years ago, I was asked to be the banquet speaker for the national conference and convention of the American Council of the Blind. That was to be on the last day of the event. I had to send in the title and topic of my speech only about 48 hours before the banquet. Because of the immediate deadline, it was obvious that I had not been their first choice and they were getting desperate, but I didn't care. I was thrilled to be asked. I had always wanted to be an after–dinner speaker, and here was my debut.

It was a perfect venue, because I would be among friends. I'd been a member of ACB for about 25 years, and for five years, I was the executive director of the Ohio affiliate. Although this would not be a paying gig, I was excited and eager to perform for my ACB friends. To be the banquet speaker was a big deal, and I wanted my talk to be funny and somewhat motivational, but mostly entertaining.

It took me about five minutes to decide on my topic. I'd do the Hen Hike speech, complete with all the parts I'd had to cut for contests that had a limit of seven minutes. Luckily, I had kept those cut–out parts, because another lesson I had learned in Toastmasters was to always have a speech in your back pocket. This was the kick in the pants I'd needed to put together an entertaining after–dinner speech.

Two days before the big night, I sat down with the speech and rearranged paragraphs and put back in the parts that wouldn't fit before. It was going to be a challenge. I needed to revise and memorize a speech I had written nine years earlier. But since I had given that winning speech on pursuing your passion and finding a way to make it happen, I had inspired myself to pursue my own passion of public speaking. And now here was my golden opportunity. It had fallen into my lap. I could have brushed it off, claiming that there was too much stuff going on in my life, but I embraced the opportunity to stretch, to grow, to grab that mike and give it a go.

Because I had already been polishing and practicing, rewriting and reworking a speech about the Hen Hike for a speech contest, it made sense to use a longer version for this after–dinner speech. The uniqueness of the Hen Hike group is that half of us are blind, a perfect subject for the ACB banquet speech. How convenient. The endearing quality of the Hen Hike is that we know how to laugh, but more important, how to laugh at ourselves. My goal at the ACB banquet was not only to entertain, but also to inspire my audience to try new endeavors and to have fun while they were at it.

To my delight, my audience was eager and willing to hear my stories and to laugh in all the right places. In fact, they did such a good job of laughing that I often had to wait for the laughter to subside before I delivered the next line. I felt like a real comedian standing up there, and I was loving it. The more they laughed, the funnier I felt. I'm sure that part of my success was due to surprising them with humor. They were not expecting the former executive director of a state affiliate to talk about 12 women in their 50s and 60s harmonizing to Girl Scout songs or hiking to the nearest liquor store to replenish their supply of wine and cheese.

What really set me up for success, though, was that most of the people in my audience were blind. Blind people naturally communicate with each other verbally. A smile or a nod means nothing unless it is accompanied by something we can hear. When I speak to a sighted audience, there may be reactions of smiles and expressions of interest, but if I can't hear it, I might think I've bombed. This audience, however, let me know each and every time when something I said piqued their interest or tickled their funny bone. The feedback was fantastic. Fortunately, they liked what I said, so everybody was happy. The best part was that they knew it and I knew it, because they laughed out loud. What a compliment! When I got home and played back the tape I had made of myself, I reveled in the sound of laughter at my humorous speech. Laughter feels good, especially when you're the one telling the jokes. I was loving, absolutely loving, this "stage" of my life.

Chapter Eight
College, Job, and the Real World

What if "the butcher, the baker, the candlestick maker" were all the same person who just took a while to figure out who he wanted to be and what he wanted to do with himself?

When I enrolled at Ohio State University in 1963, I thought I was going to be a social worker. I had no burning desire to save the world or even make life better for people who needed food or a job or someone to solve their many problems. I was there because the courses required for a social work degree seemed to be more within my reach than any others. I liked people and I was a good listener, so I guessed it was as good as any career that wasn't what I truly wanted, which was to be a dancer on Broadway. To my surprise, I did enjoy certain courses, such as anthropology, psychology, and sociology. Now that I think about it, those were the only ones I thought were relevant and of any use to me. But the course work was the least of my nemeses.

Being a blind student in 1963–1968 could have made me even more uncomfortable than the average sighted student about having to get a college education, but in the end, it helped me meet the challenges and grow into a strong, independent, and tenacious adult. I guess my parents and my BSVI counselor were right after all.

When I was in the fifth grade, and I could no longer see the blackboard or read print with a magnifying glass, my mother started reading all my homework to me at night. She worked full time as a typist and also performed all the household duties of a typical wife of the 1950s, cooking, cleaning, and doing laundry, then reading homework every night to her visually impaired daughter. She even obtained permission to read my tests to me, writing down my answers whether they were right or wrong. Later, in high school, when I was required to write papers, she did the typing for me. I would do my best at typing on my own, but it was impossible for me to correct errors, so she would take my messy paper with all its X's over my mistakes and type a clean copy.

Today, children with a vision impairment are given sophisticated pieces of adaptive technology to get their work done, and they have specialized teachers to aid in their educational experience. Because my parents didn't know I was legally blind and could possibly have received such assistance, my mother took it all on herself. And because my teachers didn't know any better, they were quite willing to let me take my tests home, I suppose because my mother was scrupulously honest. Even when it pained her soul to write down the wrong answers, she did it.

My nextdoor neighbor and best friend, Lynda, and I did our high school homework together every afternoon. For literature class, she'd read me the story, and then we'd discuss it, which was good for both of us. Studying math together was also a give-and-take activity. I understood geometry better than she did, for some reason I'll never be able to explain, except that I loved the satisfaction of writing those three letters emphatically at the end of the proof, QED. But algebra was elusive to me, so she pulled me through that course in return. Lynda was not just a study buddy.

We walked to school every morning and to football games and other school functions together, which had to be a huge relief for my parents. If it were not for Lynda's persistence, I would have been left out of the social life of high school. I was not invited to parties, for instance, until Lynda reminded the hosts that I would like to come, too. I don't know if it was because of my low vision or if I just wasn't likable, but I suspect it was the former. There was nothing particularly unlikable about me except that I was smart, and everybody knows that boys at that time did not like smart girls. I was also quiet and a bit timid, despite my love of performing.

When I was declared legally blind at age 18, in the middle of my senior year in high school, my BSVI counselor introduced me to the wonders of talking books and arranged for me to have a home teacher to teach me how to read and write braille. That was about the extent of my preparation for college studies. Oh, yes, I was taught to use a white cane, but it would be several years before I would accept it and actually use it.

Acquiring textbooks for my college courses proved to be the most challenging of all the obstacles I would face. Often the professors would not release their syllabi until a couple of weeks before the start of the quarter, which meant, for me, that buying the books, sending them off to be recorded by an organization called Recording for the Blind, and then getting them back on tape might take half the quarter. I often brought my textbooks home for my mother to record, and then she would send the tapes back to me.

Because at that time there was nothing called an office for students with disabilities, I was on my own to find readers for my class assignments and student teachers to administer tests to me in a room that was separate from the rest of the class. Thanks to the digital age, today's students have none of these obstacles. Even better, they have their materials in accessible formats, so they don't have to run around trying to just get the reading done. They can do it themselves. Sometimes I think I was born 50 years too early, and sometimes I'm very thankful I was not. My college years were difficult, but I didn't have nearly the pressure and stress that young people face today.

The social part of being a college student had its ups and downs. For the first time, I was actually going out on dates. In high school, the boys were either intimidated by me or didn't know how to interact with a girl with poor vision, but at Ohio State, I dated more in the first quarter than I had in four years of high school.

As my mother and I unpacked my clothes and tried to find a place for all my belongings in my cramped dorm room, my dad went off to do his part. He bought me a season ticket for the football games. Even then, the highlight of college life was supposed to be attending the home games, and my dad wanted me to fit in, forgetting that I had no interest in football whatsoever. Still, I wanted to do what was expected of a college student, so I dressed up in my nicest suit and high heels (as we did in those days) and clomped down the sidewalk with the throngs of kids to the stadium. I was shown to my seat, smack between two old men. Not only could I not see the players or understand what they were doing, but I had no one to talk to. At half time, I walked alone back to the dorm. Okay, I had gone to a football game and had heard the band, but that was going above and beyond the call of duty of a daughter trying to please her dad. That was the last game I went to for many years. Twenty-five years later, I went to my second game with my husband because the alumni band was playing. My husband joked that I should try to go to a game every 25 years.

As I said, there was no such thing as a service for students with disabilities, so I was advised to see Professor Loetta Hunt in the College of Education. She taught courses for students who would be teachers of "exceptional children." Professor Hunt was the only person on campus who understood what visually impaired students needed, and I immediately liked and respected her. She said that the first thing I needed was a braille writer, a monstrously heavy piece of equipment that was the equivalent of a manual typewriter. She hauled one out of the storeroom and thumped it down on her desk. Then she quickly and efficiently taught me how to use it and armed me with some braille paper. She knew there was no way I could carry that thing across campus to my dorm, so she enlisted the help of a grad student named Ray, a charming young man who was happy to walk with me and carry the braille writer across campus to my dorm.

That was the beginning of a romance that lasted for over a year. Ray was the first blind person I had ever met, and it was that common bond that attracted me. But it wasn't enough to keep us together.

In my sophomore year, one Saturday night, I went to an opera by myself. While I was standing out in the lobby during one of the intermissions, a young man started a conversation with me. We ended up dating for several months.

Professor Hunt was responsible for another aspect of my personal life that was even more important than introducing me to that charming young man. It had to do with my grooming. Certainly, I was clean and well dressed, and I tried to make my hair look nice, but I had no idea that my eyebrows needed attention. My mother had taught me to practice good posture, to hold in my stomach, to use good grammar, not to chew my fingernails, and a dozen other habits that might make me unattractive, but somehow she missed the eyebrows. Professor Hunt made an appointment at her own beauty shop and walked me there and made sure I memorized the route. The next time I needed an eyebrow wax, she tested me as we walked, to make sure I would be able to get there on my own. Ever since then, I have gone to get my eyebrows done every three weeks, first to that beauty shop near campus, and then wherever life took me.

Dorm life was a mixed bag of memory-makers. For my freshman and sophomore years, I lived at Oxley Hall, the oldest women's residence hall on campus. It was also the smallest, so it was easy to get to know most of the young women who lived there. I had two roommates my freshman year and three during my sophomore year. In spite of the limited space, I liked all my roommates. I had always wished that I had sisters, and now I was reminded of the admonition, "Be careful what you wish for."

One day during the first quarter of my freshman year, one of my roommates came back from class wearing a very attractive red skirt.

"I like your skirt," I said.

"You should," she answered. "It's yours. I hope you don't mind that I borrowed it this morning."

I had no retort, but it must have bothered me, since I still remember it all these years later.

The other roommate, who was also much sweeter and funnier, got a package from her mom one day. We both sat on the floor while she ripped open the wrapping. Her mother was Hungarian and often sent her care packages with wonderful pastries and other foods that were favorites of her daughter. She always offered to share them with me, so when she discovered a jar of homemade jam, I asked her what she was going to use to put the jam on. We had no bread, and there was no bread in the box, so she calmly got two spoons from her dresser drawer and answered in a matter-of-fact tone, "A spoon."

Sharing a room with three roommates was much more problematic. Because I had to listen to all my textbooks and notes from class on an enormous tape recorder with headphones, it was a little hard—okay, really hard—to study while my roommates had a popcorn party one Friday night. They sang and danced to records without so much as a glance at how I packed up my reel-to-reel tape recorder and lugged it out of the room. The problem was, I had nowhere to take it where it might be quiet. I finally decided on the restroom down the hall, because there was a slightly comfortable chair in the shower room, and there wasn't a whole lot of activity right then. Ignoring the occasional flush, I soldiered on with my assignment, feeling very sorry for myself.

For taking notes in class, I used a portable reel-to-reel recorder with three-inch reels, which I would usually have to turn over in the middle of the lecture. One snowy morning, I was so busy concentrating on making sure I was on the sidewalk and not wandering off the path, since the snow covered up any

difference between the grass and the sidewalk, I didn't notice
that the full reel on the left side had completely unwound. As I
walked, I was dragging the tape like a loose thread on the hem
of my skirt. When I found a seat and prepared to wind the tape
onto the right–hand reel, I was devastated to discover that the
tape was a tangled mess, and it took me almost the whole hour
to straighten it out. So much for notes for that class.

My usual routine was to take the tape recorder back to my
room, listen to the tape, and make braille notes on the braille
writer that Professor Hunt had procured for me. Thus, I had
always heard the lecture twice—except for that day, when I had
missed almost the entire thing.

On the whole, I enjoyed dorm life. Even though I had no
sisters at home, I felt that the girls who lived at Oxley Hall were
like sisters. I had no desire to join a sorority, but we did observe
a few ceremonies that were somewhat like a sorority house, and
that was close enough for me.

Whenever one of the girls "got pinned," that is, when her
boyfriend gave her his fraternity pin, we'd all gather in the
lounge after hours, which was probably around 9:00, and turn
off the lights. A single candle was passed around the circle until
it came to the "lucky girl." Then she would blow out the candle,
and we'd all squeal with delight.

If the girl had received an engagement ring, the ring would
be attached to the candle with ribbon, and the girl would let it
pass by. The excitement grew as the ring made its way around
the circle for the second time until it reached its owner. She'd
blow out the candle, the lights would be turned on, and
everyone would laugh and cry and gather around her with
congratulations. I became engaged to Mike Hiland during my

sophomore year, so I had the thrill of being the center of attention in the ring ceremony.

This sort of intimate tradition could only happen in the smallest dorm on campus, so even though it was old and among the most remote of buildings but still considered on campus, my memories from living there are mostly good ones.

By the time I reached my junior year, I was finally granted a single room, which I had needed from the beginning. With all the equipment I needed for study— which included a huge reel-to-reel tape recorder, a smaller version of the same, a braille writer, a box of braille paper, and a record player for reading books from the library for pleasure, to say nothing of quiet and privacy so I could use all these devices—I needed a room just for me. Besides, the powers that make these decisions thought it best for me to have a single room, since I was now married, whatever that had to do with anything. My husband was in the submarine service and would be at sea for almost exactly the same time that I would be doing a quarter at school.

One evening, as I was setting my hair in big fat rollers for the night, one of the girls from down the hall knocked on my door frame. (My door was usually open when I wasn't studying.) She invited me to come to a room two doors down for some popcorn. At first I said I would be going to bed soon, so thanks, but I just wanted to get some sleep. She insisted, so I reluctantly followed her into another girl's room. Then about six girls all yelled, "Surprise!" It was a little bridal shower they were throwing in my honor. Because they were all "poor college students," the gifts were modest, such as dishtowels and a cutting board, but it was touching and sweet. They all knew it was really a surprise when I showed up in my nightgown with half my head covered in pink foam rollers. Somebody in this world might have the photo they took of me that night, opening my gifts.

In these days of smartphones and all sorts of communication gadgets, it's fun to reminisce about the single telephone booth on each of the three floors of Oxley Hall.

The receptionist at the front desk would call that phone, and whoever heard it ring would run and answer it, hoping the call would be for her. Then if it wasn't, she'd open the door to the phone booth and yell out the name of the girl for whom the phone had rung. If she didn't respond, the girl would either try to find her or just tell the guy to call back later.

In my junior year, we had phones in our rooms, but they were only instruments for paging the girls who lived in that room. If the phone rang in my room, I would answer and be told which line my call was on. Then I'd run down to the hall phone to talk to my caller. If that phone was in use, I'd have to run to another floor to find a phone that was not in use. Phone calls in those days were reserved for matters of importance, like an invitation to go out or to make plans for a study date. We didn't run all over the place just to say, "Hey, wassup?"

Sunday afternoons were the only time a male visitor could come behind those closed doors to the dorm corridors. And if a male friend was invited to come into a girl's room, the door had to be at least ajar. The time limit was two hours on Sunday afternoons only. At all other times, we could run around in our slips, nightgowns, or bathrobes. If we didn't have a bathrobe handy, we would just pull our half slip up over our bustline for some modicum of modesty, but on Sunday afternoons, we had to be fully dressed or stay in our rooms if we didn't have male company.

Men were allowed to visit in the living room area any time, but they had to leave by certain times on weeknights and a little later on weekends. And we all had a curfew according to our status. Freshmen had to be in by 11:00 on Friday nights and midnight on Saturdays. Seniors were allowed out until 2:00 a.m., but only a certain number of times per quarter. We had to sign in and out each time we left the dorm at night. Nobody minded. That was just the way it was. I'm sure our parents were very pleased with those rules.

On Sunday nights, I would call home to touch base with my parents. There was one pay phone at the bottom of the steps in the basement. It cost a quarter to make a phone call and many quarters to make a long-distance call. So I'd call my house, let it ring three times, and hang up. Then my mother would call me back immediately on that number. Most people used a similar system to avoid paying long-distance charges. And long-distance calls only lasted three minutes, because after that, the rate would go up. I guess we were lucky we didn't have to crank the phone and talk to the operator as they did in the TV show *Lassie*.

For the first two years of college, my life as a visually impaired student wasn't as noteworthy as I had feared it would be, but my luck would eventually run out.

It was while I was carrying my dinner tray through a crowded dining room that my vision impairment could no longer be ignored. I was not using a white cane, nor was I being guided by a sighted friend. I thought I saw a spot just past some girls sitting near the end of a table. I turned sideways to squeeze through, but I didn't quite make it and slammed the edge of my tray into the side of the head of the girl sitting nearest to me. I was mortified. She was only mildly irritated, considering that it must have been painful. I apologized profusely, but it caused me to face reality. From then on, I asked for help.

Marriage

It was Christmas night of 1964 when my quiet evening with my parents was interrupted by the ringing of the doorbell.

"Who on earth?" I said, a little annoyed and a little hopeful that it was a Santa delivering a present he'd forgotten the night before.

In a way, that's what it was. My friend Lynda and her friend Carol from college, with Carol's older brother, Mike, in tow, had come to see if I wanted to go to a movie.

"No, thanks," I said. "It's Christmas night. I just want to stay home." What I meant was that I thought my parents would disapprove of my running off to go see a movie on Christmas night.

So they came up with a Plan B. The purpose of this invitation, I learned later, was to make an opportunity for me to get to know Mike, who Carol and Lynda thought would be a perfect match for me. The only thing we had in common was that we were both short, but I guess that was good enough for a perfect match.

The next evening, Lynda hosted a basement party, with Cokes and chips and records to dance to—and also a mother who made an appearance periodically throughout the evening. These basement parties were a popular form of entertainment in the early '60s. Couples danced, girls gossiped, and at least one couple made out under the stairway.

The match–making worked, because Mike and I went out every night for the next week, until he had to report back to the Navy for duty and I had to go back to school for winter quarter. Whenever possible, which meant once every three months, Mike drove from Charleston, South Carolina, a 15–hour drive back then, to see me on Saturday, before heading back on Sunday. A lot of our time was spent "watching the submarine races" by the Olentangy River. This popular sport among college couples kept the campus police busy shining their spotlights into the startled faces of amorous "spectators."

By December 18, 1965, Mike Hiland and I were married. But he was still in the submarine service, so for three months at a time, he would be at sea—or under the sea, I should say. During those times, I would be allowed to send him three messages of no more than 15 words each. They were called "familygrams," and I would spend hours trying to edit my words of love down to 15. I also spent a great deal of time making tapes (still reel–to–reel) of our favorite songs, especially those that expressed how I felt, and I'd give them to him the next time we were together. He'd play them over the P.A. system of the sub so the whole crew could enjoy them.

When Mike's tour of duty was over, he joined me at Ohio State. I was finishing my college education, and he was starting his, on the GI Bill. We rented an apartment within walking distance of campus, bought a secondhand bed and some other basic furniture, and began a more normal life together.

First Job

Because I had done an internship for my social work degree at the Vision Center of Central Ohio, it was a natural step to apply for a job there. I was hired immediately and fired six months later.

My title was case worker, and I enjoyed teaching braille and homemaking skills to women much older than I who had lost their vision. But I was not a very good teacher and not a good example of accepting my blindness. At least that's the way I remember my poor performance review. I wish I could crawl back into that time period, just for a minute, and observe myself and see how different I am now. I say "just for a minute" because my present life is so much better.

One of the highlights of the year for the teenage clients of the Vision Center was a two–week work–and–learn session in the summer. The best part of all was a camping trip in southern Ohio. Because I was the youngest member of the staff, I was sent along to help. I don't know if that was meant for me to gain experience with teens who were blind or to punish me for not being the case worker they'd expected. I absolutely hated camping, and everyone knew it. But I went.

The kids had been divided into two groups. The more active and courageous ones were allowed to sleep in tents, swing from tree branches, and go on long hikes. The younger and less adventurous kids were to sleep in a big farmhouse, play jump–rope, and sing songs. Those were my kids.

I was happy to teach them how to play Jacks and jump rope, and I was so glad to sleep in the big farmhouse instead of a tent. But my charges were disappointed with being treated like little kids, so the next night, they were allowed to sleep in the tent.

Meanwhile, there was only one camper who cried—me. I was miserable. It was hot and humid, and I really and truly had a migraine headache, so they let me sleep in the farmhouse, and I was excused from the hot and buggy hikes through the poison ivy–covered woods.

I was told that on Wednesday night of the camping week, the counselors went into town to have a beer for a midweek break. When Wednesday evening came, my headache was gone, and I was more than ready for a break. It turned out that the only counselor who wanted to go was John, so the two of us went, and I was as happy as a lark. John and I sat across from each other in a booth at a local bar, and I poured my heart out to him.

I had called Mike from the privacy of the farmhouse the day before and had begged him to come down to the camp. "You'd be so good with these older boys," I pleaded. I really missed him. But he insisted that he had to stay in Columbus and study. And besides, he had his job of unloading trucks at night for UPS. I understood, but I was disappointed that he didn't take pity on me and come to the camp.

I was deep into baring my soul to John when I felt a hand on the top of my head. It was Mike, surprising me and embarrassing me at the same time. Here I was, sitting in an air conditioned bar, drinking a beer with a man, when I had been whining that I was miserable and needed Mike so badly. To my surprise, he was not upset at all, and he and John had another beer together.

Later that night, Mike and I were the only people sleeping in the old farmhouse. But sometime during the night, we were serenaded by the other counselors and some of the older boys.

That was another moment of embarrassment.

The next day, I was allowed to go home with Mike. After all, I wasn't much use to the campers and certainly no help as a counselor. A couple of months later, I was let go.

"That's fine," I said proudly, "because I have a much more important job to do now. I'm pregnant."

Mary with friends in front of Oxley Hall, OSU 1963

Grandma and Mary on her wedding day, December 18, 1965

Chapter Nine
On Being a Blind Parent

Parenting as a blind person may sound nearly impossible. I did have many questions and doubts at first.

My husband, Mike, changed the first diaper for our newborn, Stephen. As the oldest of twelve kids, Mike had had plenty of practice, but as an only child, I had none. I hadn't even babysat for infants, so I felt I was going into this new career as a mommy with no experience. But as with many new jobs, I learned as I went along, with one exception.

I had decided unequivocally that I would breastfeed my baby. It made so much sense. The milk was always ready, always just the right temperature, came in its own reusable containers, and it was free.

I was watching some daytime show on TV when I heard about an organization that promoted breastfeeding called La Leche League. I memorized the phone number given and immediately called it. It was the home number of the woman who had started the Columbus chapter. She was warm, personable, encouraging, and inviting. I promised I would be at the next meeting, and I was. I met a woman there who was expecting her child almost exactly at the same time I was, and we became close friends. She not only coached me in starting a La Leche League group in Gahanna, but we also remained friends for the next 50 years as of this writing.

In those days, we had no way of knowing the sex of the baby until the moment of birth. When I woke up from my C–section and was told I had a beautiful baby boy, I have to admit that I was apprehensive. What on earth was I going to do with a boy? Of course I was in love the moment they placed him in my arms, but the real moment of deep motherly love came about a month later. I remember it as if it were yesterday, and yet it's such a seemingly insignificant event in a person's life.

I had just finished nursing him and had burped him over my shoulder when he laid down his head with his sweet little face turned toward me, took a deep breath, and sighed with the most peaceful satisfaction I had ever heard and would ever hear again. He slept there on my shoulder as if he had finally found the spot in this world where he was meant to be.

Stephen soon became Steve, although both sets of grandparents tried out the name Stevie with no success.

When Kara came along three years later, I had the same reaction when the whole operating team breathed a joyful "Ah" when the doctor announced, "It's a girl." I was awake for her birth.

Unlike Steve's entrance into the world, which took 28 hours, Kara's debut was much more orchestrated. Since I'd had a C–section for Steve, back then it was mandatory to have each subsequent baby the same way. So we set a date. I got my hair done, shaved my legs, and checked into the hospital the night before. I had planned to nurse her on the operating table, but by then, I felt pretty rotten, even though everything went according to plan.

But I couldn't help thinking, "Oh, no, what am I going to do with a girl? I only know how to take care of a little boy."

Now, so far, you're probably thinking that being a blind parent isn't so different from being a sighted one. Doubts, fears, joys, and the deepest love a mother can ever experience are common among parents, whether blind or sighted. But the practical side of parenthood can have a few more points on the challenging side and a few more points on the positive side.

Changing diapers became a matter of course with practice, and today it's much easier with disposable products. Because I gave my babies the best nutrition God could have created for newborn humans, there was no need for spooning baby food into a tiny mouth until age four months or so. My husband, feeling left out of the feeding part of being a father, was eager to start with the cereal at night, so we might have started a couple of weeks early for both babies. But when it was my turn to spoon in the mashed peas and sweet potatoes, I usually got more on Steve's face than in his mouth, so by the time it was Kara's turn to be fed solid food by her mother, she was content to wait until she was given soft foods she could pick up and eat herself, like small bits of banana instead of mashed banana on a spoon. I always said that fingers were invented before spoons, anyway.

As with children of sighted parents, the real challenges began when Steve learned to walk. Chasing after a toddler when you have 20/20 vision is exhausting enough, but add blindness, and life becomes a bit more complicated. Jingle bells on shoes were the first line of defense, and that worked fine for inside the apartment. But as he grew older and stronger and needed to run around outside, my fears increased by leaps and bounds. What if he wandered off into the parking lot, or worse, into the street?

He had little riding toys that he could use on the sidewalks along the inside of the apartment complex, and there was the possibility that he would make a wrong turn and get lost. A hundred worries could have plagued me, but I chose to spend his outside time right along with him. Our neighbors probably got used to looking out their kitchen windows and seeing me lurking around, then realizing that I was just watching my child.

At that time, I was not totally blind; I just had terrible vision. Two vivid memories stand out from that time in my life.

Although I was diligent in my vigil, there must have been a minute when I had to duck inside to answer the phone, or put the clothes into the dryer, or perform some other urgent task. Having lost track of Steve, I started running toward the neighbors' apartment where he liked to hang out, playing with the toys they left outside. The next thing I knew, I had run headfirst into a clothesline pole. Stunned, literally, my first thought as I reeled from the blow was, *Oh, no, I can't move, and I don't know where Steve is.* I clung to the pole to stay upright, but God must have known I would need my hard head. Miraculously, a neighbor had seen what had happened and rushed over to help me to a lawn chair and to tell me that Steve was fine and not far away.

As Steve became a few months older and his vocabulary grew, so also did his awareness of my inability to see him from a distance. Sometimes I would give him a little more freedom and let him roam while I sat on a chair outside our door. If I couldn't hear him, I'd call out, "Steve?" and he'd answer me, "I'm over here, Mommy." There were times when all I'd have to do was look his way, and he'd affirm his location even if I hadn't called out for him. "Here I am, Mommy." He couldn't possibly have really understood why I needed affirmation, but it just became the way we did things when we played outside.

Steve was three when Kara was born, and by then we had moved into a house, where I still reside. It's a split-level house, with three bedrooms on the uppermost level. At that time, all the floors upstairs were hardwood, so when Kara was old enough to scoot around in her "Hulacoop," the biggest danger was the threat of the steps leading down to the living room. We kept a baby gate at the top of the steps, but for short periods of time, Steve would stretch his little body across the steps and announce, "I'll betect her."

Often, my next-door neighbor, Mary Lou, and I would sit in the front yard with a playpen nearby, with both our baby girls in it, and I could relax, knowing that Mary Lou had her eye on them.

When Kara reached the age of wanting to play outside and not just in her own back yard, once again I was trailing along behind her, close enough that I could either see her or hear her. I recall with embarrassment following my daughter into the back yard of our next-door neighbor to play on their swings. We did not have a swing set in our back yard because I didn't want the responsibility of watching neighbor kids play on it, but ironically I had no problem with my child playing on the neighbors' swing set. But I never left her alone.

Later, when Kara was older and she played with Kristy, a little girl across the street, Kristy's mother and I would set up our chairs in the driveway of their house. We'd talk for hours on end as the kids, both boys and girls, would ride their bikes or play basketball in the cul–de–sac. It was a golden time for me, bonding with other mothers while my kids were safe in their play. So many times over the years, I have longed for the days when our children were small and were the means by which we knew our neighbors.

As the kids grew into school age, they became involved in many activities that required transportation. They could walk to school, but dance lessons, football practice, cheerleading practice, swim lessons, piano lessons, church youth group, parties, and play dates required my being on the phone for hours each week, arranging rides—not only for my own outside activities, but theirs as well. By this time, my husband had his own CPA practice in Gahanna, so he could sometimes take a few minutes away from the office and drive them to where they needed to be, but I didn't want to abuse that convenience.

Mike loved sports and instilled in Steve that same enthusiasm. Steve played ice hockey for a few seasons, and this was one time I was glad I couldn't drive. The only time they could get ice time at the one arena we had was 4:00 in the morning. I felt sorry for both of them as they dragged their sleepy bodies out to the car on cold, dark Sunday mornings, and then I'd feel resentful because Mike would have to sleep most of the rest of the day after they got home. But now I'm glad they had that experience. On the few days that they had their games at a reasonable time, I got to be there as my son skated with the skill and grace that I had admired when I watched the Cincinnati Mohawks when I was a kid.

I'm glad Steve didn't really get into football all that much, but he and his dad were involved with Little League baseball from the time Steve played T–ball all the way through his sophomore year in high school, and later in softball teams at work. Mike was the Little League coach, and he enjoyed planning which kid would play which position at each game. I was expected to have their dinner on the table by 4:00 p.m. and to attend the games. Mike would set my lawn chair up along the first base line at a spot where I was least likely to get hit in the head with a foul ball. I am very thankful that even with sitting through hundreds of games, I never got hit.

Of course Kara came with us, and she was pretty good at entertaining herself through these long and boring trials of her patience. One game was held at a school where an enticing playground was just a few hundred feet away. I agreed to walk over there with her, and she was climbing the ladder of a slide when I heard eight–year–old Steve calling to me from the nearby outfield. "Mom," he yelled, "you're supposed to be watching me!" I was busted. Surely he knew that I couldn't really "watch" him, but he wanted me to be in my chair on the first base line. But there might have been a little sibling rivalry going on there, too.

No, my kids were not exempt from sibling rivalry. I remember having to count the meatballs in the SpaghettiOs to make sure that each bowl had exactly nine in it. On Christmas Eve, I made sure that both stacks of gifts were equal in height. Okay; I put that burden on myself, but it stopped the year we gave Kara a piccolo. Even as a freshman, she was quite talented as a flutist in the high school band. Because a piccolo is much more expensive than most sports–related apparel, Kara's pile of presents was much shorter than Steve's that Christmas.

Kara confessed to me years later that she did wonder why her stack of gifts was so much smaller than Steve's that year, but she never said anything. She didn't need to. She was ecstatic with the piccolo and secluded herself up in her room and practiced all day. At first, I thought I had just bought her a $300 whistle, but by the end of the day, she was playing a tune that I could recognize as actual music.

After sitting through baton competitions, where I was just a presence on a hard bench in the bleachers for hours on end, while recorded marching music played and I had no idea what talented moves my daughter was making, I could finally enjoy a performance that I could hear and appreciate. Kara brought me countless hours of pride and pleasure as she excelled in the band and at competitions. She often accompanied the church choir, particularly for special music at Christmas and Easter. As an adult, she joined a community flute choir, and I loved going to rehearsals with her. I have always enjoyed rehearsals of any kind at least as much as the actual concerts.

Kara is also a good singer, but I didn't fully appreciate that until one summer when she invited me to visit her for a weekend at Club Med in Florida, where she worked for a while after college. While she had to be at her job, I swam in the pool or lounged on the lanai of my spacious room. But in the evenings, we went to the bar, where karaoke entertained the guests. To get the guests in the mood, some of the staff would get up and sing. I was in conversation with one of Kara's friends when I heard a voice that was vaguely familiar, but I wasn't sure who was singing with that confidence and style. Suddenly, that voice broke through my consciousness, and I asked if that could possibly be Kara. To my delight, she had surprised me with yet another talent.

My son and daughter have both brought me moments of

pride that far outweighed the struggles of being a blind mother. When my own mother had to be moved to assisted living, they both played a huge part in that transition. Steve, who lived nearby, made time to visit his grandmother regularly and made a big deal of her birthday, allowing her to feel pride in her caring and loving grandson. Kara flew in often to give me a break from the stress of having a mother with dementia. And the proudest I have ever been of Kara was the day I stood by her bedside and observed her cradling her firstborn in her arms. This exhausting feat of strength and will surpassed all the dance recitals and flute competitions, her wedding day, and the kindness she has shown to me.

Grandma/Grammie

Steve's firstborn, Meghan, made her appearance in October of 1998. She was the first of my five granddaughters. When she was about a month old, Kara, her then-boyfriend, Scott, and I offered to babysit while Steve and Tammy went out for dinner and a movie, their first outing since the birth of their child. They were nervous about leaving her, but we assured them that three adults could handle a one-month-old baby.

We took turns holding her, cooing to her, and rocking her, but when Steve and Tammy tiptoed in, expecting crying, I was the one in the rocking chair with a sleeping baby on my shoulder. We were peacefully chatting as the baby slept on, and Steve was pleased. I hoped that this tableau would convince them that I could be a suitable grandma.

When Meghan was about a year old, and Kara, Tammy, and Meghan were going somewhere, Meghan decided she wasn't going. She proceeded to fling herself down on the floor and kick and scream. Tammy was embarrassed and didn't know what to do. Finally, I decided to take charge. I scooped up the child and handed her to Tammy.

On one occasion two years later, when McKenzie had joined the family and they all came over for "Grandma night," the once-a-week dinner that I prepared for them, Meghan had a meltdown the minute they came in the door, which apparently was my fault. First I called out hello to Meghan, and then I said hello to McKenzie, not wanting to appear that I was ignoring the new baby. I was in the kitchen, so I hadn't been making a fuss over McKenzie, but Meghan was totally incensed and began wailing. Steve explained to me that she didn't like McKenzie to get any attention. This is pretty typical of very young children, so again, I scooped Meghan up. But this time, instead of handing her off, I held her close and snuggled her, letting her know that I still loved her just as much.

Again, I agreed to babysit, this time for two children, and this time alone. Was I crazy? McKenzie cried on and off the whole two hours that her parents were gone, and the only way I could calm her was to stand and sway back and forth, back and forth. What parent doesn't know this trick? Meghan had fallen asleep, even through all the crying. Tiring, I finally sat on the edge of the bed, and ever so slowly and gradually, I lay back, with my feet still on the floor, and McKenzie fell asleep on my chest. That's how Steve found us when they returned. It was an awkward position to be in, but it had worked. Steve apologized, but I hoped he would see that I would do anything for his kids. Now, I'm pleased to say that these two sisters are the best of friends, and they are a delight to be around.

My first opportunity to babysit Michaela, Kara's firstborn, came when she was about six months old. Kara and Scott went to a friend's wedding where children were not invited, but they could take Michaela to the reception. Before they left for the wedding, we agreed that an easy way for me to entertain her would be to take her for a walk. Using a stroller would not be safe, since by then I had no vision at all. So we strapped her into a contraption that holds the baby secured to your chest but facing outward, so she can see the world. Then I hooked Sherry, my Seeing Eye® dog, into her harness, and we set off for a walk.

I was immensely grateful that Kara and Scott trusted me to walk with my guide dog with their precious baby on my front. They had every confidence that I would not trip and land with Michaela on her tiny, fragile face. If I had tripped, I assure you, I would have twisted my body to prevent that from happening. But I was extremely careful, and I think Sherry knew how important this was and was diligent in letting me know about every crack in the sidewalk.

We walked around the block, and because Michaela had no gloves on, I worried about her hands getting cold. As a woman approached me from the other direction, I stopped her and ask if my granddaughter looked like she was happy. The woman said she looked fine, except that her hands were getting red. Fortunately, we would be home in minutes.

Taking the contraption off was a lot easier than getting it on, thank goodness. I put her in her little bouncy seat and sprinkled some Cheerios on the tray. Then I sat with her and chatted and sang to her, so she was happy when her parents walked in.

Whew. Success.

Singing to my grandchildren was a soothing talent that I inherited from the women in my family who preceded me. It was no surprise, because I remember my beloved Aunt Lynn, and my cousin Carolyn, too, making up songs to familiar tunes but with personalized words to put my younger cousin, Johnny, to sleep.

Kara and I had been to visit my mother, who lived 50 miles from the nearest airport. Kara had flown in and then rented a car, having carried two car seats and a baby, with a very young Michaela in tow.

The drive out to Mom's was uneventful except for having to pull into an old farm road so Kara could nurse Brianna, who was not going to wait until we got to Great-Grandma's.

On the way back to the airport, Kara asked me to sit in the back seat between the two children to entertain them for the hour-long drive to the airport. I began to sing, first a few songs with real words, like "The Eensie Weensie Spider" and "Old MacDonald Had a Farm." Then Kara noticed in her rear view mirror that both children's eyelids were drooping.

"Keep singing," Kara said softly from the driver's seat. So I did. I began with the same songs, and then I started making up words as I went along, softly crooning away, sometimes rhyming words, and sometimes just singing a story about my darling little babies.

"Keep singing," Kara said when I paused to take a breath. It was a concert we will never forget, as it made for a very peaceful ride to the airport.

Another precious moment of Grandma success happened when Michaela and Brianna were very young. Kara and Scott with their children, and Tammy and Steve with theirs, all went with me to visit my mother in Indiana. We spent the night at a casino in Louisville, and I had an adjoining room with Kara and Scott. The parents all went to the casino while I stayed in my room with the adjoining door open. The children were all asleep, but after a while, Brianna woke up and began to cry.

I wanted to call Kara and Scott, but cell phones were not allowed in the casino part of the hotel, and I didn't want to have them paged, because this was not an emergency. I was going to have to handle this myself.

I had not even set foot in their room earlier—a mistake, I realized, when I heard the crying and did not know where to find the child. But I used my sense of hearing, found the source of the crying, lifted Brianna out of the crib, and carefully made my way back to my room. I was amazed that she allowed me to pick her up without being able to see me in the dark, but I'm told that babies can sense who is safe and who is not. She seemed happy to play with me on my bed, and that's how Kara and Scott found her when they returned. They were not at all surprised that I had managed to find her and bring her safely to my room.

When Meghan and McKenzie were not babies anymore but young children, I struggled to think of ways to entertain them on Grandma nights. Then I pulled out of my memory bank a game I used to love as a child, and although some adjustments had to be made, it was a huge success.

Did you ever play Rock School? Both kids sat on the bottom step. I held a penny, in lieu of a rock, in one fist and then held out both fists for the first child to choose from. If she chose the fist with the penny hidden inside, she got to move up to the next step. Then it was the other child's turn. If she picked the wrong fist, she had to stay on her step. Whoever got to the top first got to be the "teacher," the one who hid the penny behind her back and then presented her hands to the other child and me.

Here's where the adaptation came in. By this time, they had learned that I couldn't see, so when I tapped the fist that held the penny, the "teacher" would have to tell me if I had picked the right one.

Grandma is not the nickname I would have chosen, but Steve started using it before we had a chance to discuss it. My friends had cute names like Nonnie or Geema or Nana. But I was stuck with Grandma—that is, until Kara's third child was born. It seemed a good time to make a change, so to Bethany, I'm Grammie.

I am not the kind of grandmother who is thrilled to care for babies, but I do enjoy the kids as they get older. I don't think blindness has anything to do with that. When Michaela was 16 and her whole family was visiting here, Michaela chose to stay home with me while the rest of the family went out to lunch and to do something fun for Bethany, the toddler in the family. Luckily, I had fresh spinach on hand, and Michaela, who follows a vegan meal plan, was happy to join me for a spinach salad.

We talked easily and frankly about our thoughts on politics and other weighty matters of the day in our world. I sensed that she needed some quiet time, so after lunch, we both sat in the living room in companionable silence, she with her book and me with my laptop. It was one of the most pleasant times I've had with one of my grandchildren.

As for Steve's two girls, I've made a point of taking each of them out to lunch once a month. Now that they can both drive, it's easy and the best way to get to know them. I quickly discovered that taking them both at the same time was a mistake, as they often just talked to each other. But when I take them one at a time, we have great conversations, and it's been very helpful in forging good relationships with them.

As adults, Steve and Kara have both been a source of pride and support. Kara is the more nurturing of the two, but Steve will come to my aid immediately if I need him.

When I was hospitalized for two back surgeries, it was Kara who reversed our roles and became my caregiver. As women who are mothers, we bond over parental worries. And when I had to reverse roles with my own mother as she developed dementia, it was Kara I turned to for advice and comfort. When my mother fell and broke her hip, it was Steve who drove me to the hospital in Indiana, and then again eight years later, when she broke the other hip at the assisted living home near me.

I wouldn't say that there were benefits for my son and daughter in having a blind mother, but they learned some lessons and values that they've passed on to their own children. Sensitivity to and acceptance of people with disabilities are two of the most important. As young children, their vocabularies were extraordinary, because they knew that pointing to something they wanted would not work. As adults, in my opinion, they are shining examples of kind and caring people.

I'll close this chapter with an example of how Kara dealt with a sensitive situation at her wedding.

She and Scott wanted to have their mothers light a unity candle together. Typically, the mothers walk up to the altar, take a lighted candle, and touch their flames to a single candle, signifying that the two families are now united. Kara's dad was able to walk her down the aisle, although he was very sick with cancer, but we were no longer married, so for us to walk up to the altar together would be awkward at best. Kara solved the dilemma by having Steve walk with me and assist me with the candle. To make it look like this was the way they had planned it all along, Scott's mother was assisted by Scott's brother, too. To me, this gesture of allowing me to participate without making it look contrived was a tribute to Kara's sensitivity that permeates her very being.

Is it no wonder that I feel so blessed? In some ways, I wish that I had had more children. But then, maybe it was good that I quit while I was ahead—way ahead.

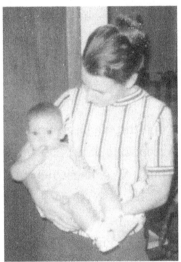

Mary with baby Steve

Mary with baby Kara

Mary with her granddaughters Brianna and Michaela, 2004

Chapter Ten
Dogs Are My Favorite People

After my children and grandchildren, my favorite people are dogs. As of this writing, I'm working with my fifth Seeing Eye® dog, Dora. She's the one on the cover of the book, and I've included photos of all five of my guide dogs at the end of this chapter.

Not all guide dogs are from The Seeing Eye, but they all have the same job, to guide people who are blind or visually impaired. Many training schools around the world have the same mission, but I like to quote from the website of The Seeing Eye: "...to enhance the independence, dignity, and self-confidence of people who are blind through the use of specially trained Seeing Eye dogs."

Introducing My Seeing Eye Dogs

I was 37 when I finally made the decision to get a guide dog. Because I worked with a man with a wonderful dog from The Seeing Eye, I was convinced that it was the best guide dog school in the country. I still believe that, although nowadays there are several schools in the U.S. that do a fine job of training their dogs and their students.

It was a huge step for me to take, but I had almost no vision left except for a little light perception, and I hated using a white cane, mostly because I wasn't very good at it. I had always had a dog, ever since I was a little girl, thanks to my dad, who loved dogs and who taught me to love them, too. It was natural for me to progress to the security and efficiency of traveling with a guide dog.

So off I went to Morristown, New Jersey, to discover the freedom I hadn't known I was missing until I took those first thrilling steps with my new best friend.

Mindy—1982–1992

It was 1982 when I went to Morristown to train with my first Seeing Eye dog. While I was there, the rest of my family were celebrating the 4th of July. It was the first time I had been away from home on a holiday. I would be missing the Little League tournament game, the annual parade in Gahanna, the traditional cookout, and the fireworks to follow. I could have been sad for missing all that, but I wasn't. In fact, I felt a little guilty for enjoying the time away so much.

The 4th was a beautiful day, sunny but not oppressively hot. I had been there for about two weeks and was midway through my training. There were about 20 of us in that class, and we were all celebrating our own Independence Day.

We had all arrived on a Saturday and had been given lunch and a tour of the grounds. The instructors took each of us on what they call a Juno walk. The instructor holds the front end of the harness, which would later be worn by the dog, and the student holds onto the handle, as if they had a dog out in front. In this way, the instructors can judge what kind of pace the students like, observe their gait, and chat about their lifestyles.

Then, while we got settled in our rooms, we got to know our roommates. We attended our first and only lecture without a dog lying at our feet. The instructors huddled, compared notes, and came up with perfect matches of students with dogs. Some students had a preference for one breed over another, but I just hoped to be matched with a dog that my family would love. As for me, I could love any dog. We would be given our dogs the next afternoon, an eternity away.

I didn't sleep at all that night, and the next morning, when I heard the dogs barking in the kennels across the parking lot, I knew that one of those barks was meant just for me.

At last it was Sunday afternoon, and we were gathered in the lounge for the matching announcements. The instructor would say the name of the person, then the breed of dog and the dog's name. When it was my turn, he said, "Mrs. Hiland, your dog is a Golden Retriever, and her name is Mindy."

I choked back tears of relief and joy. I had secretly hoped for a Golden Retriever, and with a name like Mindy, she had to be adorable.

She was. It was love at first sight for both of us.

The instructor told me later that he knew it was going to be a perfect match 30 seconds into the training. I'll never forget the first time I picked up the harness handle and we started walking at a steady but very brisk pace down the sidewalk in a residential neighborhood.

Oh, my God, I thought, *I'm putting my life, literally, in the hands of a dog! And it's wonderful! Look at me, just walking down the street on my own, just me and Mindy!*

I felt a big, goofy grin spreading over my face, and I felt a little silly, but I couldn't help it. Mindy really knew her stuff and responded promptly to the slightest correction. She was all about pleasing me.

When we weren't tromping around on the sidewalks of Morristown, we were encouraged to walk on the "leisure path," a paved walking trail on the beautifully manicured grounds of The Seeing Eye, where there would be no curb ramps or traffic to negotiate. It was just an easy, no–stress walk where we could unwind. I would often stop at the gazebo about halfway around the path and relax with one or two of my classmates. That's where I spent my favorite 4th of July, hanging out with my fellow students and my new best friend, Mindy.

Mindy and I were starting a new life together. For the next 10 years, we would have a partnership of dignity, freedom, and independence.

Of all the dogs I've had over the years, Mindy was the most serious worker, and yet she brought me happiness and laughter in many ways.

Being a Retriever, she loved to carry things in her mouth. One day, when I walked to the bank, and I had done what I needed to do and was heading back out the door, a man called after me, "Ma'am, he dropped his shoe."

Thinking he was talking to someone else, perhaps a mother with a baby, I kept going. But he ran after me, repeating, "He dropped his shoe."

He held out to me a plastic shoe that was clearly a dog toy. Mindy had carried it a mile up to the bank, and while we were standing at the counter, she had dropped it but hadn't picked it up, and I was not aware of that at all. On the way home, I carried it in my pocket.

I was working at the radio reading service while I had Mindy, and one of her most endearing habits was to pick up her leash whenever someone came into my office. Because she had to have something in her mouth whenever she got excited, and there was nothing like a toy or a shoe to pick up, she'd grab that leash, and wagging her tail like a flag, prance around with it in her mouth. At home, whenever someone came to our door, she'd run and grab a toy or a shoe. On one occasion, she was frantically trying to find something to carry, and I could see she was getting frustrated. So I just took off my shoe and handed it to her, and she was fine.

She loved to collect shoes and hide them behind the chair in the living room. She never chewed them up, just stashed them behind the chair. Whenever one of us couldn't find one of our shoes, we learned to first go look behind the chair, and most likely it would be there.

When I first told my husband, Mike, that I wanted to get a guide dog, he hated the idea. He said he didn't like the thought of my "running all over town alone." The truth was that he enjoyed my being dependent on him.

I changed his mind by surprising him one Sunday afternoon with an unforeseen benefit to my having a guide dog. He was a CPA, it was tax season, and he often worked on Sunday afternoons, taking advantage of the quiet. His office was about a mile–and–a–half–long walk from the house, but I knew the way. So Mindy and I left the kids at home (they were young teenagers by this time) and set out for the office with sandwiches and cookies that were still warm from the oven. Mike was impressed, and we celebrated with the picnic lunch I had brought, even though he was up to his elbows in work. From then on, he approved of my being able to walk all over town on my own.

Because Mindy took her work so seriously, we had to teach her how to have fun. At the time, we had another little pet dog who had the run of the back yard. For a month, as prescribed by The Seeing Eye, Mindy was always at my side, either in harness or on a leash. One sunny afternoon, Mike and I took her into the back yard to run around with the other dog, but she stood stock still. We had to coax her, but eventually, she learned that romping around was acceptable and even fun.

She also got to go canoeing with us. By this time, Mike was almost as much in love with her as I was. At first, she was terrified, trying to hide under my seat in the canoe. But when we stopped at a little beach and encouraged her to get out of the canoe, she discovered that wading around in the water was way more fun. After we were sure she was comfortable in the water, we began to paddle on down the river in a very slow and easy manner, and she swam along with us. But after a while, she tired, so she hooked a front leg over the side of the canoe and let us take her for a ride the rest of the way. When we pulled ashore, we bought her an ice cream cone as a victory celebration, and she slept in the back seat of the car all the way home. It was one of the best days in her doggy life.

Although Mindy was 11 at the time, old for a Golden Retriever, her death was sudden and heartbreaking.

When she became seriously ill with no warning, I took her to her vet. He told me that she had a tumor on her liver and he thought it best to be aggressive and surgically remove it. He should have known she was too old to undergo that kind of surgery. She died that night as she came out from under the anesthetic.

Aside from losing my precious girl, I was angry and hurt that they hadn't called me to let me know she was in danger of not making it. Instead, they waited until midnight to call me to tell me she had died. It is always very sad to lose a pet, but it's tragic to lose a guide dog, and it was unforgivable to not be there to comfort her as she left this world.

Sherry—1992-2004

When I returned to The Seeing Eye, this time I prayed for a Golden Retriever, and my prayer was answered.

Sherry was a little shy at first, but when I sat on the floor with her and stroked her tummy, she decided that I would do. She was just as talented as Mindy, but she had a playful streak that entertained my family and me. She could turn on her work mode as soon as the harness came on and then revert to play mode as soon as we got back home and the harness came off.

One of the questions I'm often asked is if my dogs ever get to play. You bet. At home, they're pets who get extra love and attention because they have become part of me.

I had a lot of fun with her name. While in training at The Seeing Eye, my instructor would often get our names mixed up, as in, "Sherry, please have Mary sit." When I called my friend Sherry to tell her about my new dog, we laughed, imagining that I would give my dog Sherry a command, and my friend Sherry would think I was talking to her, as in, "Sherry, forward." And of course, since Sherry loved her tummy rubs, I would sing to her, and her tail would beat the floor in time to The Four Seasons' hit from the '60s, "Sherry Baby." It was "our song," and even now when I hear it, my heart swells a little with the love I had for my Sherry Baby.

Sherry loved my kids and always greeted them with exuberance, even though Kara was away at college and Steve had moved out. Generally speaking, Sherry would not even try to get on the furniture because I discouraged it from the beginning. But one day, when Kara was home for a few days, we were both lying on my bed a couple of feet apart—just talking, you know, as mothers and daughters do sometimes—when Sherry walked into the room, saw an opportunity to join the girl talk, and leapt onto the bed. She settled in between us as if to say, "Go on. What were you saying?"

Sherry was a sweetheart, but she was not the angel that Mindy was. She was the number one chewer. I still have a hole in my carpet at the foot of my stairs, a little reminder of Sherry each time I reposition the throw rug I have there to cover it up.

When I went away for a ski weekend early in Sherry's career, I left her at home with a friend of Kara's, who stayed at our house to take care of Sherry. But the girl had to go to class one of the days I was gone, and when she returned, she discovered that Sherry had chewed a hole in the arm of the couch and another hole in the arm of the matching loveseat. Kara's friend was mortified, but it wasn't her fault. Fortunately, both pieces of furniture sat against the wall, so the arms were re-covered with material from the backs of the pieces.

This happy dog loved a party. Whenever anybody had a birthday at the office, we had pizza or some fast food that the birthday person chose, as well as cake. The radio reading service is a non–profit organization, so there were no lunches out or bonuses or gifts. But Sherry always made it a festive occasion. After we had eaten our cake and had scraped our paper plates clean with our forks, I would let Sherry lick the plates, and she thought this was the best party ever.

We also had staff meetings in the break room, and Sherry always joined us, even though she was out of harness most of the day. One staff meeting got off to a hilarious start when somebody, probably me, noticed that Sherry hadn't joined us. So we all sang Happy Birthday, and here she came, galloping down the hall, thinking she was about to miss out on the cake.

Sherry had a pretty traumatic time at the vet's, too, but in her case, she was a TV star, and it had a happy ending. A tumor had developed on her thigh and the vet wanted to try to do a new laser surgery that had just been developed for animals. She told me that there would be no cost to me if I gave permission for TV cameras to film the procedure and produce a story about it.

While Sherry was in surgery, another crew from the same station came to my office to interview me. I didn't mind until they wanted me to walk down the hallway so they could film what it would be like without Sherry. I flatly refused. I was not going to be part of a pity production, so all they got from me was an interview about how important she was to me and how much it meant to me for Sherry to have this operation.

She recovered just fine and lived to be 13.

One of the best Thanksgivings I ever had was when Kara, Sherry, and I went to a posh hotel in a town about 30 miles away for dinner.

After our meal, we changed into jeans and tennies in the car and took a good, long walk on the bike trail that ran near the hotel. When we reached the outskirts of town, I took Sherry's harness off and let her run. Her nose was like a little shovel as she plowed through the leaves. She'd romp ahead of us and then run back to check in, then take off again, sometimes looking over her shoulder to make sure we were coming. She never got out of sight, and there were no other walkers on the trail.

It made my heart burst with love for this joyful dog and my kind daughter, who made sure Sherry was safe. As Kara said, "This is making her little doggy day." Mine, too.

Sherry could be quite the character and surprise us with behavior we would never have expected.

During Sherry's tenure, I was dating a man named Tom, and one summer, he invited me to go with him to his Michigan home for the 4th of July. I decided to leave Sherry with Kara, since there was no place to walk there, and I wouldn't really be needing her.

Kara and a friend took Sherry with them to a park where there was a large pond. Her friend suggested that Sherry might like to go swimming. Kara told him that she didn't think Sherry would enjoy that, but she'd give her the opportunity, just in case she would. To their amazement, Sherry not only went into the water, but the first thing she did was stick her whole head under water.

Later, they went to the 4th of July parade, and they took Sherry and our other little pet dog, Jeanie, with them. Jeanie loved it, getting pets from everybody and trying to run out and grab the treats that the people in the parade tossed to her. But Sherry would have none of it. It was clear she hated the whole thing, because she turned her back on the parade and sat down.

It was as if she were saying, "I told you I didn't want to go, and I'm not going to watch it. I want my mommy."

The end of Sherry's life came suddenly and without warning. I was getting ready to go home for the day from the radio reading service when she collapsed in my office. Luckily, I knew a vet who made house calls, and he came quickly and drew blood. He told me he would be taking the blood sample to an emergency veterinary hospital, and they would have results by the following day. Meanwhile, I had missed my ride home. I knew I would have to take Sherry to the vet the next day, anyway, and I didn't know how I was going to get her home, let alone get her to the hospital the next day, so I asked the vet if we couldn't just go with him.

When we arrived at the hospital, he carried Sherry in, leaving me to find my own way in without so much as a cane. But when your baby is in crisis, you do what you have to do, and I made it into the waiting room. Eventually, with the support of the kind and understanding hospital vet, I made the decision to end her pain. When they brought her into the private room where I was waiting, she was walking on her own. I thought I had made a terrible mistake, but the vet told me that they had just given her fluids so she could walk. She immediately lay down beside me on the floor.

This time, I was there with her and held her as she took her last breath. This was the night before my birthday. The office staff was prepared to have pizza and cake and to let Sherry lick the plates, but there was no party that year.

Pippen—2004-2013

Pippen's story has a much happier ending. She was three-quarters Yellow Lab and one-quarter Golden Retriever, but her personality was 100% Lab. She was a little squirt, weighing only 39 pounds, and she could charm even those who thought they didn't like dogs.

Our training at The Seeing Eye lasted for only 11 days, not the typical 18 days for returning students. I had signed up for the "Home and Away" program so I wouldn't have to use so many vacation days, but I later realized that was a mistake. Our schedule of training walks and lectures was so accelerated that I felt I had no downtime or time to socialize with other students. I'll talk more about what happens during training at The Seeing Eye later in this chapter. For now, I'll just say that I made a vow never to do that again.

The "home" part of the program meant that an instructor came to our homes after our training at the school, and that's part of the attraction. We got to practice with our new dogs on the streets where we would actually be traveling, not just on the streets of Morristown, New Jersey.

When Pippen and I were done with our training at the school, it was Easter weekend, so we were on our own for about four days before the instructor came to help us. It was cold and pouring rain, but he was there, so we had to go out and do it. It was not an auspicious start, so it's no wonder that Pippen really didn't enjoy working that much. Oh, she was a good little worker and learned new tasks quickly, but she had her own ideas of when it was and was not time to work. For instance, when it was raining, even just a little, and we'd step outside the front door, she'd turn around and face the door. It was like she was saying,

"I'm not going. Take your own self for a walk."

One evening early in our time together, as we were walking on the school track about half a mile from my house, a thunderstorm kicked up out of nowhere, and it began to rain in buckets. We were on the far side of the track, and Pippen came to a dead stop. "I don't do rain," she said, in a silent language only I could understand.

"You can't quit now," I shouted to her over the thunder and pouring rain. "We've got to get home."

She must have understood, because we scurried around to the other side and through the gate just as the Little League game was called off by the storm. I couldn't hear anything because of the thunder and the stampeding rain on the pavement. We needed to walk beside the cars to get out of the parking lot, but I couldn't tell if I was in the path of a car or not. That night, I had to put my faith in God and just move forward.

If you are a guide dog user, you might say, "Why didn't you put your faith in your dog?" Remember, this was a very young dog, and she was terrified of rain, so this night, it was up to God—not only to get us out of the parking lot, but also across the busy street. Pippen was so eager to get home that she crossed the street on the diagonal instead of going from corner to corner, and it was only the grace of God that kept us from getting hit. When we reached the far corner, still alive, albeit soaked, I thanked God profusely. *From now on*, I vowed, *if it looks like rain, I'll listen to my dog.*

Pippen was a cuddler, which pleased me immensely. Each afternoon, after I changed jobs and could work from home, we took a nap together. I'd lie on my side, and she'd arrange the front half of her body in the hollow between my ribs and my hips. In the evenings, as I watched TV, we'd share SunChips, and then when the bowl was empty, she'd hop up on the couch and drape herself over my lap.

If I ever get too old or infirm to use a guide dog, I'd like to have Pippen reincarnated to be my pet.

As I mentioned in a previous chapter, I was in Toastmasters for many years, and one of the speech project manuals concentrated on "The Entertaining Speech," including one that is supposed to be a touching story. Here's the one I gave, which stars Pippen.

Pippen Meets Mary

August 23, 2004

This story is told by Pippen, but because her New Jersey accent is so strong, Mary will interpret.

Mr. Toastmaster, people,

I met Mary on March 29 at The Seeing Eye in Morristown, New Jersey, where I had just completed three months of basic training as a Seeing Eye dog. I didn't like it at first. I never said I wanted to be a Seeing Eye dog. I was perfectly happy being a stay-at-home dog. However, when I was two years old, somebody decided I should go to work. *Work!* I thought. *Whatever happened to "It's a dog's life" or "the dog days of summer"?* Nonetheless, there I was at The Seeing Eye, learning to be a working dog.

My teacher's name was Pete—a nice guy, who taught me things like how to walk on the sidewalk, stop at curbs, and turn right and left, and words like

Forward, Hupp up, Leave it, and the dreaded Phooey! Phooey is a German word they use at The Seeing Eye to correct the dogs when they screw up. It means, "You screwed up." I got lots of phooeys, but in time, I learned all my stuff, and it was time for me to be matched up with my own real, blind person, who would be my new boss.

When it was my turn, Pete led me into the big house where all the people lived. We walked down a long hallway where all the doors were closed. I could hear my doggy friends behind those doors, wagging their tails. I heard laughter and murmurs and even little whimpers. Oh, I hoped my new boss would be nice.

Finally, we got to the right door, and Pete knocked. I heard a woman's voice call sweetly, "Come in." Pete opened the door, and there she was! Mary was kneeling on the floor with her arms spread wide open. "Pippen, come," she said. It was her first command to me. I obeyed immediately, ran and climbed into her lap, and licked her face. If she was going to be my new boss, I'd better start kissing up.

That afternoon, we just hung out together, but the next day, our real training started at 5:30 in the morning. All day long, every day, until 8:00 at night, it was work, work, work. When we weren't out walking the streets of Morristown, I was learning how to sit, lie down, stay put, and be quiet, as well as don't bark, don't sniff. That was the hardest part for me, the don't sniff part. I was the nosiest dog in the class. But you see, for me, sniffing is like reading the mail. I just can't help it. It was phooey this and phooey that, all day long. I also got a lot of "Good girl, Pippen," and "Atta girl," and "Good job, Pippen," and "That's the way, Pippen," because Mary was supposed to encourage me and praise me whenever I did something right.

Now I'm going to tell you about the day Mary started to trust me. We were crossing a street when we had a terrific traffic check. I learned about traffic checks when I was in basic training. Pete and I would start to cross a street, when a car would—and this was all planned—swerve around the corner and almost hit us. At that time, I didn't know that cars were a bad thing, so the driver would lean out the window and bop me on the nose with a rolled-up newspaper. It didn't hurt, but I didn't like it, so I'd back up. We did this over and over, until finally, when I saw that car coming, I'd stop and back up right away, because I didn't want to get bopped on the nose.

On this particular day, Mary and I were starting to cross the street when there was an unplanned traffic check. This guy came out of nowhere and turned right in front of us, so of course I slammed on the brakes and backed us both up. Mary was so pleased and so proud and so grateful that I had saved both our lives that when we got to the other side of the street, she knelt down on the ground, put her arms around me, and hugged me and kissed me. I don't know what the big deal was. I was just doing my job. She was so choked up that she couldn't say her words in a cheerful voice like she was supposed to. Instead of saying, "Good girl, Pippen," she just whispered "Good girl, that–a girl," all the way down the block. I guess she recovered, because by the time we got to the end of the block, I smelled something I wanted to sniff, and it was Phooey! The honeymoon was over.

We did lots of neat things in our training walks, like escalators. They're a blast! Mary was afraid to try them, because she had never taken a Seeing Eye dog on one before, and she was afraid I'd get hurt. But Pete knew I could do it. We went to a department store, rode up two flights, then down two flights. By the time we got to the bottom, Pete was smiling real big, and I was wagging my tail, and Mary said, "Whew, I need a drink."

All too soon, it was time for Mary to go home. But wait a minute! I was going with her. It was sad to think of leaving all my friends at The Seeing Eye, especially Pete, but exciting, too, because we were going on a plane to some place called Ohio.

The first thing we did when we got to Mary's house was that she let me sniff all over the house without a single phooey. Later that afternoon, we took our first walk in the neighborhood, nothing complicated. Keep it simple, they told her. We just walked up to the end of the block and came back. But when we got up to the end and turned around, I thought, *Uh, oh. I don't know where I live. I have no idea which house is mine.* But Mary is smarter than she looks. She had put a radio out at the end of her driveway, so she could hear where to tell me when to turn in. It worked. We did this lots of times, and then finally, Mary left the radio inside. It was time for me to turn in on my own. The pressure was on.

I did very well until the day that the mother robin built her nest in the bush right outside our front door. Every time we went in and out of the house, that bird would come shrieking out, flying into Mary's face and trying to attack me. One night, when we came back from our evening walk, I saw that bird. I was not going to turn into the driveway, so I just kept walking past the house. *Maybe she won't notice*, I thought. She noticed. We turned around, and I passed the house again. Up and down the street we walked, back and forth, and I could feel Mary getting madder and madder. So I thought, *Let's just turn into this other driveway. Maybe she won't notice.* She noticed. I can't tell you what she said, because nice ladies don't say those words, but I sure got a phooey for that. I decided I'd better just grit my teeth, put my tail between my legs, and head on home.

We've had a lot of adventures in our first five months together. It takes a lot of work to build a team. I think that Mary is really trying hard, and I think that in time, she'll get the hang of it, and in time, I'll like being a working dog.

Years later, after we had been a team for nine years, Pippen began to show signs that she was tired and needed to stop working.

The day I knew the time had come was the day she almost refused to walk home from an appointment we had in downtown Gahanna. Promises of a cookie, a treat, feeding time, some SunChips—all meant nothing to her. We walked at a snail's pace, and I never asked her to walk that far again. When we got home, I wrote this letter to the people in our lives I knew would care.

I made the call. I've been putting it off for weeks. I knew it had to be made, but I didn't want to do it. And when I did it, I couldn't believe the words I was hearing myself saying. "I'm calling to talk about returning for my fourth Seeing Eye dog."

How could I do that to Pippen? Here she is, lying at my feet, happy to be near me. She's snoring gently, and she sleeps much of the day. I have to face it. She is old, ten and a half, which is old for a Lab/Golden cross. She's certainly not able to work as she used to. We no longer take two or three walks a day, walking at three and a half to four miles per hour. No longer do we walk to the center of town for coffee or lunch. Jogging together on the school track is a distant memory. She's content to limit her exercise to sniffing trips around the back yard and brief walks in and out of the assisted living residence where my mother lives or at doctors' offices.

But am I content to hang up my independence and my active lifestyle along with her old, worn-out harness? No. I need to stay active for my own health. Sure, I can use my treadmill and my ski machine, but there's nothing as refreshing and beneficial as a good, brisk walk outside. I enjoy the feeling of accomplishment when I can walk to a destination to meet a friend for lunch or get myself to a meeting at church. That's why I chose using a guide dog over a white cane in the first place.

My first dog, Mindy, was 11 when she died, as a result of surgery she shouldn't have had. My second dog, Sherry, was 13 when she collapsed in my office at the end of a workday, just before we were to go home. By 8:00 that night, I had made the decision to put her down, because she was very, very sick, and I wasn't going to put her through surgery, like Mindy. During the time of each of their slow declines, I took them for brief walks, and I turned to other forms of exercise. My cane travel technique is awkward at best, and I missed the independence I feel when I travel with a dog.

So, here I am again, following the same pattern.

Whenever I show up somewhere without Pippen, she is always missed—not just by me, but also by the person I came to see, whether it's the doctor or the hairdresser. She's still able to walk to church, about half a mile, but she's motivated because she loves her church friends. Some of them have snacks for her, which fuels her love affair with them. I look the other way, because after all, she's almost retired. When I get a new dog, we'll all have to push the reset button by following the rules. No feeding the new guide dog. No talking to the new guide dog. No petting the new guide dog.

I imagine that Pippen will be relieved to have the new dog take over the duty of guiding me. ("You take her. I'm tired.") But she'll wish she could go with me, just not work for me.

If I decide to keep Pippen as a pet, it will be hard work: dividing my affection between the two dogs, caring for an elderly dog, and keeping up the training for the new, young dog. It will be expensive, too, especially if Pippen's health declines. The other option, that of asking someone to adopt her, is equally hard to imagine. How can I say goodbye to my little buddy? Will she pine for me? Will she be sad? I don't want that either.

Nobody said this part would be easy. It's part of the deal. Because the classes at The Seeing Eye are full until the end of the year, it's not likely that I'll have to face this dilemma for a few months, but it will come. It always does.

It turned out to be much easier than I thought—that is, to find someone to adopt her. I didn't even have to ask. A friend of a friend made an offhand remark that if I ever needed a new home for Pippen, she'd like to be first in line. So one day after I had made the decision to retire Pippen, we made a visit to what would be her retirement home. Here's a letter I wrote about that visit.

As Pippen jumped out of the car, she sniffed the country air and immediately wagged her tail in happy anticipation. Were we going on a picnic? Were we going for a romp through the cornfields? Were we going for an adventure in the woods? Were we going to play with that dog that was racing toward us with equal anticipation?

Her first clue that this was a special outing was that I unsnapped her leash, so she was free to take off in any direction she chose. I knew she wouldn't go far, because there were wonderful aromas right there in that five-acre lot about a mile off the road near Johnstown, Ohio.

The other dog, Molly, greeted Pippen by making her mark of piddle nearby. She was happy to have the company, but she made it clear that this was her territory. After a few minutes of gleeful romping, Pippen squatted in the exact same spot as if to say, "I know this is your territory, but I'm the guest." The next order of business was to flop on the ground and roll around in the grass. Pippen was so happy to be out in the country, without a leash and harness, and with so many opportunities to sniff to her heart's content. Then Molly ambled over to where Pippen had rolled, flopped down, and rolled right where Pippen had. Yes, these two had decided to be friends. They chased around the yard, alternating between sniffing and squatting. Suddenly, I felt Pippen bump into my side— not hard, just enough to say, "Here I am, Mom, but I gotta go. This is way cool. Just wanted you to know I haven't run off."

After a while, our human hosts and I climbed up the four steps onto the porch to chat and to talk about Pippen's acceptance of the home she would have when it was time for her to retire from being a guide. Pippen followed us by skipping the steps and leaping onto the porch. I was stunned. How could she do that at her age? Maybe she wasn't ready to retire after all. It's typical for guide dog handlers to waffle between decisions as important as this. One day, she acts like she can hardly put one foot in front of the other, and the next, she takes the porch in a single bound. Meanwhile, the husband of the family, seeing that the dogs were panting and obviously needing a drink, brought out a big bowl of water. Molly drank eagerly, but when Pippen approached the water, she sniffed and backed away. "What is this stuff? It stinks." It was well water, and this city dog wasn't so sure about it. But her thirst drove her back to try it again. She took a tentative lap and then stopped, considering. "Is this really water? Oh, the heck with it. I'm thirsty, and Molly seems to think it's good."

Then back out to the yard she leapt, skipping the steps again. Country living seemed to suit her. The humans in the group continued to visit, with the husband checking on Pippen occasionally to make sure she hadn't decided to go exploring in the adjacent woods. No, she was just around the corner of the house, smelling something wonderful, like where the cat had peed, but she readily came when I called her. I asked her if she was ready to go home, and to our amusement, she stood at the front door and whined. She wanted to go inside. "If I'm eventually going to live here," she said, "I want to see the house."

After a quick perusal of the kitchen, she trotted up the stairs on her own. "Where will my room be?" seemed to be her question. Satisfied that any room would do, she ran back down and was happy to have her leash snapped back on. This was a really cool place, but for right then, she'd be happy to curl up in the back seat of the car and go to sleep. It was a happy day for us all.

After Pippen moved on, from time to time, I'd send a message to Pippen's new mom to see how she was doing. The report was always the same. Pippen loved finding a patch of sunlight and would lie there watching her new mom work in the garden, or she'd wander off into the field, taking her sweet old time coming back for supper. "Just one more sniff, and I'll be there," she'd say. This was my girl, and it was heaven on earth for her. Occasionally, she'd seem restless, as if she didn't know what to do with herself. So her mom would invent a task for her, and then she seemed happy and pleased with herself. Once a working dog, always a dog who needs some sort of job to do—but not too much, not all day, and only things that she likes to do.

Pippen lived to be 15, surrounded by a loving family. I was not there for the end because I was not notified, and it's probably just as well. She might have been confused, and I know that emotionally, I would have been a mess.

Cisco—2013

The day I sent Pippen away to her retirement, my heart was broken in a million pieces, and I cried all day long. Guilt and longing kept surging through my soul, even though I knew it was best for her and for me. I was back at The Seeing Eye only two days later, and I couldn't shake those feelings. Preparing for a new life with a new dog felt like a betrayal to Pippen. I had to keep choking back tears as I sat at the table for lunch, meeting other students and instructors. It should have been a time of happy anticipation, but it was an extreme effort for me to be optimistic and hopeful. How could I love another dog as much as I loved Pippen? Maybe I had come back too soon. Maybe I should have taken more time to grieve, as I did after Mindy and Sherry.

Enter Cisco.

He was an absolutely gorgeous Golden Retriever, large and regal in his stature, but it turned out that it was not a good match. It happens sometimes, but it never occurred to me that this was the problem for us.

I tried so hard to fall in love with that sweet face that is so typical of Goldens. His demeanor was gentle and easygoing, which was a clue that maybe he was not the best match for me. I had told the visiting instructor, when she came to my house to interview me about my next dog, that I liked a dog who was affectionate and enjoyed being petted. I told her that I loved Goldens, but I could love any dog, even a German Shepherd, if they found one that met my criteria. She told me I wouldn't be getting a German Shepherd, but she didn't say why. My guess is that she thought I was not physically able to keep a Shepherd occupied and therefore happy. She picked Cisco for me, because he was a lover and easygoing. At the time she did the interview, I was suffering with back issues, so my pace was much slower than usual, and I believe that was another reason she chose Cisco.

In class, the moment I picked up the harness handle and began to walk with him down the hall to the dining room, I knew there was something wrong. His gait was odd, but I chalked it up to his being twice the size of Pippen, and I thought I would get used to it. That was my first mistake. Each time I felt there was something wrong, I thought it was my fault. There were many signs throughout the training that this was not the right match, but I kept thinking I was the one making the mistakes. In retrospect, I realize it wasn't working because this instructor had also been Cisco's trainer, and his bond with her and her alone was way too strong. On the last evening before we all went home, we took pictures, and it was impossible for me to smile as I held back my tears. I was sad and felt guilty that I was taking Cisco away from his true love, the instructor. It was absurd to have those feelings, so I fought them back.

I worked with Cisco for six months, trying to overcome the difficulties he had with the simplest tasks. First, I couldn't get him to walk faster than an old man. He seemed to forget what to do when a car was parked over the sidewalk, which is simply to guide me around it. He ran me into obstacles, and he would not finish a destination walk. I liked to walk to a coffee shop, and he would get within a few yards of the door and then act confused. I kept sending email messages to the supervisor at The Seeing Eye, not wanting it to sound like I needed an instructor to come out and troubleshoot, because I knew that would be expensive for the school, and it didn't feel like an emergency.

After six months, I had had it and finally asked for help. An instructor came and walked with us, again in the rain, and saw firsthand what I had been struggling with for far too long. He said after the walk around the neighborhood, "It's totally up to you, but this looks like a mismatch to me." That's all I needed to tip the scales in favor of sending him back.

The last I heard, he had been placed with someone else who, I suppose, didn't have the varied and energetic lifestyle I had. Before I got Cisco, it hadn't occurred to me that I would ever get a dog that was not a good match for me. My first three dogs were perfect for me, and I hadn't known anyone who had experienced getting a dog that wasn't right for them. I felt as if I had gone through a failed marriage, but I knew I had done my part. I wish him well.

The Match

Before I tell you about my current dog, my wonderful Dora, I think this is a good place to talk about how Seeing Eye dogs are matched with their people. Here's a journal entry from the day I was introduced to Dora and we began our life together.

"Matchmaker, matchmaker, make me a match," goes that wonderful song, playing over and over in my head as I wait to be called to the common lounge, where I will meet my new Seeing Eye dog. Typically, we arrive at The Seeing Eye campus on Monday, and we're given our dogs, one by one, on Wednesday. For the first day and a half, we get oriented to the campus, meet our fellow students and instructors, learn about new techniques, receive our new leashes and harnesses, and of course take that Juno walk around the campus. We're expected to give this pretend dog regular commands, such as, "Juno, forward," and "Juno, right." We talk a lot about our lifestyle and what we expect our new guides to do.

My instructor already knew what I was looking for in a dog, since my previous dog hadn't worked out for me. Among other problems we had was that I couldn't get him to walk at a brisk pace. He simply refused. So at the top of my list was a dog who would pull, a dog who liked to work, and a dog who loved to be loved. Cisco was affectionate and beautiful, but the match just wasn't right for us.

This match business is a very delicate and fine-tuned process. Before I arrived, sometime within the previous weeks, each of the current string of dogs ready to be placed with someone was considered for me and for each of the other 19 students scheduled for the February class. Each of us has a slightly different need or preference. The dogs are trained for eight weeks before they are considered for placement. Dora was evaluated, not only by my instructor, but also by the training supervisor, who happened to have been my first instructor back in 1982, so he knew me well.

They agreed that Dora had just the right amount of spunk for my preference. She's sharp enough to learn the routes I travel and calm enough to sit through my meetings and other activities. She'll pull like crazy when it's time to do an exercise walk, and she'll lie still when it's time to watch me as I swim laps in the pool or work on my laptop. She'll be able to figure out which door is the one for the coffee shop and where we need to stand to wait for the light to change. All the dogs have all these skills by the end of their training, but some are better than others. They are each rated with a number score on the various skills, but when it comes right down to it, the sighted instructor takes the dog out for a spin, under blindfold, and that's the final test.

So now it's Wednesday, and we get to meet our dogs. Up until this time, we are not told which dogs are being considered for us. "Dog day" is always an emotional time for me. It's like having a baby or getting the best Christmas present ever. I sit down on one of the chairs in the common lounge. This is it, the moment when I meet my new partner for the next eight or ten years.

My instructor brings a dog over to me and says, "Mary, this is Dora. She's a Lab/Golden cross." Then she describes what Dora looks like, but I'm not listening. I put my hands on each side of her sweet little face, and she sniffs my mouth, ever so gently. Then she takes a very tentative little lick at my nose, and I'm in love!

Many people have the mistaken idea that when you get a guide dog, you just go to where they are trained, pick one out, and then take it home with you. Here is an excerpt from the letter that The Seeing Eye sends out to first-time students. It's the daily schedule of what the students do after they've received their dogs.

Although there will be many other details, the general schedule for weekdays will be:

Arise at 5:30 am to feed and park your dog ("park time" is the name we give to the process of leash relieving your dog)

Breakfast at 7 am

A half–hour to one–hour lesson in town sometime between 8 am and 11 am

Park time late morning

Lunch at 12:10 pm

A half–hour to one–hour lesson in town sometime between 1 pm and 4 pm

Feed your dog and park at 4:30 pm

Suppertime at 5:10 pm

Evening discussions between 6:30 and 8 pm

Last park at 8 pm

It is a busy day, but there will be plenty of downtime to read, groom your dog, study, or visit with your classmates. This downtime in the dormitory is just as important as learning to work with your dog in town. Your dog will be lying at your feet, learning that you are the new, most important being in its life.

In other words, from the moment the instructor hands over our dog's leash, we are in charge of its care, feeding, training, and socializing, 24/7. The training starts with our first walk to the dining room for dinner, although the dogs are only on leash, not in harness. Everyone is excited and a little nervous, and that first meal might be an exercise in getting our dogs to sit back down and lie quietly under the table, but that's part of the training, too. The harness goes on the next day.

Dora—February 2014–Present

Because it was February when Dora and I began our training on the first day, it was impossible to get into town for practice walks on the sidewalks of Morristown. There had been a huge snowstorm, and the streets had not been cleared. Our first walk together was to the end of the long driveway, which had taken all morning to clear enough for walking. I almost had to run to keep up with Dora, and I was out of breath by the time we returned, but I was laughing with joy, happy to have at last received a dog who was going to keep me in shape.

The next day, we were driven into town to work on sidewalks that had been shoveled by hand, making a path just wide enough for a person and a dog. Thirty seconds into our walk, I tripped over a two-foot high wall of snow, because Dora, only 18 months old at the time, had not yet learned how to judge if a path was wide enough for both of us. It was just a trip and a tumble into a snowbank. I wasn't hurt, just a little embarrassed. It took only that first fall for her to get it, and from then on, she was meticulously careful that both of us would clear a narrow opening. She still is. Once, in a crowded restaurant, she stopped as we encountered an aisle where two chairs were blocking the way. A person would have had to turn sideways to pass through. A man seated at one of the tables asked me why she stopped. "She's afraid we can't get through," I explained.

"What? You mean the dog makes the decision?"

"Yes, indeed," I said, "because she's the one that can see."

Major decisions like where we will go that day are mine, but navigating decisions are hers.

During that first week of training on ice and snow, Dora learned to slow down when she saw black ice and to find the best way to get through those mounds of snow that the snowplows leave as they turn the corners.

Taking her out to empty was the toughest part of our training. Standing in the whipping wind with my hands freezing while I waited for her to find just the right spot was not fun, but if I had it to do over, I'd do it again in a heartbeat.

For the first time in my training of over 32 years with five different dogs, we had to stay indoors all day because of the weather. Now I know what a true nor'easter is. Because of an overnight blizzard, the instructors got creative and set up obstacle courses in the hallways, food distractions, and unfamiliar routes through the basement where not even the dogs had been before. After the streets were passable, but it was still dangerously cold, we did a lot of what they call "freelance" work in town—a lot of shopping, tours through the mall, and for me, a trip to an assisted living home.

My mother was a resident in one here in Gahanna, and I was concerned that Dora might walk too fast through its hallways and knock elderly people over. I needn't have worried. She was the very definition of cautious. We even encouraged a woman in a wheelchair to pet Dora, so she would not be afraid of wheelchairs.

When we got home, we had the same conditions, so much so that I worried that when the snow finally melted, she wouldn't be able to recognize the bare corners and crosswalks. Again, I needn't have worried. After working with a sluggish dog that seemed not very bright, I found Dora refreshingly sharp and quick to learn each new task I asked her to do. Here's an example of what a success story in training looks like.

The grocery store where I sometimes shop is one mile from my house. It's mostly a straight shot once I get out of my neighborhood, except for the very end of the route. This is where it gets a whole lot more complicated for a dog, and it's the place where Cisco never got it. For that reason, I'd been very careful to introduce this route well after Dora and I had established our relationship. I also prepared myself better this time for success with the training session.

First, I asked my friend Eve to help me with this project. Before we left the house, I engaged Dora in a short refresher clicker session, while Eve observed in amusement. It's pretty funny to watch a dog get so excited about dinging a bell with her nose and then getting a treat, which in this case was just a piece of kibble. But a piece of kibble from a hand is even more exciting than one from a bowl. I would be needing the clicker for the final destination, the customer service counter at the store.

Next, we drove to a spot about two thirds of the way, since Dora already knew that part, and we left the car there. The first part of the new route was to cross the interstate on a bridge. It's terrifying to me, but a wall prevented Dora from seeing the traffic below us, so she marched on fearlessly. We then had to cross two side streets. Not a problem, but they needed to be observed with a full stop and a wait until I gave her the command to cross.

Now here was the first really tricky part. When we turned toward the parking lot, we had to cross two islands. In order to execute this route to the door of the store, the dog needs to not wander into the parking lot but to stay on course and take me to each island. I have absolutely no vision, so it is essential for the dog to do this right. On our training session with Eve, I came prepared with treats for each success. Before I asked Dora to guide me to each island, I took Eve's arm, and I heeled Dora and treated her when we got to each island. Then it was her turn to do the guiding. It took a few tries, because she remembered that once upon a time, we had parked in that section of the parking lot, and she was probably looking for the car. That's just a guess, but dogs do remember even one occurrence of an event.

After mastering the two islands, we strode ahead to the door. Again, I took Eve's arm, and she led us to the customer service desk, which involved making a wide left turn around a display and then another left turn to the counter. Then I pulled out the clicker gear, and we practiced targeting that counter, moving back a few more feet several times with a treat with each success.

Soon a little group of onlookers had gathered to watch this process with fascination. No problem. Dora was focused on those kibble treats, and she was determined to please me.

Finally it was time to start from the door and find our way to the counter on our own, with Eve trailing behind my right shoulder and trying not to help with hints. I have to congratulate Eve for not interfering with Dora's learning process. On this final trip, I suspected that she had become distracted and was way off base, but I hung in there with her, and Eve never said a word. In a couple of seconds, I could sense that Dora was thinking, *Oh, I get it now. I've got this, Mom.* She then zoomed around to the left and came to a screeching halt at the counter. As if it had been planned, there was a cart in the way, so she had to take a detour, but she got us there.

Dora works hard and plays hard. She's the most athletic dog I've ever had. For the first five years of our working life together, I'd have to take her out in the back yard and play ball with her to burn off some of her energy before we'd go for a walk or go to church or the Y, where she would be required to lie quietly and wait.

Here's how the game goes.

I sit on a lawn chair, but I don't get comfy. Dora drops the ball into my lap. She lets go of it reluctantly, but she knows that if it's going to go anywhere, she's going to have to give it up.

"Drop it," I say, and she finally does. I stand up and throw it as hard as I can, but it doesn't go very far, because I throw like a girl. But Dora doesn't care. She races after it and often catches it before the first bounce. Unlike any other dog I've had, she then rushes back to me, slamming into my knees, as if she's going too fast to stop, like sliding into home plate. Then I coax her to drop the ball into my lap again. I pick the slimy thing up again, stand up, and pitch it into the back yard. Each time, she barrels into me with the fervor of a nine–year–old making his first home run.

We do this routine about 50 times before she begins to slow down.

It's amazing to me that this creature who acts like her very life depends on getting that ball back to me in record time is the same creature who guides me safely across the street. It's like it's her second job. But everybody needs a break from the seriousness of life. And I have to say that playing ball with Dora brings me a whole lot of joy. When I fasten the jingle bell onto her collar, so I can hear where she is in the back yard, and I say,

"Want to play outside?" she gets so excited that she can hardly contain herself. It's not just watching Dora run free. It's not just the amusement of knowing she's caught the ball like an outfielder. It's the interaction between us that's just for fun.

Lest you think that Dora is all work and no play or all play and no work, here's one more story about this impressive girl.

One Saturday afternoon, my friend Dan took us to a sporting goods store to buy tennis balls for Dora. She has a wonderful toy called a Canine Cannon, a gift from "Uncle Dan." You put a tennis ball in the end of a rifle–like contraption and then shoot it out across the yard. She absolutely loves this game, and if you don't shoot the ball fast enough, she nudges the end of the gun with her nose as if to say, "Shoot the darn thing already!" As she dashes back with the ball in her mouth, she chomps on it vigorously in her excitement, and it doesn't take long for the ball to be destroyed.

It was time to buy replacement tennis balls. When we got to the store, we were directed to the second floor. After getting off the elevator, we zigzagged all over the place and finally found the tennis balls. After we made our selection, I said, "Okay, let's go," and that's all Dora needed. She took the lead, zigging and zagging across the store, without any hints from Uncle Dan, and without hesitation, she proudly took us directly back to the elevator. It's as though she says, "Follow me, everybody. I know the way."

Dan is one of the few people in my life who get it that the dog can do her work best if they stay one step behind my right shoulder. That way, it's clear to the dog that she's in charge.

When we strode up to the elevator, he said, "I'm so impressed with her confidence, I could almost cry. She is just so awesome."

Back at home, we replaced the old, ratty ball. As I shot the new ball out over the yard from my chair on the patio, Dan took pictures of this gloriously happy girl, sitting in rapt attention as I aimed, and then leaping up to catch the ball as it sailed over her head. I hope you can see the pure happiness in her play and that I've conveyed the pure pride I feel in her work.

Myths and Magic of Guide Dogs

What Guide Dogs Do

Whenever there are three or more blind people gathered, it is very rare that they all have guide dogs, which is contrary to popular belief. The truth is that a very small percentage of people who are blind use guide dogs. Why is that? Those of us who use guide dogs would never go back to using only a white cane. Yet most people who are cane users will argue that using the cane is the only way to go.

It's a friendly debate, like the one that involved two of my visually impaired friends over dinner one evening. One has been a guide dog user for many years, while the other would never consider it, mostly because she has never cared much for dogs in the first place. She does quite well with a white cane. She enjoys being able to fold it up and put it away when she's reached her destination, something you can't do with a dog. However, those of us who are seasoned guide dog users are pretty good at tucking our guides neatly under the table or desk, so that it's often a surprise to others in the room when we get up, and the dog suddenly appears.

My cane–using friend never has to worry about dog hairs on her clothes, arranging her schedule around feeding and relieving times for the dog, getting the dog groomed, or taking it to the vet. Canes are very low–maintenance tools, but to my knowledge, no one has ever said, "What a beautiful cane you have!"

My beautiful dog has been the catalyst for many conversations with people who ordinarily would pretend I wasn't there. Of course, the initial conversation is with the dog, not me, as in, "What's your name, you pretty thing?" With this opening, I always know they're not directing their words to me; at least I hope not. Then follows a teachable moment. "I'm sorry, but she's on duty. She's a working dog, and she's not allowed to be sociable when she's in harness. But you can talk to me." Over the course of five dogs, each of whom has enjoyed a long working life, I must have said these words a thousand times. Am I always to be the first person with a guide dog these people have ever met?

Annoying as this is, I'm one who would never go back to using a white cane. Whenever I'm ready to leave a meeting or a restaurant, all I have to do is pick up my purse and stand up, and my dog heads right for the door. If there is a crowd of people blocking the exit to a restaurant, she finds a way to go around them and still get to the outside door. It's awe–inspiring to watch Dora work. When we're crossing a street, she stays inside the white lines of the crosswalk. If a car is blocking the crosswalk, she won't start across the street even if I tell her to. This is called "intelligent disobedience." If a car comes careening around the corner in front of us, she stops and sometimes backs up if the car comes too close. When we approach a flight of steps, she slows down and then stops at the top step, only starting down when I have found the edge of the step with my shoe and have given her the forward command. She leads me around obstacles, including construction sites, in a graceful and efficient way. She knows certain words I use when I want to go to a location that would be hard for me to find on my own. For instance, when we approach a store in a strip mall that I frequently patronize, I just say, "Right, right inside," with a gesture with my right hand, and she finds the door and places her nose right under the handle.

It's pretty funny what misconceptions people have about what a guide dog can and cannot do. They usually err on the side of assuming they are almost human.

What Guide Dogs Do Not Do

Guide dogs are not guard dogs. They are not trained to protect their people with their teeth or a growl. They protect their people by guiding them around or stopping at obstacles.

One day when I was in a medical lab, getting ready to have my blood drawn, the technician was afraid to come near me. I told her my dog would not bite her, and then I couldn't resist a little teachable moment. "Why would I bring a dog that would bite in here? How would I ever get any help?"

A guide dog is very smart, but it cannot think like a human. For that reason, it cannot discern how fast a car is coming toward us and if we have time to cross the street before it gets to us. It is up to me to listen and make that judgment myself. The dog is trained to stop and back up only if the car is already in front of us.

Contrary to popular belief, the dog cannot read traffic

lights. Misinformed people should think about that one for a minute. Even if it were not the case that dogs are colorblind, how on earth would you teach a dog to read traffic lights? That's like asking the dog to read street signs.

Guide dogs do not make the decisions on which way to go on your way to a destination. In other words, I do not say to the dog, "Go to the beauty shop." When I get to the end of my street, I tell my dog which way to turn, and at the end of the next block, I give her the next direction, and so it goes until we get there. If the beauty shop, or wherever it is that I want to go, is just one store among many in a row, the dog might pause at another door, as if to say, "We went here once. Is this where we're going today?" It's always amusing to see how they remember all the places we've been.

Rules About Guide Dogs

Talk to the Person, Not the Dog

As I mentioned earlier, people have a tendency to talk to my dog. What they don't realize is that distracting the dog from keeping her mind on her person can actually be dangerous. Several times, my friends who love Dora have called out to her just as I was about to go up or down some steps. I know they were just being friendly, but their greetings could have caused a fall. Keeping their greetings directed to me, not the dog, is always better, no matter whether I am dealing with stairs or not.

Never Feed a Guide Dog

Another rule that most people do not understand is to never, and I mean never, feed a guide dog. You should never feed someone else's dog, especially a guide dog. You don't know if that dog is allergic to something or will have to relieve itself as a result of eating food off schedule.

Don't Give My Dog Commands

Never call to the dog to make it turn in one direction or another. Talk to the person. And never grab the harness or the leash of the dog. If you want to help by giving a blind person directions, just use words.

I've heard an analogy that illustrates this rule beautifully. If you are riding in a car with someone else who is driving and you want them to turn right at the next driveway, you say, "Turn right at the next driveway." You don't take the steering wheel and turn it yourself.

There may be a very good reason why the dog has stopped, hesitated, or taken a circuitous route. If the blind person and her dog are clearly headed in the wrong direction, again, talk to the person, not the dog. Calling to the dog or telling her something different from what her person is saying can be confusing and is detrimental to her training.

Don't Stare at My dog

It's tempting to want to stop and stare, because of course guide dogs are fascinating to watch, but staring can sometimes spook a dog, and they will stop in mid-stride. Then the handler wonders if there's an obstacle or some other danger, like a big hole in the sidewalk. Besides, it's rude.

It happens in restaurants all the time, but at least my dog has her mind on finding the outside door, so she's rarely distracted. When it's most annoying is when a parent points to the dog and tells the child, "Look, that's a working dog. Don't pet it." To me, that's teaching the child to stare. And even worse than that is to tell the child, "That dog is that lady's eyes." For a small child, this is impossible to understand. How can a dog be someone's eyes? Children are very literal, and speaking in metaphors is only confusing the issue. It's better to say, "Yes, that's a dog, but it has a very special job to do, so let's leave it alone and keep going." A more detailed explanation can come later.

I love having a guide dog, and I have loved every one like a child. Indeed, I feel like each one is my baby and I am offended when anyone says that she has done something wrong, when in fact, that person doesn't understand how a guide dog works. For instance, I have heard many times, "She almost ran you into that sign (or wall or whatever)," when actually she walks right up to it and then turns to avoid it. After all, the dog is not blind. People just don't understand how a guide dog is trained, and making inaccurate judgements is annoying. But let them say how beautiful she is, how well-mannered, how obedient, how smart, and I'm bursting with pride.

To learn more about Seeing Eye dogs, visit seeingeye.org .

Mary and Mindy, 1984

Mary, Sherry, and the Olympic Torch
January 2, 2002

Pippen, 2013

Cisco's graduation photo, 2017

Dora waits for Mary by the pool

Mary, Dora, and Dan in a 5K walk

Chapter Eleven
How Do You Do It?

In my first book, *The Bumpy Road to Assisted Living: A Daughter's Memoir*, I devoted one brief chapter to how I live life as a blind person, just to give my reader a glimpse into the setting in which I played the part of a daughter without sight who took on the responsibility for her elderly mother. Living without sight is no picnic. I won't try to claim it is. But I don't wake up each morning thinking, "Oh, God, I'm blind. How am I going to get through the day?" In fact, I don't give it a thought. As I said in Chapter One of this book, it's not as though I suddenly became blind overnight. My blindness was caused by a progressive eye disease, which means I had years and years to become accustomed to it, to learn to deal with it, but not necessarily to embrace it.

The difference between embracing blindness and accepting it is that the person who accepts it allows herself to be angry, to feel cheated, to wish to be treated like everybody else, but she does not allow herself to be beaten down by blindness. She pushes it aside to make room for achieving goals, accomplishing tasks, and even having fun.

If I embraced blindness, I would cheerfully tell you that it's fun to be blind. I get to read with my fingers in the dark. I get to take my guide dog everywhere. I can love someone who doesn't have a pretty face. But if I accept blindness, I understand that I am required to find different ways to solve problems that wouldn't be there if I could see. I understand that these solutions are not burdens but workarounds. They are sometimes difficult, but they are doable.

You might have noticed that I avoided using the word "challenge." I abhor the label of "visually challenged." "Challenged" is a negative word that doesn't make me feel any better about being blind. Other negative terms that set my teeth on edge are "sightless," "visually handicapped," "handicapable," and "differently abled." These are all euphemisms that defeat their purpose of trying to accept blindness. I am blind. It's a straightforward term that tells the truth and is not ashamed of it.

As the title of this chapter indicates, I'll address the practical issues of blindness, and then in the next chapter, I'll address the perceptions, both imagined and true.

How I Get Through a Typical Day

Let's start with getting out of bed.

Some people, both blind and sighted, might use a smartphone or Alexa to serve as an alarm clock, but I use one of the earliest pieces of technology, a Sharp talking clock. It can be used to tell time by pressing a small button. It can be used as a timer, as a reminder of a half hour's passing, or as an alarm clock. As an alarm clock, it plays a Boccherini tune that you'll recognize if you're a classical music lover. It's a very pleasant way to wake up. But often, I either wake up on my own or my dear Seeing Eye® dog, Dora, pads over to my bed, puts her pretty face near mine, and either gives me a kiss or shakes her collar if I don't start moving immediately. That's the best alarm clock of all.

After taking Dora out to empty, the first business of the day is to make my tea. A few years ago, my daughter gave me a single-serve coffee maker, made by Keurig, but it can also be used for making a cup of tea at just the right temperature. Until I received this gigantic piece of equipment (but well worth the space it takes on my counter), I insisted that the only civilized way to make tea was to pour boiling water into a teapot and then serve the tea from the pot. Although I'm good at pouring liquid, I often scalded myself with this method or missed the opening of the teapot by just a hair, and I'd have water all over the counter. Most of the time, holding a finger of the other hand at the rim of a mug or a glass is the best way to tell when the liquid reaches near the top, but not when you're handling boiling water.

Reading the Paper

After I've made my tea, Dora and I settle on the couch in the family room to "read" the newspaper.

It's possible to use a computer or a smartphone for this purpose, but I prefer a touch-tone phone, because it's easy. There's no having to jump around, back and forth from article back to menu and on to the next link, and then repeat the process. I realize this makes me old fashioned, but at least I've graduated from the radio reading service—not to minimize its value to many older folks with vision loss.

I must say that the radio reading service played a very important part in my life. When it was first introduced in Columbus in 1975, I was absolutely elated. Volunteers read newspapers, magazines, and other print material, such as grocery and department store ads, voter information, and even the comics. I was so grateful for this service that I volunteered as a host for one of the talk shows and spoke to Lions Clubs and church groups to recruit volunteers and of course to inspire donations. I even jumped at the chance to work there as director of volunteers, and I held that job for over 21 years. For many elderly people who are not able to or prefer not to deal with technology, listening to a closed circuit radio station where volunteer readers bring the news to them is like having a window on the world.

But when the National Federation of the Blind, NFB, created its *Newsline*, I felt liberated to read what I wanted when I wanted. It's all synthesized speech, but the tone and speed can be adjusted to the comfort level of the listener. By dialing up *Newsline* on the phone and then pressing various buttons, I can choose which newspaper I want to listen to, which section I like, and which article interests me. If it doesn't appeal to me or if I've heard enough after the headline, I don't have to sit through it. I just press the 3 button, and I'm taken to the next article. Pressing Star gets me out of that section or out of that newspaper, and I can choose something else. I have a favorites list, which I access by pressing 4. Then I can choose from *The Columbus Dispatch*, the AARP magazine, *USA Today*, and many other publications. I can also access a comprehensive weather report that gives me the current conditions, the hourly forecast, and the daily forecasts for the next seven days. I can choose what I watch on TV that night by pressing 8 and then following the prompts to choose a time or a network, including cable channels.

More about TV later.

Using a Computer

After reading the paper and having breakfast, I settle down with a cup of coffee to check my email. I use a laptop computer that has a screen reader with a speech synthesizer called Window–Eyes. Another program is called JAWS, but I've stuck with the Microsoft product because when I first learned to use a computer, it was called Vocal–Eyes, made by the same company. I didn't want the hassle of learning new commands. Instead of using a mouse, as sighted computer users do, I use arrow keys and certain combinations of keys to perform tasks, such as reading a sentence in full, reading word by word, reading letter by letter, or deleting any of these. I can also delete or move whole paragraphs, whole pages, or even whole documents. All of these functions are performed with the action of pressing certain keys. The way I have my computer set up, I hear the name of each key as I strike it, so theoretically I can hear typos as I make them. "Theoretically" is the operative word here. That's why I have an editor for anything I intend to sell. My email friends make plenty of their own typos, so I do the best I can and then don't worry about it.

Reading a Book

In my leisure time, I love to read for pleasure. The National

Library for the Blind, which is part of the Library of Congress, produces thousands upon thousands of titles, either in braille or as what are called "talking books." Although I use braille for labeling and for making notes for speeches or for recipes, I have never been comfortable using it for pleasure reading.

The first talking books were produced on long–playing records, to be played at 16–2/3 speed on a specialized talking book machine that looked like an old record player with a manual arm. We had to place the needle in the first groove, and it played only one record at a time. The next generation came on flexible disks, smaller versions of records. Next came cassette tapes, followed by digital recordings on cartridges.

All these recorded books were sent to patrons through the U.S. mail. When we were finished with them, we just dropped them in the nearest mailbox or simply left them out for our mail carriers to pick up and lug back to the post office. These days, library patrons who are comfortable with using a computer or other device that connects to the internet download books from the Library for the Blind onto our specialized devices, such as the Victor Reader Stream. I now use a Victor Reader Trek, which also has a GPS feature.

Using Technology on My Walks

As I mentioned above, I currently use a piece of equipment called the Victor Reader Trek, made by HumanWare. This handheld device not only plays talking books, podcasts, and internet radio, plus notes that the user records, but it also serves as a GPS for traveling outside the home. I never leave home without it. When I'm walking around the neighborhood with

Dora, it keeps track of where I am, how fast I'm walking, in which direction, and how far ahead the next intersection is.

I know my neighborhood like the back of my hand, but on a rare occasion, my guide dog will decide that rather than climbing over that snow bank that's blocking the crosswalk, it would be much easier to turn the corner and go in a different direction. She's a smart little girl, but like the rest of us, she's not perfect. That's when I pull Victor out of my pocket, and I press a couple of buttons to find out which direction I'm facing and what the next intersection is.

When we get home, it tells me how far we walked and at what speed. I don't use it for reading books while I'm walking, because I need to pay attention to my surroundings and exactly where I am. By the way, I also carry my iPhone with me, in case I want a little background music as I go, but mostly just in case I run into a bigger problem than being disoriented. I might fall and break a bone, or I might have to call the police if a dog attacks my dog. This actually happened one time, but that's another story.

Okay. Because most people want to hear all about it, I'll tell the story here.

My former Seeing Eye dog Pippen was a little Lab/Golden cross. One day, she and I were walking in the neighborhood when suddenly a big dog rushed out of his yard and attacked Pippen. He started biting her, and I screamed and screamed for help, but nobody appeared.

Then he had her on her back, and she was screaming. I hope to never hear that sound again. That was my cue to jump in and do something instead of just standing there screaming. I straddled that dog and grabbed his collar and pulled his head up and away from Pippen, thus allowing her to jump up and run away. Finally, the owner came out and led his dog back into the house, but not until I was done with him. I gave him a lecture about not having complete control of his dog that he will surely never forget.

Meanwhile, the police arrived, checked on Pippen's wound, which was minor, and gave a severe warning to the owner of that dog, which I later learned was a nine–month–old Mastiff puppy. His idea of play was actually not only an attack on a smaller dog, but it was also a misdemeanor by law. Interfering with the work of a guide dog is illegal and can be punished with a fine.

Walking My Dog

An essential part of each day is to walk at least two miles with Dora.

When I first started using a Seeing Eye dog, I was working full time at the radio reading service. I'd take Mindy (1982–1992) for a walk at 5:15 in the morning and then again as soon as we got home. There was no place to walk her at noon, but she never seemed interested in emptying until we got home to her own back yard. Later, when the office moved to a neighborhood where it was safe to walk at lunch time, I could take my dogs for walks midday.

I recall being very frustrated when I first took Pippen (2004–2013) out for lunchtime walks, because in the interval between retiring Sherry (2003) and bringing home a new puppy in 2004, the neighborhood streets had been reconstructed to include roundabouts, which completely flummoxed me. It took weeks of frustration and finally sighted help to figure out what had happened.

Now that I am retired, Dora's life is not so complicated, but she is required to help me get safely to certain destinations, such as the grocery store, the bank, and the beauty shop. Unfortunately, all other destinations, such as doctors' offices, church, and shopping, are not within walking distance.

A Little Help from My Friends

So how do I get there?

I am blessed to have a team of volunteers from my church who are willing to drive me to appointments and take me shopping for groceries, clothes, and household items. After getting to know the strengths and interests of each of them, I have learned to ask them individually for certain errands. One loves to shop for clothes, so she's the one I ask to help me find an outfit for a speaking engagement. One is good at finding obscure places, so she's the one I ask to drive me to doctors' appointments. One is not shy about telling me I need to replace my window dressings, so she's the one I ask to take me for buying curtains.

Another volunteer is comfortable with computers and smartphones, so she's the one I ask to help me order on Amazon. I know blind people who manage Amazon on their own, but as of this writing, I haven't yet learned how to do that.

One volunteer, Sherri, from an organization called Volunteers Express, has taken me grocery shopping since 1991, so she knows what brands I like and how green I like my bananas. In fact, she often goes without me and then calls me when she has questions. She puts me on speaker phone, and via her phone, I ride around the store with her, so she can talk to me as she goes. Of course, I like it better if I can go, but when I was recovering from back surgery, this was the perfect solution for me as I stayed home to recuperate. I would make a list and send it to her via email. My impulse buying was greatly reduced with this method, but the trade–off was that I could shop for groceries from my recliner. Another way I shop from my recliner is to use an app on my phone to order groceries and have them delivered, but it's not as personal as doing a "proxy" shop with my friend Sherri.

Homeowner Blues

As a blind and single homeowner, I could be facing one nightmare after another. In fact, I did, to the tune of many thousands of dollars over the years, paying for repair after repair in addition to paying for maintenance of the house and the yard.

Among my most treasured blessings is the friendship of a man who happens to be a handyman, so all my homeowner woes are solved by him. He has replaced my garbage disposal, repaired my garage door when it wouldn't close all the way, replaced screening on my patio, planted grass seed and then fenced off the area, replaced light bulbs and fixtures, and performed a hundred other chores around the house. He takes me to the hardware store to buy the right products for a job. After a visit to the pet store, he carries the monstrous bag of dog food. A bonus is that he adores my Dora. The feeling is mutual, so sometimes it's a challenge to get the jobs done without her insisting he throw the ball instead.

Cleaning House

I confess that I have my house professionally cleaned once a month. Unfortunately, I have to do a little housework between times, but back when I had a family to take care of, too, I did it all.

The first rule for a blind housekeeper is to try to keep the house in order. I had a volunteer from an organization that matched volunteers with people with disabilities come into my house, and he was immediately surprised by how tidy it was. He expected clothing and dishes to be tossed everywhere. What an absurd notion. If that were true, how on earth would I keep track of my belongings? My mother taught me, "A place for everything and everything in its place," which seems like a stodgy old rule, but it is a truism that I try to follow.

Next, I tried to keep a schedule for each task that I might not notice needed doing. For instance, on the first weekend of the month, I used a cobweb duster to swipe at every corner in the house, just in case a cobweb happened to be there. And if I thought of it, I'd take a swipe at the ceiling fans and light fixtures as well. Each Saturday, I washed the sheets and returned them to the beds. Why Saturday? Even though I am retired now, I still maintain that schedule, mostly because that's how my mother did it. Mothers come in handy when it becomes necessary to establish a habit.

Running the vacuum cleaner has its own challenges, but it can be done by a blind person. First, I have to walk around in my bare feet to detect dog toys, a forgotten ball of yarn, or objects that might have fallen off a table. Then I use the sweeper like a lawn mower, trying to make straight lines back and forth over the room.

Once someone asked me if I liked my new vacuum cleaner. She wanted to know if it cleaned the carpet well. I have no idea. I just do my job and hope it does its job. You might say it's a matter of blind faith.

Sweeping the kitchen floor with a broom is done with a little different routine, starting at one end, making short swipes toward the other side of the room until I get to the other end of the room, and repeating this routine until all the crumbs and dog hair are on one side. Then with short swipes, I eventually get to make a little pile of dirt and whisk it into the dustpan.

All that being said, now that I don't have so much traffic in my house, I use one of those soft cloths that are attached to a stick, and the cloth picks up the dirt in no time. Then I just remove the disposable cloth and attach a new one, and I'm ready for the next spurt of cleaning energy.

Dusting must be done carefully, or I'll wind up swiping everything onto the floor. This is one reason why I don't have any knickknacks sitting around on tables. In this particular case, I don't want to be like my mother and have dozens of unnecessary things to have to dust around. The tables in my living room are made of glass, so I just use a paper towel with a bottle of glass cleaner and work my way around the room.

Cleaning the bathroom is not really that hard, given the new products for convenience that are available to us. When I was first married, I cleaned the toilets with toilet bowl cleaner and a rag, using my bare hands. What a dope I was. I eventually saw what that was doing to my hands and bought a brush. Now I use those wonderful little sponges that clip onto a stick. You swipe around the inside of the bowl, hope you did a decent job, and then flick off the sponge into the trash, without touching a thing. I try to clean my bathroom and kitchen sinks each night before I go to bed so I wake up to cleanliness and a tidy bathroom and kitchen. It makes finding what I need so much easier if everything is in its place and surfaces are pleasant to touch.

I used to wash windows myself because I have the kind that tilt inward, so I could wash the outside as well as the inside. I had no way of knowing if I left streaks or not. I just wiped the glass in one direction and then did it again in another direction with a good glass cleaner and lots of paper towels. I had the same philosophy for mirrors.

No matter how hard I tried, I would still miss spots on the walls or on the countertops that were impossible to feel. When my kids were little, I handed them a tube of toothpaste and offered them a nickel for each spot they cleaned off the walls. Now the kids are grown and gone, so the spots just have to wait for the monthly housecleaners, and they have those wonderful little sponges that easily remove the spots.

Remember how housewives used to wash on Monday and iron on Tuesday, week in and week out? I used a similar routine for keeping the house clean throughout the week. For a while, I was on a kick of taking 15 minutes out of each day to do a chore. For instance, maybe Monday would be vacuum the living room day, and Tuesday would be clean the family room day. That way, I wouldn't have to do everything all in one day, and the day before, the house wouldn't look like a cyclone had hit it. I must admit that sometimes now, when I come home late from an evening out, I don't always hang up or put away everything I've worn that night, but I try to, because I don't enjoy getting up to a mess.

Speaking of clothing, I'm often asked how I walk out the door with clothes that match or are well coordinated. First, I keep my closet organized. Dresses and skirts are hung together. Winter clothes are hung in one closet, and summer clothes are hung in another. Long sleeves and warmer garments are at one end of the rod, gradually progressing to sleeveless and cooler items. Scarves are hung on the hanger with the dress or top that they accessorize. If I've bought jewelry to go with that particular item, it goes around the neck of the hanger, too. I can usually find the garment I want by feel, but if a top, for instance, has several colors in it, I'll make a braille note and clip it to the garment or the hanger to remind me what it is. I am a firm believer in the "one in, one out" rule. When I buy a new top, I find one that I haven't worn in a couple of years or one that I never liked in the first place and it goes in the giveaway bag.

My coat closet is arranged with the warmest coat at the far left and the lightest jacket at the far right. I keep my shoes in shoe organizers and try not to get two pairs of the same style but in different colors, because like anybody else, I hate being caught in public with two different shoes on. For the same reason, I use safety pins to keep my socks paired when they go into the wash. I also use safety pins to mark dish towels and good hand towels as ones I will actually use in my bathroom or kitchen, as opposed to the ones that have been relegated to the dog towel basket.

Speaking of washing clothes, I should mention here that most of the time, I cannot feel a stain. At the beginning of each clothing season, I ask a friend to look at every piece of clothing I have worn over the last year and check for stains. If the stain won't come out, then out it goes. I'd much rather be told if there is a stain on my shirt than to go around all day looking like a slob. It might be cool to do that in some sectors of our society, but for an older woman, it's not so cool. If you had a smear of mustard on your cheek or spinach in your teeth, wouldn't you want someone to tactfully and privately tell you about it?

Occasionally, when someone takes me shopping, they remark that it probably doesn't matter to me what color something is or if it goes well with the rest of my outfit. What an insensitive assumption. Of course it matters to me. I might not be able to see it, but the rest of the world can. It's just as important to me to look well put together and to wear colors that are complementary to my skin and shape as it is to anyone else.

Applying Makeup

Many women who are totally blind shy away from using eye makeup, because they're not sure if they're using the right colors, shades, or amounts. Just like many women who are sighted, they simply might not want to bother, or they don't need it. I've learned that wearing makeup does improve my appearance, so I have made it a practice to consult an expert and buy quality products.

The best way to start is to go to a department store where free makeovers are offered at the cosmetics departments. I pay attention to how the technician applies the makeup on one side of my face, and then do the other side myself with her supervision. She might get nervous when I move an eye liner pencil toward my eye, but because I have a good sense of the location of my features, and if I move slowly and cautiously, I'm usually successful and wow the technician on the other side of the counter. She might even hand me a mirror, forgetting that I really am blind.

I'm pretty proficient at applying eye makeup except for mascara, so I only wear it if I'm going to be with someone who can check it for me before I leave the house or get out of the car. Once again, it's essential to have a trusted friend tell us if we've accidentally made a mistake with the makeup. Better to fix it with a little spit and a tissue while we can than go through the evening with a dark spot where it doesn't belong.

Using the iPhone

After a busy day of writing, reading, walking, and taking care of errands and tasks, I like to watch some mindless TV show to wind down. I am an Amazon Prime and a Netflix subscriber, but instead of using my television, I use my iPhone. I have a gizmo that I can talk to, and it can find the channel I want on my television, but it's getting hard for me to hear dialog, and as of this writing, I haven't yet purchased a sound bar. I find it more convenient to just use my phone. I don't need a big picture. They could make the picture as big as a house, and I still wouldn't be able to see it. So I get into my fleecy robe, lean back on my couch, put the phone on my shoulder, and enjoy my shows after tapping on certain areas of the phone's screen. That took a while to master, and I must admit there were times when I wanted to just stomp on the thing, but evenings around here no longer sound like a crazy woman yelling at her phone.

When I first got my iPhone, it reminded me of when I first got a computer. It has been a struggle for me to keep up with the changes in technology, but I continue to struggle, because if I don't, I'm going to be left behind by the world.

I read manuals, and friends helped. I took cabs to blind friends' homes for tutoring, and after months of frustration, I finally learned the basics. It had to be friends who were blind who could teach me, because the commands with voiceover are different from those executed by the sighted user. Swiping doesn't work for us, when double–tapping does. But in certain cases, swiping does work. Tapping with two fingers does something entirely different from tapping with three fingers or four. When the speech suddenly disappears, and I am about to have a meltdown, I suddenly remember that if you tap twice with three fingers, it magically comes back on.

I believe that blind users of smartphones are going to have better brains as they age than sighted folks will because we have to use the phones so much more. I think about all the times sighted people use pictures to navigate a page on a computer or phone screen, when the blind user has to remember a certain command. And then there are the webmasters who have still not recognized the need to have a word accompany the picture or the graphic in order for the blind user to find it. I applaud the websites that use words instead of pictures when you have to prove that you are not a computer. I am so grateful when the word "link" is heard when I get to one, so I know where to press Enter to go to that link.

Audio Description

One particular advancement in technology has greatly enhanced the world of entertainment for people who are blind. Audio description or video description (the terms seem to be interchangeable) allows the visually impaired viewer to hear a description of scenery, costumes, and actions that are not evident from dialog or sound effects. TV, movies, plays, and operas are all made more meaningful to those of us who would be missing an important element of any performance were it not for audio description.

When the concept was first introduced for use in theaters, all the description was done by a person sitting in the audience or in the sound booth, speaking softly into a microphone. His voice would be heard only by the blind patron, who held a small receiver with an earbud. Now, since the technology has become more sophisticated, moviegoers can hear the descriptions that have already been scripted and recorded right on the movie disk on a separate track.

We still use a small receiver or headset, depending on the theater, and there are some snags in the system that still need to be worked out as of this writing.

The first problem we encounter at the movie theater is that we must insist on getting a receiver that has been programmed for the visually impaired. Because the deaf community has made deeper inroads in getting their needs met, and closed captioning and enhanced listening devices have become much more prevalent, we are often handed a receiver that has been programmed for a person with hearing loss. Once I was actually handed a device that produced closed captioning, even though I specifically asked for a receiver for the visually impaired and I was standing there with my Seeing Eye dog.

The next obstacle to overcome is that even after we are assured that this is indeed the right receiver, we sit through a half hour of trailers, which cannot have audio description, and then when the movie starts, there is no audio description, for one reason or another. Perhaps it's a dead battery. Perhaps it's the wrong receiver. And what makes it even more maddening is that the manager tells us, "If you have any problems, just bring it back to me, and I'll make it right." That means sending a companion back to the front, tracking down the manager, and consequently missing the first 15 minutes of the show. I have sat through many movies without the promised description because I didn't want to inconvenience my friend.

On the other hand, I've been so entranced by the audio description at a live theater production, and even more so at an opera, that I have vowed to never go to another opera without audio description. I had no idea how much I had been missing without it. For the same reason, I usually don't watch a TV show without audio description. Some of the streaming services offer it for most of their original programming, and some broadcast shows make it available on a secondary audio programming (SAP) channel. The caveat is that the SAP channel is accessible only by using a menu, which ironically is not accessible for blind viewers. However, certain newer televisions have remedied that problem by including the right technology that can be accessed by everyone.

As of this writing, I don't own one of those televisions, so most of what I watch, I watch on my phone. After all, I don't need a big picture, or any picture at all, for that matter. But since I only watch about an hour of TV each night, it's not a big problem.

My Friend Alexa

One of my favorite ways to entertain myself, after reading, writing, and watching shows on streaming services, is to play the games offered on Alexa. If you like trivia, which I do, it's a constructive way to have a little fun and learn something, too.

Because I don't use my Echo Dot for music, I have purchased five less expensive units and have placed one in each of five rooms of my house. Mostly, I use this service for a quick check on the time or the weather, but I also use it extensively for checking on spelling and definitions. It's much easier to ask Alexa than to sort through websites to find what I want. In the good old days, I used a handheld talking dictionary, but having Alexa as my personal assistant is much more fun.

Although I like playing trivia games with Alexa, my favorite games are played with real, live people and without technology. Give me a braille Scrabble game, and I'm happy for the whole afternoon.

My love of Scrabble was developed when I was a little girl, because my mother, my cousin, my aunt, and I often played it on holiday afternoons. We were never that interested in playing cards or Monopoly, but the thrill of capturing a triple word score with a Q or a Z in it kept the interest and even excitement going for hours. The ultimate entertainment for me is to play a game of Scrabble with real people sitting around a real table, hands on the board, conversation in the air, and strategies in our minds.

Practical Matters

When You Can't Drive

Let's talk about transportation.

For a person with any disability that prevents him or her from driving, getting from one place to another can be the biggest handicap of all. If I ever win the lottery, the first thing I'm going to do is hire a full-time chauffeur.

Fortunately, there are options other than having a private chauffeur. In years past, the only options were city buses and taxicabs. Both of these were either inconvenient or too expensive. Then along came paratransit systems, such as Project Mainstream, operated by our city bus service. This is a curb-to-curb service, which sounds great until people experience the many flaws. Among them are the rigid rules that favor the drivers, not the passengers. A driver is allowed to be up to 30 minutes late for an appointed pickup time, and yet we passengers may not be more than five minutes late in appearing at our doors, ready to go. We must make reservations up to a week in advance, and even then, we may not get the pickup time we want, and we might be on the bus for as long as 80 minutes. There are more, but I'm not going to bore you with my complaints. I'll just say that when I used it for getting to work, my 20-minute drive in a car was a 90-minute ride on Project Mainstream.

So when Lyft and Uber came on the scene, it was almost as good as having a private chauffeur. Well, that might be a stretch. First, I have to deal with an app on my iPhone that keeps changing with every update. Then my driver may claim that he is in front of my house, but he's actually on the next street, because he doesn't know how to use his GPS. Or he might not speak English so well, and worst of all, he might not accept my service dog. This, of course, is against the law, but I have had the experience of standing with my guide dog outside a building, waiting for my Uber driver, hearing a car approach, and then hearing it drive away. The next thing I heard was my phone announcing that my ride had been cancelled.

Aside from having a friend take me where I need to go, the very best service is from the Red Cross. Most people don't know that the Red Cross in my county will provide transportation to doctors' appointments or other health–related activities. They take me to the Y twice a week, and they are almost always exactly on time, very courteous, helpful, and friendly. They come to my door when they arrive, and usually they will walk me to the door of the building where I'm going. The best part of all is that it's free.

A Little Education Goes a Long Way

At first, I did have to do a little educating about transporting a person with a guide dog.

When I first requested a ride with the Red Cross to the Y, my driver wasn't sure he was allowed to have a dog on board. He said he would have to call his supervisor, so I went back into the house to wait. He came to the door and said his supervisor said I couldn't take the dog.

I was so incensed that I replied, "Then I'm not going."

He explained that other passengers might be allergic to dogs, and even if they weren't riding at the same time, they might have a reaction after the dog had been in the vehicle.

I called The Seeing Eye, because I knew their community

relations person would have the right words for me to say. She did. She told me that one disability cannot trump another. Then she called the director of my local Red Cross and explained to him my right to have my guide dog travel with me.

Not only was I allowed to bring my dog, but also, the director of the county office of the Red Cross called me and apologized profusely. They even sent out a note to all drivers to not distract the dog and to respect it as a working partner for me.

I was irritated with that driver's lack of knowledge about the rights of service dogs, but I was pleased that we could resolve the issue with just a little education.

Cooking

One of the most frequently asked questions when I give presentations is, "How do you cook?" Basically, I say I use my hands a lot.

As I look around my kitchen—that is, mentally look—I see an ordinary kitchen, but you as a sighted person might notice some significant differences.

Starting with my seasonings and spices, you'll see that they are all labeled in braille and in alphabetical order. They're stored in little shelves that are attached to the inside of a cupboard door, both for easy access and to keep them from being stuck any old place on the inner shelves. My brown sugar and Bisquick also have braille labels because they're in identical Tupperware containers. I use containers of many different sizes and shapes for other baking ingredients that I can recognize easily, so they don't need braille labels.

Next are my glass stovetop and oven. When I first started

shopping for the glass–top stove, I wanted one that would let me feel the burners when they weren't turned on so I could center my pan in the right place. I paid an extra hundred dollars for one that I could sort of feel, but in reality, I just turn it on, and when it heats up, that's when I place the pan on it. I just hold my hand above the source of heat, and if I have to make an adjustment, I use my sense of hearing. If I'm boiling water, and the boiling sound gets louder if I move the pan a little to the right or left, I know it's centered. Since electric stoves take a while to heat up, I have plenty of time to make the adjustment.

My favorite feature of glass top–stoves is that they're so easy to clean. No more scrubbing burner wells or burnt food on the coils. In my opinion, it's also a safety feature, because you'd have to spill a lot of food to make it burst into flames. Yes, I've slopped food out of a pan onto the glass, and, yes, it burns and makes a mess, but I use a special cleaner, one that usually wipes the mess off quite efficiently. If that doesn't do it, I very carefully use a razor blade to chip away at the burned–on mess, being careful not to scrape the glass, but to approach the mess from the outside edges and work to the other side of the stubborn mess. I try to prevent these spillovers by using a larger pan than I think I need. I measure food such as pasta into a bowl and then dump it into the boiling water, instead of breaking up the spaghetti over the pan.

My oven is self–cleaning. However, I do need the assistance of a sighted person to set the timer, because it's impossible to mark that dial. I've marked the other dials with various tactile substances, such as High Marks and stick–on dots meant for that purpose. If I were to buy a new stove, I would get one with a default temperature of 350. You press up or down arrows to change it. After you memorize how many taps on the arrows to make, the temperature will be accurate.

Because I've been cooking for many, many years, I don't use one of those huge pot holders shaped like a mitten for a giant. I find them awkward. I prefer a smaller version with the same design. You just need to be aware of where your arms are when you reach into the oven and be careful to keep them in the same vicinity they were when you reached in.

It's also important to try to keep the pan or cookie sheet level. Most important, don't be in a hurry. If the phone rings when I'm in the process of using the oven, I either let it ring, or I answer quickly and tell the person I'll call her back.

In my first book, I described the time I was removing cookies from the oven while talking to a friend on the phone. Being distracted by the conversation, I forgot that I had used parchment paper to line the cookie sheet, and when I yanked out the cookie sheet, the cookies flew everywhere. Then I had to turn off the oven to prevent a fire and try to grab the cookies that had made it to the floor before my dog could gobble them up.

What did I do with the ones on the floor? You've heard of the five–second rule, haven't you? Baking cookies is not my favorite thing to do, so I wasn't going to let my work go to waste.

Speaking of baking cookies, I'm often asked about measuring ingredients. Before I begin a baking project, I line up all the ingredients I'll need. This practice ensures that I actually have all the ingredients. I'm famous for deciding to make chocolate chip cookies and then discovering that I have no chocolate chips. Measuring dry ingredients is easy. Just hold the spoon over the container and slide your finger over the top to make a level amount. Cooks on TV would never do this, but my philosophy is that God made fingers before He made spatulas. Measuring liquids can be a little trickier. I use nesting measuring cups, and I crook my finger over the edge to determine when the liquid has reached the top. Measuring oil is often messy at my house, because it's room temperature and a little harder to detect, so I hold the measuring cup over the sink to catch any overflow. I do the same when measuring other liquids, such as milk. Another way I save on cleanup is to use a large cookie sheet or jellyroll pan to do all the preparations on. It's much easier to wash than a whole countertop.

A favorite appliance is the microwave, which I have brailled. It's amusing to me to watch someone else stand in front of my microwave, completely baffled as to how to work it, because of the dots on the numbers. It's just easier for me to tell them to step aside and I'll do it myself. I have braille numbers on the number pad, and bigger stick-on dots for commonly used functions, like "Start" and "Beverage." It really isn't rocket science, but when you're not used to seeing all those extra bumps, it must be confusing.

My new microwave, which is fun to demonstrate, is connected to the Echo Dot, so all I have to do is tell Alexa to "cook" for a certain number of minutes, and away it goes. I can even tell her at what power to cook, something I have always found frustrating on a standard touch pad.

Now we come to the last appliance in my kitchen. Just like any other mother or grandmother, my refrigerator is adorned with lots of handmade magnets from grandchildren's artwork, but in addition, the side of the fridge is covered with about 50 magnetic labels that I've used for canned goods. Once the product was used, I'd slap the label on the fridge, and then on the next grocery day, I'd place the label on the lid of the new can.

People who don't use braille have devised other ways of identifying their canned food, such as using rubber bands placed in creative ways around the can. If I have a product that I'm probably not going to use very often, I just use a label I've brailled from a product called Dymo Tape. I use this method exclusively for products that go in the fridge, such as salad dressing, sauces that I use so rarely that I'll forget what they are, and the spicy mayonnaise, which is in a container that feels very much like the mustard.

I try to keep the food organized on the shelves in a way that makes sense to me. For instance, I keep the soft drinks that have caffeine in them on the top shelf, because I should drink them only early in the day. The ones on the bottom shelf have no caffeine in them, so I can drink them in the evening.

Dining Out

Every blind person I know has experienced the humiliation of having the server ask his or her companion what the blind person wants instead of asking him or her directly.

It's not just a restaurant annoyance. It happens wherever there is a counter in a store, at the doctor's office, or any other time when some interaction is needed between the blind person and the employee. But it happens most often in restaurants. Here's how my friends and I have handled this situation.

When the server asks if we are ready to order, I order first, because if my friend orders first, the server will look at me for my order and will be silent instead of saying something like, "And for you, ma'am?" We avoid that awkwardness by my going first.

I was with a group of friends the other night, and the server made her way around the table and took our orders behind the right shoulder of each person. This was excellent, because I could hear her, and I could ask questions of her because she could hear me. It's really difficult when the server stands on the other side of the table in a noisy restaurant and I have no idea when it's my turn to order. This particular waitress has served our group many times, and she even remembers what we're likely to order. But she has a habit of setting down my glass of wine and not telling me. The same thing happens when she presents the bill. Consequently, I sit and wait and wait for my drink, not realizing that it's right there in front of me. So I finally decided I needed to ask her to tell me when she sets my drink down, and she happily did so. She also told me when she set down my bill, so that time, I didn't have the embarrassment of not knowing that everybody else had paid but I didn't even know the bills had been passed out. Keep in mind that besides being in a noisy restaurant, we are a noisy bunch of women. My favorite server in the world not only knows what I'm going to order, but she is also a tremendous help when she brings my change. She tells me, for instance, "The five is on the top, and then you have four ones under that."

When I have to deal with a person behind a counter in a shop, it's very tempting for that person to talk only to my friend who can make eye contact, even though I'm the one making the purchase. It's even gone so far as when I've handed her the money, she returns the change or the credit card to my friend, probably because she's the one who can see that the clerk is extending the card. To avoid this awkward and annoying situation, I've coached my friend to look away or even walk away, so that the clerk is forced to talk to me. Sometimes, if I'm in a sassy mood, I'll say, "I speak English. You can talk directly to me." Or my friend will say, "Hand the change to her. She's the one making the purchase."

Then there are the ones who think they are being helpful by grabbing my hand so they can put the change into it. All they need to do is say something like, "Here's your change." It sounds so simple as I write this, but you'd be surprised at how difficult this apparently is. It's very rare that I don't have to deal with this, simply because I can't make eye contact. But when it doesn't happen, I'm thrilled. Imagine having to be thrilled when someone treats you like a human being with a brain.

Participating in the Community

When you have a disability such as blindness, it's easy to retreat, withdraw, or come up with a hundred excuses for staying home and letting the world go by. If you don't have a friend who is willing and eager to drive you to meetings, activities, and entertainment, if you feel awkward and invisible when you're in a crowd of non-disabled people, or if you just don't feel like putting forth the effort, then that's your choice.

I've often been praised for being like "popcorn in a hot skillet," or "never letting the grass grow under my feet," but the truth is, I like being around people, and I don't like missing out on what everybody else is getting to do. Sometimes I get lucky, like when my friend Janet invited me to come to Bible study, and without hesitation, she said she would pick me up each week. But more often, I need to work a lot harder at getting involved than most people realize.

Here's the story of how I managed singing in the church choir. I was one of 68 singers in the annual cantata. It was a lot of work for me to do that. First, I had to have someone come over and dictate the words to nine songs so I could transcribe them into braille, being careful to insert page numbers. That's because at rehearsals, the director would often skip from one piece to another, telling us to turn to a certain measure on a certain page.

Then, if I could manage it, I'd have a friend come over and sing the alto part with me, along with the CD we'd been given to practice with. One year, no one was available, so I had to rely on just listening very hard to the CD. During rehearsals, I recorded the whole practice, hoping to catch just the altos, so I could learn that part.

I must have spent a hundred hours practicing at home. Yet by the time we performed on Sunday, I still didn't feel confident about the alto part. After praying about it, I realized that I didn't have to know this thing perfectly. So what if I didn't come in exactly on time. As long as I didn't sing out whenever everybody else was silent, and as long as I did sing out when I was confident about my part, then it should be a good experience. I had been ready to quit several times, but then my friend Kathy reminded me of the joy I felt when I sang at the last concert. She was right. I did feel joy.

So I ironed my white blouse, gathered up my brailled music, and took my place in the second row beside Kathy. We had been moved several times because one person or another couldn't see the director, but Kathy insisted that we were a unit. She was the one who tapped my leg when it was time to stand up, and again when it was time to sit down, which wasn't always at the beginning or ending of a piece.

It is indeed more work for me than for any other member of that choir, but the joy I feel when I'm singing makes it worth the effort.

Shopping

"Who picks out your clothes for you?" I'm often asked by people who are curious about how a blind person can be well-dressed with coordinating tops and skirts. It's an innocent question, but on first hearing it, I was a bit taken aback. I pick out my own clothes, and I dress myself each morning—because, contrary to public conjecture, I don't have a staff to do that for me.

It's actually two questions. What they mean is, "How do you select your clothes at the store?" and "How do you know which top goes with which skirt when you get dressed?"

Shopping for clothing can be a challenge for someone who's totally blind.

How I select my clothes depends on several factors. When I start shopping, my companion or store associate will say, "What color would you like?" This is not an unreasonable question. I used to be able to see, so I have my own preferences, but what I'd like and what they have in my size are not always the same. Often, the only thing they have in my size is black, and I don't like wearing black. I like colors, and I have my favorites from when I could see. I'm also subject to the opinion of my shopping helper, sometimes inadvertently, and sometimes by my choice.

"Does this make me look fat?" I ask. "Is this too bold a print?" "Is this a good color for me?" "Does it look like I'm trying to look younger?" In other words, I need an honest human mirror. In the end, the choice is mine, but in a subtle way, you can almost tell who took me shopping that day. I'll never forget going shopping with a woman who was 20 years older than I. What I had been told were stunning outfits turned out to be clothes that my mother would wear.

My absolute favorite helper for clothes shopping is my daughter. I think I can safely say this is true for many blind women who have sensible and sensitive daughters. Kara already knows what I like, as well as what will work for me and what won't. She knows what is fashionable, but she doesn't waste time showing me things that would look all wrong on me.

I have a few rules for myself when shopping for clothes.

1. Never buy a skirt, pants, or a top without having something to wear with it to make a complete outfit. Sighted people have the luxury of being able to keep an eye out for the coordinating garment as they shop on another day. I do not. Clothes shopping is always a one–day event, so if I don't find something to go with the odd–colored garment that day, I don't buy it.

2. Always ask your helper, "Would you wear this?" Many times, when I'm trying to match a top with a skirt, she'll say, "Well, that's not bad." And that's when the red flag goes up. Not bad? Would she wear it?

3. No matter how trendy or cool they say a particular garment is, if I don't feel good in it, it's not for me.

Now to answer the second question. I manage to keep from wearing stripes with plaids or colors that clash by keeping my closet very well organized.

I hang all my black skirts and pants on a multiple skirt

hanger, and the same with the brown pants and the gray pants. If I have pants and top that only go with each other, I hang them together. Then I must be sure to put the corresponding clothes back on the same hanger. Often, I can tell which dress is which by touch. No, I can't detect color with my fingers, but I know that the dress with the ruffle in the front is green, and the dress with the wide belt that feels like a sweater is red.

I also have a secret weapon called a talking color identifier. It says "black" when I hold it next to a pair of black socks and "brown" when I put it next to the brown socks. Sometimes it gets pinks and purples mixed up, and it has no idea what to say when the garment is khaki, but it's still one of my favorite pieces of technology. It's a blind woman's best friend when she's getting dressed. And if a person doesn't have a color identifier or doesn't trust it, she can use an app on her phone called Be My Eyes. By tapping on a certain spot, she can be connected with a volunteer from anywhere in the world who will identify a color, a setting on her oven, or any number of small tasks that require a good set of eyes.

How I would love to be on *What Not to Wear*! Then when I'm asked who picks out my clothes, I'd have a great story to tell.

Money Matters

I'm often asked, "How do you know that's a $5 bill?" It's a good question, because in this country, all our bills feel the same. You can feel the difference between a quarter and a nickel, a dime, and a penny. There are ridges on the edges of quarters and dimes, and a nickel is bigger than a penny, but it's impossible to detect the difference between a $1 bill and a $20 bill. One hundred and eighty countries have a monetary system that is accessible to blind people. You'd think that the U.S. would be among them.

To make up for this oversight, the U.S. Government has issued every legally blind person in the country a small device that will detect and announce the denomination of the bill. It's not the perfect answer, so we who are blind have developed individual methods of keeping our cash organized. There is no one right method, so I'll tell you about mine.

I keep all my ones flat in my wallet. I fold my fives in half from left to right. I use a lot of five–dollar bills for my transportation, so I try to use cash for lunches out and get change whenever I can. Besides, I try not to use a credit card if the card is going to be whisked away out of the sight of my luncheon companions. However, if I do have a ten, I fold it like a five and then fold it over again. I fold my twenties over like a five and then down from the top. In this way, I can easily tell which bill I have plucked out of my wallet. The trick is to get them stashed properly in the first place. Here's where some issues of trust and honesty come into play.

When I make a cash purchase with a $20 bill, and I'm expecting change that includes a higher denomination than a dollar, I always ask the person handing me my change to tell me which bills are which. I don't mind taking a few extra seconds to do this for two reasons. First, it helps me keep control of my money. Second, it reinforces to all the fact that I am indeed in charge of my money.

Have you ever seen that TV show *What Would You Do?* They had a situation in which the blind person was cheated by a store clerk, who handed her the wrong amount of change. He thought he could get away with it, but bystanders came to her aid.

If I'm ever in doubt, I say, "Here's a twenty." That way, the clerk can never tell me that I only handed him a one. And if I have accidentally pulled out the wrong bill, my mistake will be noted by us both.

Have I ever been cheated? Not to my knowledge. In fact, it's more likely that a clerk will point out that I have handed him a twenty instead of a ten, not the other way around.

Another method I use, particularly when I'm traveling, is to keep ones in my right-hand pocket and fives in the left. That way, I don't have to fuss around with digging tips out of my purse. Of course the problem can be remembering which pocket holds which denomination. I think that one time I accidentally tipped a skycap $10 instead of $2, but that wasn't his fault. It was just his lucky day. Or maybe he thought I was Miss Moneybags and I always tip like that.

Writing and keeping track of checks can present more of a challenge. I could use a check-writing guide if my handwriting were more legible. They are made of plastic or cardboard, with windows cut out where you fill in the date, the amount, etc. I always sign my checks first and then have a third party fill them out. I was cheated once when I trusted the payee too much. The reason I sign the check first is to prevent my helper from automatically signing her own name out of habit.

I keep track of my checks by recording them in a very old piece of technology called a Braille and Speak. I call my bank regularly and check on the status of my account. Automated phone systems are great, but those who are more computer savvy than I am can do the same online.

Whether I'm keeping track of pennies or my life savings, the most important things to remember are to not get lazy and to always be in control.

Voting

I love going to my local polls to vote, especially now that there are audible voting machines. Gone are the days when I had to have two extra people in the voting booth with me, one Republican and one Democrat. It got a little crowded in there with my Seeing Eye dog, too, to say nothing of the lack of privacy. Gone are the days when I had to have a trusted friend or relative read the ballot to me and mark it for me. Now that we have audible voting machines, I just put on a pair of headphones and listen to a very pleasant female voice read the names of each candidate in each race, and I press a diamond–shaped button to "select" my choice. Then I press the triangular button to arrow down to the next candidate, race, or issue. It takes longer for me to vote than it does for my sighted friends, because I can't skim the ballot for just the races I want to vote in, so I'm not limited to five minutes in front of the machine as others are. In addition to the exhilarating sense of independence I feel at my voting place, I enjoy chatting with neighbors and friends I haven't seen in years.

When I vote early, I have to go to what was previously a department store, and there isn't the intimate feeling of gathering with neighbors. But because the workers are well prepared and knowledgeable about the audible machine, it is usually a smooth and efficient experience. It's okay with me to trade the small–town atmosphere for getting the job done.

Working Out

Let me start this section by telling you that I hate exercising for the sake of exercise, especially at a gym. As you learned earlier in this book, I have lived a very active life through dancing, skiing, skating, cycling, swimming, walking with my guide dogs, hiking, and even running. But push-ups and sit-ups have always bored me to death. I was fortunate to maintain an active lifestyle by doing activities I loved, mostly with other people. And except for the dancing and the swimming, all of them were done outside.

Because of a couple of medical issues, namely spinal fusion and osteoporosis, I've had to alter my workout routines. Following physical therapy for the back surgery, I'm trying very hard to continue those boring exercises. But increasing my weight-bearing exercises for the osteoporosis has become a new challenge.

Walking at least two miles a day with Dora is a real joy, considering that this time last year I couldn't even walk to the next house without pain. My goal is to get up to three miles at a time at three miles per hour, which is slower than when I was younger and stronger, but not bad for a person my age who has been through some very serious surgeries lately. I know I can do it because I walked in a fundraiser for an animal shelter just three months after the spinal fusion, and we walked 3.1 miles in just over an hour. Of course, we had the excitement of joining hundreds of other walkers, some with two legs and some with four, and we loved passing slower walkers. I have to confess that Dora is not the only one on this team that possesses a keen sense of competition.

Twice a week, I swim at the Y, and on those days, my walks

with Dora are not so long. After all, I'm not superwoman. But I love the overall workout that swimming creates, and my reward is a brief soak in the hot tub. If I'm lucky, I get to talk to some other folks who are also rewarding their bodies with churning, hot water. Having the tub to myself is relaxing, but I prefer to have people to talk to.

It's not always easy. About half the time, the people who are already there just stop their conversation and stare at me as I hook my dog up to the railing and make my way down the steps and take a seat. When I'm not put off by their rudeness, I try to start a conversation, but all they can think of to talk about is my dog. Well, that's okay, but I get a little tired of only being her spokesperson. And then there are the times when I feel invisible. I might be sitting there thinking I'm alone when suddenly I notice someone stepping past me without a word. Surely they can't be checking their Facebook messages in the hot tub. But then there are other times when my fellow soakers are friendly and even want to know my name, not just Dora's. It's a red letter day for me when I've added one more lap to my total for the day and had a conversation with nice people, too.

Stepping into a situation where I am the only blind person, such as at the Y, takes some planning and some courage, mixed in with a liberal sprinkling of luck.

Before my back pain prevented me from doing almost everything, I signed up for six lessons with a coach on how to use the weight equipment. While I was there, I ran into several friends from church, who immediately offered to provide transportation and to help me go through my weight routine. One of the women, Regina, organized a group of five men and women who would take turns on different days of the month being my spotter. They would set up the weight for each machine and assist me in getting from one machine to another safely. I couldn't believe how lucky I was and how much fun I was having. Thanks to Regina, who set up the schedule of helpers, I didn't have to worry about how I was going to manage my next workout session. I especially liked it when my helper would go work out on a different machine while I was on mine. That way, she was getting something out of this workout, too.

My next adventure at the Y was joining a yoga class for seniors, thanks to another woman from my church, who would meet me at the Y and then take me home after the class. If I wasn't understanding what the instructor wanted us to do, Nonie would come over and show me the pose. You might say that being a member of a church with a strong commitment to helping others was the best thing that could have happened to me at this point in my life.

Meanwhile, one of the front desk workers named Hulalor (pronounced you–lay–luh) befriended me by escorting me into the pool area and finding an empty lane for me. We'd talk and laugh as I stowed my stuff in my locker, and then she'd wait with me until a lane opened up. Sometimes she'd even go so far as to ask two swimmers to share a lane so I could have one to myself. I'm not good at sharing, because I'm not very good at swimming in a straight line, but somehow I make it up and back multiple times, even with zig–zagging back and forth to each lane-marker rope.

Dora is secured to a bench nearby, but she watches me constantly, and as soon as I climb out of the pool, she's up and ready for the next task. I need no help once Hulalor has found a lane for me. That's because Dora is so good at taking me to the hot tub, then to the locker room, then to the shower, then back to my locker, and finally out to the lobby.

If I get out there before my Red Cross driver arrives, Hulalor makes me a cup of coffee. She even brought me a bouquet of chocolate–covered fruit when I was stuck at home after the surgery.

I've appeared in two videos for fundraising for the Y and have given three talks, not only to the staff and executives, but also to the teachers and other employees. You give a little, and you receive a lot.

At this YMCA, I could use one of their family changing rooms. It certainly would be more convenient for me, because I wouldn't have to wait for a shower, and Dora would have plenty of room. But I prefer the friendly banter and conversation among the women in the locker room. They even asked about me repeatedly while I was away for about three months following my spine surgery, and when I did return, they all cheered when I walked into the pool area. They made me feel like a rock star. No wonder I love it there.

Traveling

When I'm getting ready for a trip, say to my daughter's home, my acquaintances will ask in wonderment, "Do you go by yourself?" Of course I do. I'm an adult, after all, but I do need assistance.

I know of many independent people who are blind who are just dropped off at the curb, and from then on, they manage to get to the ticketing counter, through security, to the gate, and onto the plane completely on their own. My friend Deborah is one of them, but I am not. I have been dropped off at the curb, but I make sure my driver makes eye contact with a skycap or the curbside check-in people. From there, a skycap escorts me to the ticketing counter, through security, and to the gate. Sometimes this is quicker than having a friend come and see me off, but when I have a friend willing to do that, I'm much more relaxed. My friend has to get a gate pass, which means he's allowed to go through security with me, but once he leaves the secure area, he can't get back in.

Having my daughter go with me on the return is especially efficient, because she can escort me into the public restroom. When I am with a male companion or skycap, I'm on my own, which means finding a stall and then finding the sinks without help, even if other women are there.

This is one of those times when a woman who is blind is also invisible. If I have my dog with me, she can find her way out very quickly, but then I have to go back in to find the sink so I can wash my hands. It's strange how most people will either not notice that I need help, or they stand and stare to see how I will find what I'm looking for. Here's where I have to swallow my shyness and say out loud to whoever can hear me, "Can anyone tell me where the sinks are?"

I am so thankful when a family restroom is available, but I always have the skycap peek in to make sure it's clean before I enter and lock the door.

When a skycap escorts me to my gate, that's the end of our relationship, except for my handing him or her a tip. The tip amount depends on how many concourses, trams, or buses we've had to negotiate together.

In the past, and sometimes even today, the skycap has ignored the "meet and assist" request and assumed that meant a wheelchair. I've had many arguments with skycaps about wheelchairs. I think it's particularly amusing when I have walked onto a plane with two perfectly good legs, led by a dog with four perfectly good legs, and the flight attendant asks me if I want a wheelchair when they call for a "meet and assist." I want my sarcastic self to say, "Didn't you see me walk onto this plane? Do you think I lost my legs in flight?"

When making my reservation, my daughter navigates the websites for me and actually plays travel agent. She takes into consideration the times the flights leave, which airports they use for making connections, and how much time I have to get from one plane to another. Then she looks for window seats, particularly in the bulkhead row.

I used to prefer sitting in a non–bulkhead row because my dog was small enough to slide under the seat in front of me. The only disadvantage was that I didn't have room enough to stow my backpack there as well. I didn't like the bulkhead seats because they insisted that my carryon belongings be stowed in the overhead bins. The flight attendants always promised to get down anything I needed once we were at cruising altitude, but they never did. These days, since Dora is a big and long–legged girl, we absolutely must have the bulkhead row. But in many of the smaller planes, where there are only two seats on each side of the aisle, Dora takes up all the foot room, and her feet hang out into the aisle, which is strictly forbidden. So now when I fly, I not only have to ask for the bulkhead row, but I have to make sure there is enough room for my dog, or she just doesn't get to go.

If there is room for her, I accept one of the accommodations that Delta offers. I can purchase any seat on the plane (the bulkhead seats are more expensive), but I can call Delta in advance, and they will move my ticket to the bulkhead row for no extra charge. Then the only problem to overcome is sitting next to someone who either hates dogs or doesn't want golden hairs on his pants legs.

I've been on a plane where the man sitting next to me was so angry that he was willing to get off the plane and take a later flight. The attendant handled the situation beautifully. She found a small woman sitting near the back who was delighted to trade places with that grumpy man. We had a delightful conversation for the whole flight.

If I'm traveling by myself, I don't care where I sit, except not in the bulkhead row, because I like to have my backpack accessible to me—that is, under the seat in front of me. The other seat I try to avoid is the aisle or middle seat. I always ask for the window seat, which might seem odd, given that I can't see anything. But what invariably happens is that I'm boarded early, so I'm already in my seat when the other passengers file in. When the person who has the window seat or the middle seat arrives, he stands there and waits for me to get up to allow him room to get in, not realizing that I can't see that he is glaring at me. It just saves a lot of awkwardness if I can be tucked away in the window seat.

The one problem with this seat is that when it comes time for refreshments, if I'm lucky enough to be on an airline that offers passengers a cup of coffee, the flight attendant often passes me by because I haven't made eye contact with her. One time, I was sitting in the window seat, next to a friend who was also blind. The flight attendant served him and moved on, but my friend turned in his seat and said, "She would like something, too." So now when I board a plane, and the flight attendant shows me where the call button and the nearest exit are, I tell him or her that I will want something to drink. "So please don't pass me by," I say, "even if I'm not looking at you."

One final annoyance when flying is that, as a person with a disability, I am told to stay in my seat until all the other passengers have left the plane. Occasionally, I will slip into the flow of passengers, but when I get to the front, the flight attendant tells me to sit down in the first row to wait.

My friend Deborah refuses to obey; she says it's humiliating and wrong to treat us that way. She tells me, "Don't let them plunk you down like a package. Keep going. You could miss your next flight or unnecessarily keep your driver waiting if you're arriving home."

Asking for Help

I know some blind people who would rather walk through fire than ask for help. Independence is an admirable trait, but there are times when I know it's much smarter to acknowledge a need than to try to be what is known in the blindness community as "super blind." Here's an example of one of those times.

I was reaching for a box of cake mix in my pantry when I accidentally touched a bottle of red wine, which was lying on its side. In one second, it rolled off the shelf and immediately smashed onto the tile floor. Seriously, one second.

Standing in a puddle of red wine, a puddle filled with jagged fragments of glass, I knew that this was not something I should attempt to clean up myself. I'm not afraid of broken glass. If you handle it carefully, and it hasn't shattered into shards, it's not that hard to deal with. But there was no way I could investigate the damage without making the mess much worse than it already was.

I backed out of the puddle and realized that my socks were now soaked with wine, so I had to take them off to move anywhere. I returned to my kitchen, where I sat down to ponder this situation.

It was a Sunday afternoon. Whose Sunday afternoon would I hate the least to ruin? I considered my good friend Dan, but he might cry at the sight of ruined red wine. Just kidding, Dan. I considered my son, Steve, but he was most likely involved in one of his daughter's activities. I called my friend Mary Beth, who had helped me out of a vicious glass crisis before, but her husband had just been taken to the ER. Never mind, Mary Beth.

I was relieved to reach my neighbors, Dan and Amy, who have helped me with a few other crises, like removing solid ice from my front door, raking my leaves when my back problems prevented me from doing it, and looking for a missing house key. So Dan and Amy to the rescue, even though they were just wrapping up a day with their parents, celebrating their twins' confirmation. They quickly Googled how to remove broken glass, and they came armed with slices of bread. This was going to be some crazy kind of communion. I had put down paper towels around the perimeter of the puddle to keep it from spreading over the utility room floor, but after that, I just stayed out of the way, and fortunately, Dora had no interest in the red wine.

Once again, I was reminded that there are indeed times when I just have to be realistic and ask for help. And once again, I was reminded that I'm truly blessed with good people in my life who will come to my aid, especially when it involves broken glass.

It's a good thing I don't like red wine. That empty spot in the pantry can now be used for something much better, like chocolate syrup in a plastic bottle.

* * * * *

There you have it, my manual for living life as a blind person. However, I have more stories to tell in the next chapter that show you the myths and misconceptions about blindness and people who are blind. I promise not to whine, complain, or be sarcastic. You might even find them humorous, as I often do.

Mary emerges from the pool at the Y

Chapter Twelve
Myths and Misperceptions

I'm dedicating this chapter to all the visually impaired people I have known throughout my life, who have served as role models of how to deal with being blind.

Abilities

The word disabled does a great disservice to those of us who have vision loss. It sounds like we're broken, like a disabled car. While we may be able to recite a long list of things we can't do, such as drive, read print with our eyes, make eye contact, etc., there are many gifts we can be grateful for that still remain a part of who we are.

Rather than focusing on the negatives of being a person who is blind, I'd like to trot out the positives of my life. At the risk of sounding like I'm bragging, I want to describe to you a person who has many attributes other than being blind. For people who have never met a blind person or a person with low vision, it's hard to see past the blindness, so in this chapter, it's my intention to help you do just that.

As is the case with many active blind people, my abilities

include dancing, cycling, skiing, hiking, and swimming. But you don't have to be a super athlete with mysterious talents in overcoming blindness in these sports. If you, my dear reader, are a person with vision loss, I encourage you to either continue to be active or become active. It will save your life.

Being active does not necessarily mean being an athlete. It means keeping your mind and body engaged in your surroundings and seeking ways to keep growing and developing your strengths, because you do have strengths. You don't have to be a mountain climber or a pole vaulter to say you have abilities. Consider some simple everyday tasks, functions—and yes, talents—that you might be overlooking.

Everyday Abilities

Although I had to struggle with mastering the computer, I write every single day. I write letters. I make lists. I keep a journal. I read emails. I write for a blog. Writing is a talent I did not have to give up with my vision loss.

I love singing. I used to sing with a volunteer singing group and with my church choir. Doing that was a lot more work for me than it was for my sighted friends because I had to transcribe the words of the songs and anthems into braille and learn the music by rote. But it was a passion I didn't have to give up.

I studied dance when I was young and hoped to be a ballerina someday, but with the onset of RP, I had to give up that dream. But I didn't have to give up dancing. I enrolled in private ballroom dance lessons so I could use that talent with the help of a dance partner.

I belong to a book club because I have the ability to enjoy, comprehend, and discuss a variety of books, which I listen to via talking books from The National Library Service for the Blind.

Over the years, I have developed organizational skills for my personal life. Arranging for rides, making appointments, and budgeting my time are all abilities that allow me to live independently.

I'm not a great cook, but back when my family was young, I did the meal planning, the cooking, and most of the cleanup. My husband hated grocery shopping. He paid someone to drive me so I could do that, too.

I like to knit. While I used to make sweaters, these days I make simple things like scarves and dishcloths. It's very relaxing to me, and it's easily done by feel. I use patterns that I have transcribed into braille.

I walk every day. I have a very athletic guide dog who helps me keep a brisk pace, and because she needs the exercise, too, we go out even in the cold and the rain. The two conditions that keep me indoors are wind and ice. I could tell you that then I use a treadmill, but the truth is, those are the days I curl up with a good book.

I hire a person to clean my house once a month, but between her visits, I run the vacuum cleaner, dust the furniture, do the laundry, and clean the bathrooms myself. I might miss a stain on the kitchen counter or a blob of dog hair in the corner, but that's why I hire someone to help occasionally.

In the winter, I used to love to shovel snow, and in the fall, I enjoyed raking leaves. With the onset of medical issues, I've had to give those activities up, but both can be done by feel. I used to put a portable radio outside my door to make sure I didn't get disoriented if I was out in my yard.

Doing for Others

I admit there have been times when I wondered how I could help others when I'm not able to do typical volunteer jobs. But lately, in addition to writing instructional pieces on my blog, I regularly give blood. This is about the easiest way you can save somebody's life. Lie back on a lounge chair and squeeze a little rubber ball for about 15 minutes, and the next thing you know, you have a pint of blood to donate to someone who might need that blood to survive. It's a great feeling. You don't need vision to do this important good deed.

Recently, I started visiting a World War II veteran at his assisted living home. He enjoys my visits, and I might even get more enjoyment than he does, hearing all his stories. Here, I'm not the blind lady needing a favor. I'm a friend who's enjoying a visit to ward off loneliness.

Even as a person who is blind, I have more abilities than disabilities. It's just that blindness is the big one, and the biggest disability of all is to get people to see beyond it.

Braille Is Not a Language

A few years ago, I wrote an article for *Toastmaster* magazine. It was printed pretty much the way I wrote it, with the exception of one glaring word that I never would have written in this context.

The article as I wrote it started this way: "It's 7:25 on a Monday night, and my Toastmasters meeting will be starting in five minutes. The voices of my fellow Toastmasters blend around me as I check the agenda, which I have entered in braille in my note taker." Note that I said "entered in braille." What they substituted, without my permission, was "translated into braille." Braille is transcribed, not translated. You don't need to translate English into braille. Braille is English, at least in the U.S. It's not a foreign language. It is a tactile way of writing.

Think of it this way. If you write something in cursive, often called script, it is not a different language from writing the same thing in print. I used the word "enter" in my article because I was using an electronic device. I could have said "typed." The point is, I did not say "translated." It didn't even occur to me to use the word translated. That was the editor's choice and evidence of her misconception about braille—and probably about blind people, too. Blind people speak the same language that sighted people do.

Am I Really That Scary?

This is the question I ask myself each time I encounter someone who, upon discovering that I am blind, suddenly loses the power of speech and the ability to have an intelligent thought. Words are suddenly elusive, so apparently, a silent expression of terror is the default. They might as well say it out loud. "OMG, she's blind! What do I do?"

In an issue of *The New York Times*, validation of my observations appeared in an article by Rosemary Mahoney, called "Why Do We Fear the Blind?"

The author, who is a teacher of students who are blind, wrote about a conversation she had with an otherwise intelligent woman who wondered how you can actually talk to a blind person. "In her mind there existed a substantial intellectual barrier between the blind and the sighted. The blind could hear, yes. But could they properly understand?"

It's a barrier that I'm continually butting my head against. It seems that I spend an inordinate amount of time trying to prove to the world that even though my eyes don't work, my brain does. It irritates the heck out of me each time someone implies that because I'm blind, I'm in the dark about the meaning of a word, a current event, what colors are, or any number of commonplace concepts, definitions, or experiences.

Ms. Mahoney went on to say: "The United States has one of the lowest rates of visual impairment in the world, and yet blindness is still among the most feared physical afflictions. Even in this country, the blind are perceived as a people apart."

Boy, did she ever get that right! That's why when I'm in a room full of people who are afraid to engage with me, I often feel invisible. I want to tap them on the arm and say, "It's okay to talk to me. It's not catching."

Ms. Mahoney quoted blind author Georgina Kleege, a lecturer at the University of California at Berkeley, when she said this: "Even the most brilliant sighted person can take a stupidly long time to recognize the obvious: There is usually a perfectly healthy, active, and normal human mind behind that pair of unseeing eyes." In other words, just because the curtains are closed, it doesn't mean nobody's home.

Then, once in a while, I'm blessed with an experience like the following one. I was dining with friends at a restaurant when a former client of my ex–husband came over to me and engaged me in pleasant conversation. First, I was gratified that he recognized me after not having seen me for over 20 years.

But what was more important to me was that he treated me like any other old acquaintance. There was no fear, no awe, no insensitive curiosity. It was just a natural exchange of pleasantries. How refreshing!

I get the same feeling of joy when a clerk in a store talks directly to me, not expecting my companion to be an interpreter. It's rare, but it does happen. For that brief time, I'm not "apart." I'm not invisible. The barrier is down. I'm not perceived as having a contagious disease or other-worldly powers.

While everything written in that article is true, I'm so thankful for times, like that night, when it's not.

Some of the funniest and at the same time most annoying stories come from my experiences in doctors' offices. You'd think that nurses and medical technicians would be trained in communicating with people with disabilities, but apparently they're not. You know how I constantly preach, "Don't talk to the dog. Talk to me." You wouldn't think this would be an issue. Of course you would talk to me, not to my dog, except when you're saying to my dog, "I know I'm not supposed to talk to you, and I'm not petting you, but you are just so pretty and such a good girl."

No, you don't do that because you know better. But here's a funny situation I had never encountered until I went to get blood work done the other day.

The blood technician led me to a room and correctly told me to go into the room on the right, or maybe she said, "Turn right here," but I heard how her voice was directed to the right. Upon entering the room, I had no idea where I was supposed to sit, since I go into a different room each time.

"Sit in this chair," she said.

"I'm blind," I replied, "so I don't know where you're pointing."

"Right over here," she said.

So far, this is a very common scenario, the dreaded "right over here."

"'Right over here' isn't very helpful to me," I said, in my gentlest, non-irritated voice.

"But I was talking to the dog," she said.

She was actually pointing to the chair and looking at my dog as if my dog had the responsibility of dragging me around. I gently told her that it really works better if she talks to me. I'm the human with a human brain in this relationship. I give the dog directions by using words like right and left. It's so tragic that medical personnel who deal with people all day can't think to say, "Please have a seat in the chair to your left."

Speaking of forgetting how to use words: Last Sunday at church, when I was trying to find the comfortable chair I always sit in for Sunday school, a very kind woman tried to assist by putting both hands on my shoulders and turning me. She actually thought I needed to be placed so that all I had to do was bend over and sit.

"Please don't turn me," I said. "I like to put my hand on the seat so I know where it is, and then I can sit down all by myself. I'm not a doll that you put on a chair. I'm a thinking human being. Please don't handle me."

No, I didn't say this to her. After all, she was only trying to help. But it's just another of a thousand ways I have to educate people every single day of my life. You would be appalled at the number of times I've had to say, "Please don't push me."

Again, I'm a person who understands English, not a thing

you have to place somewhere.

In another doctor's office, I had to say, "Please use words."

The nurse actually said, "What words do you want me to say?"

I replied, "How about the chair is on your right?"

Good thing she wasn't the one who was going to give me a shot. She was a bit irritated at my response.

Killing Me with Kindness

As I've mentioned many times in this book, I like to take long walks with my Seeing Eye® dogs.

I live in the perfect neighborhood for such an avocation, because you could walk for hours on my sidewalks and never have to retrace your steps. It's a quiet neighborhood with little traffic, but I do have to cross streets on most of my routes.

Unlike in big, bustling cities, the drivers are not rude, but almost too polite. When I hear a car approaching the corner where I'm about to cross, I wait. Then the car waits. We're at a standstill, both waiting for the other to go, until I motion for them to go ahead. What drivers don't know is that I prefer not to have the noise that the engine makes blocking my ability to listen for other traffic. They think they're doing me a favor, but in reality, it would be much better for them to move on so I could hear.

The new electric cars that are almost silent pose an entirely different problem. My heart stops every time I do cross, thinking there's no car waiting there, and then when I reach the other side of the street, I hear them pull away. I thank God they were paying attention and didn't run over me.

Taking a walk in the neighborhood can be a scary experience. Cars that are idling in driveways are some of the biggest hazards. If I hear them in time, I stop and wait. I don't know if they are soon to back out across the sidewalk and into the street, or if the drivers are just checking their texts or directions on their phones. I lift my right arm up and down like a railroad crossing to catch their eye so I can go ahead and walk behind the car. This may look strange, but I have been hit a couple of times before I caught on that it's better to look silly than to be flattened.

Open Doors

Chivalry is not dead, but it can be deadly for guide dog users.

Everybody wants to open the door for me and will even sprint to reach the door first. When I'm approaching the glass door of a restaurant, sometimes my friend Janet will say, "Stop, Mary." That's because the hostess has leapt to the door and opened it out toward me just as I was reaching for the handle. If I had not stopped, she would have clobbered me with the door. I can't see the door opening toward me, but the hostess doesn't seem to understand that. She's just trying to be welcoming. But for me, it's much safer to open the door myself. Here's why.

My dog is trained to show me the handle of the door. I don't want to break that training because I'm not always going to have a gallant observer to come and rescue me from a closed door. When the door is partially open, my dog is hesitant to move forward. She's trained to make sure we can both fit through, so a partially open door is an unfair test of her judgment. In addition,

I can't tell how far open the door is, either, so I'm left trying to find the door with my right hand or the other side of the doorway, to reassure my dog that we can go in. If I don't do this and insist that she go forward, I could run into the edge of the door.

The absolute worst scenario is when the door opens to the right, for example, and the helpful person is standing to the left of the door with his arm over my head to hold the door open. Now we not only have to discern how far open the door is but also whether or not we can clear the overhead obstruction. This is all too complicated to try to explain to a stranger, so I just deal with it and let it go.

I've educated all my friends, however, about opening car doors for me. I really prefer for my dog to show me the handle. I am perfectly capable of opening my own door. Opening it for me without telling me is the most dangerous "helpful" thing they can do. More than once, I've not known that the door was partially open and I've run right into the corner of the window. If the door is held wide open, I still have to run my left hand alongside the outside of the car to find the opening and then give my dog the command to get in. I could avoid all this if I would do as I was instructed and get in first, then tell the dog to get in after me, but the way car seats are so awkward and tight these days, it's not practical.

Another reason for allowing me to open the door myself is for me to be oriented to which way the car is facing, which is obvious when I open the door myself. Some drivers prefer to back into my driveway and some do not. It's especially a problem when the vehicle has a sliding door. I have to reach inside and put my hand on the seat to determine which way the seat is facing. Once again, it would be oh so helpful for the driver to use words such as, "I've backed in."

I know all this "open door policy" is counterintuitive to people who want to help, but I'd like for them to think of it as making an accommodation.

Speaking of backing in, I noticed one day that an acquaintance was having a little trouble backing into my driveway. It was his first time giving me a ride to church. I had a feeling he was doing this to be helpful to me, but I assured him that he really didn't need to do that. After all, he was only saving me about six steps, which was totally unnecessary. He knew that I walk about two miles a day, yet he wanted to save me six steps.

If someone wants to push my hot button, they can ask me if I have a "handicap sticker." These days, I just say "No," but back in the day when I was cycling 50 miles in a day, walking three miles at a brisk clip, and cross–country skiing all day, I would say, "You've got to be kidding." I have two perfectly good legs, heart, lungs, and a guide dog. Why would I need a parking spot to save me a few steps? Now I realize that my driver is only trying to usurp the privilege of a convenient parking spot through the use of a "handicap sticker" that they assume I have.

Super Powers

It's a common misperception that blind people have superior hearing. That may be true in individual cases, but it's more likely that we are just paying more attention to what we hear. I'll often comment on a sound I hear, like a church bell or the conversation of people walking behind me, when my companion didn't hear it. But if we could rewind the tape of that incident, the sighted person I was with would most likely hear it, too. He or she had the distraction of seeing what was around us or concern about making sure I didn't step off a curb or bump into something, and they just didn't notice. Too many stimuli at once can block out a person's ability to hear a particular sound.

On the other hand, when I'm in a situation where there are many cacophonous sounds, I can get disoriented and not be able to discern which sound I need to pay the most attention to. Noisy restaurants are the worst environments for people who can't see. This is one time when I'm glad I'm not young and expected to go with friends to noisy bars and eateries.

Another misconception is that blind people have an extraordinary sense of touch. Again, this may be true on an individual basis. However, touch is indeed often more important to us than to sighted people. I like being touched as much as the next person, but I resent the notion that people have the right to push, pat, pull, or even caress me when I don't know them.

Here's a setting where a brief touch on the arm is extremely helpful. When I'm at a gathering of a lot of people, the noise level is high, and I'm talking with someone, a very embarrassing situation can occur. My sighted acquaintance sees someone else to talk to and leaves me and doesn't let me know. I'm left talking to the air until I realize she has gone. A brief touch now and then from that other person is reassuring that she's still there, and then a word to me that she has seen another friend and is going to go talk to her ends our conversation naturally.

Assumptions

One particular assumption can cause unintentional

embarrassment. It happens most often at church, where there are literally hundreds of friendly people with hundreds of different voice inflections.

Many times a well–meaning person will say, "Hi, Mary," assuming I can tell who it is, and then move on to greet someone else. Unless I'm given a few more words or a hint as to who they are, I'm left wondering who just spoke to me. Just saying "Hi" back to them seems a little inadequate on my part, but I don't have the extra clues of being able to see their faces, and unless they have a very distinctive voice, it's almost like that old prank we used to pull on each other—putting our hands over their eyes and saying, "Guess who."

It would be so helpful if they'd just say, "Hi, Mary. It's (insert name here.)" Maybe it's assumed that I have the power to recognize anybody anywhere just by their saying, "Hi, Mary." When it happens while I'm grocery shopping or just walking down the street, it's even more puzzling. I actually had someone beep their horn as they drove by as a way of greeting. I said to my guide dog at the time, "Who was that?" and she said, "Darned if I know."

One assumption that I find amusing is that blind people don't have to go to the bathroom. I know that sounds absurd. I'll be having lunch with a friend, and we'll be getting ready to leave, when she announces she's going to the restroom and will be right back, and she rushes off. Didn't it occur to her that I might like to go, too?

Speaking of public restrooms, going in alone is like a treasure hunt without using your hands. Airport restrooms can be the most frustrating because of noisy hand dryers and multiple stalls to choose from— assuming you can even find the section where the stalls are. I have been known to wander around, getting trapped in dead-ends, until finally, by accident, I find a stall. Going in with a sighted person is a lot more efficient unless they guide me to an oversized stall, even when I don't have my dog with me. Then they start to guide me straight out the door, and I have to say, "Wait, I want to wash my hands." Do they not wash their hands after using the restroom?

What To Say

Conversations with a blind person do not have to center around vision loss. It seems that many people are curious about the cause of my blindness and how long I've been blind, and then that's all they can think of. We have much more to talk about, and frankly, it's rude to begin a conversation with those questions. Besides, the cause of my blindness is not a fascinating story, so to avoid disappointing them, I just say it's a progressive eye disease. Most people don't know what that means, anyway, and since the story doesn't involve a gunshot wound, a fire cracker gone wild, or a vicious dog attack, we're both bored before I get very far.

Why not begin the way they would with any other person at that event? "How did you like the speaker?" or "Is this your first time at this conference?" Another popular conversation starter is, "What's your dog's name?" After I either tell them or choose to explain to them that I don't normally tell people her name and why, or I just make up a name, that seems to be the end of it.

It's obvious to me that the assumption is that my dog is all I can talk about. This is the prime example of how for some people it's very hard to get past the blindness.

Living With a Blind Person

When I first started to date a man I'd met online, he was kind, seemed interested in knowing me as a person, and truly enjoyed being with me. Eventually he fell in love with me. He was unique in that he accepted my blindness but didn't patronize me. Best of all, he knew how to handle social situations that could have been awkward were it not for his sensitivity. For instance, we once visited a church where his friend was the pastor. When it was time to greet other members and shake hands and pass the peace, as so many modern churches like to do, he very surreptitiously nudged my elbow when someone was holding out a hand for me to shake. He knew instinctively that I was uncomfortable holding out my hand when I wasn't sure it was going to be shaken.

After we'd been seeing each other for about two years, he confessed to me that at first he wondered if he would get tired of always having to be the one to drive, to read the menu at a restaurant, or to read the map on a trip. Then, as he got to know me better, he realized that those were unnecessary worries. It didn't matter.

People Say the Darndest Things

Remember that old TV show, where Art Linkletter interviewed little kids in a segment he called "Kids Say the Darndest Things"? You've probably seen lists in magazines such as *Reader's Digest* and church bulletins. For your enjoyment, here's my list of unbelievably odd things people have said to me. After each question or comment, I'll share with you my silent response.

"What's your dog's name?"

Why is it so important for people to know her name? If I tell you, then you'll start talking to her, and if you're guiding me to some place, you'll talk to the dog instead of me.

"Does your dog sleep with you?"

I know this is going to disappoint you, but, no. If you must know, she chooses to sleep on the floor, sometimes not even in the same room with me. Maybe I snore too loudly.

"Oh, I wish you could see this beautiful view."

Me too. How about just describing it to me?

"You can't see this, but..."

Thanks for pointing that out. Couldn't you just leave off the first part of that statement? Just tell me what you see that's so interesting.

From a woman standing near me in front of a fireplace: "This fire really feels good. Can you feel it?"

Yes. You don't need vision to feel warmth on your backside.

From a preacher at a little country church: "You can tie your dog up here on the porch."

What? This is my guide dog, and she goes where I go. She doesn't get tied up like a homeless mutt.

From a young girl in the pool at the Y: "Is your dog blind?"

Now why would I bring a blind dog to the Y?

"Do you want to feel my face so you know what I look like?"

Ick. That only happens in movies. I don't care what your face looks like.

"Did you see...er...listen to that show last night?"

You don't have to avoid saying "see" or "look" or "watch." I see my friends often. I watch TV. I look at the dresses on the rack. How awkward it would be for me to say, "Let me feel that dress." "I'm going to listen to TV tonight." "I heard that movie." You can even say, "Watch your step here." Or "See you later." Or "Look at this gorgeous sweater." This is the way Americans talk. Please don't segregate me with your words that point out that I can't see.

In a doctor's office: "Do you need help getting dressed?"

No. I'm a big girl now. I got dressed all by myself this morning.

At a buffet table: "Here's some green stuff, but I don't know what it is. Do you want some of that?"

Would you choose something described as green stuff without knowing what it is?

From someone amazed that I cross-country ski: "I can't even do that, and I can see."

Here's a news flash. Skiing takes strength in your body, not your eyes. The reason you can't do it is probably that you've never tried it.

From someone I had just danced with at a party: "I thought you were blind, but I didn't want to say anything."

That's okay. I've known it for years.

I am well aware that most of the strange if not ludicrous things people say are meant to be kind, but it seems that the harder they try to pretend they're thinking past my blindness, the more they prove that they can think of nothing else. If there is a theme to this book, this is it. Blindness is only part of who I am, not the definition of my life.

Afterword

Legacies from the Women in My Life

I can't help it that I am tenacious, creative, stubborn, and goal–oriented. I come from a long line of strong and independent women. I had no choice. This chapter is dedicated to educating my grandchildren about where they came from and why I wrote this book.

My family has been dominated by our women for as long as I can remember, because they knew what had to be done and they did it. I loved the men in my life, and they were strong and dependable, but it was the women who made the decisions. They exercised their right to think on their own and believed in their own abilities. In the final chapter of this book, I intend to tell you some stories that illustrate why I am who I am today.

Grandma
Eva May Emmons Hagen
1893–1976

My memories of my grandma start with the first Thanksgiving I can remember.

She lived alone in a little cabin in southern Indiana, with no running water or electricity. In those days, she didn't even have a phone. A wood–burning potbelly stove in the middle of the house heated the dining area and the living room. The kitchen kept warm from the cook stove and the half dozen women who crowded in there to help make the meal.

The men made whiskey drinks and told lies to each other while the women sweated in the kitchen. Of course the men were called on to carry in more wood, keep the fire burning, set up extra tables, and carve the turkey.

Meanwhile, as a little girl of about three, I spied a bowl of chocolate drops in the center of the table. These were dime-store candies with a white center and covered with milk chocolate. I was allowed to take two, but then I told my mother I needed to go to the bathroom. No doubt she was dreading introducing me to the unpleasantness of an outhouse, or the "privy" as it was known then. Of course it was smelly and scary, but the worst part of all was that I accidentally dropped my candy down the hole, which was very upsetting for a three-year-old. My mother assured me that I could get more from the bowl on the table.

Through the years of my childhood, I came to love that little clapboard house and the grandma who came with it, but never the outhouse. My cousins Carolyn and Johnny, who were close to my age, and I spent summers there, as our parents all worked outside the home and accepted Grandma's generous offer to keep us during summer vacations.

Grandma was a round and sturdy little woman, almost as wide as she was tall. The crown of a thick black braid she wore wrapped around her head gave her a formidable persona, but her heart and soul were as soft as the voluminous breasts that were wonderful for taking a nap on. She didn't have much of a lap, but I was welcome to curl up there any time I wanted, with my thumb in my mouth and my head resting on the soft pillows of her bosom. She never told me she was too busy to hold me, but now as an adult I know that there were chores to do all day.

I'd often finger the safety pins she always had stuck to the front of her dress. Now, as an adult, I sometimes have a safety pin attached to a pocket because I found it on the floor and needed someplace to put it until I could put it away. When that happens, I always think of my grandma with her supply of safety pins at the ready.

Grandma rarely had time to sit down until the late afternoon or evening. She kept a garden, canned fruits and vegetables, cooked three meals a day for us kids when we spent the summers there, kept her little house neat as a pin, visited people who were old and sick, went to church regularly, and helped shape our futures.

We had no swimming pool, no ballet lessons, no youth groups, no soccer games, no television, and no neighborhood kids to play with, but our imaginations flourished with made–up games and entertainment in the yard around Grandma's house in the country. We made delicious pretend pies and cakes from the natural sand pile under the poplar tree in the back. From one of its branches, my dad had fashioned a tire swing, which brought us many hours of fun. A cherry tree in the back yard might have produced fruit for real pies, but what I liked best was to climb it and share private conversations with Carolyn.

The best tree of all was the huge oak that stood in the side yard. My great–grandfather, that is, Grandma's father, had built a rope swing on its lowest branch. A double length of rope was looped around the branch and held a wooden slat at the bottom for a seat. Like most kids, we weren't satisfied with just a swing, so we turned it into a boat. We found a rickety old ladder and placed one end over one loop and the other end over the second loop, which had been pulled out away from the first loop, thus forming a platform that we covered with many pillows and blankets to make a comfortable sailing ship. We spent hours out there, either reading or taking naps. It broke my heart when one summer many years later, lightning struck that tree and shattered our childhoods.

Bath times during those summers were held on Saturday nights on the back porch. Grandma would heat water on the stove and pour it into the largest roasting pan she had. Then either Carolyn or I would go first or second with the same water, followed by poor little Johnny, who always had to be last, since boys were naturally dirtier and had boy germs.

We all wondered how Grandma ever took a bath, but we concluded that she waited for a good rainstorm and took a shower on the back porch at night. She had no neighbors, so it was sufficiently private out there, anyway.

The back porch was used as an extension of the kitchen, especially in canning season. Usually, Grandma planned her canning day for when my parents came to visit, so she would have help with this monumental project. Peaches, green beans, tomatoes, and cabbage all had to be washed and sliced and otherwise prepared before being packed into the glass canning jars for their baths in boiling water.

Another big cooking project was much more entertaining. When Grandma decided to make fried chicken for dinner, she'd catch a hen, plant her foot on its head, and swing that hatchet right down on its neck. We always worried a little that she'd miss and chop off her own foot, but we needn't have worried. Grandma had been doing this for years. Then the wonderment began as the chicken flopped around the yard headless, even though it had died swiftly and efficiently. As kids, we thought it was funny to watch but a little hard to eat when it was served for dinner that afternoon. I always respected my grandmother for being so strong and brave, knowing that if we were going to have fried chicken, this was what needed to be done.

Each morning late in the summer, as I lay in the featherbed with Carolyn, I could hear Grandma trudge by the open window on her way to the garden. Most mornings, I'd just snuggle deeper into the featherbed, but sometimes I'd slip out and follow her down the path to the garden to help. Thanks to her, I learned how to dig potatoes, pick tomatoes, and harvest peas and green beans.

I suspect that many people even my age don't know what pole beans are, much less why they're called that. These beans like to climb up a pole. The poles were positioned in the ground to form a structure much like a teepee.

When we helped in the garden, our reward was to pick a big juicy tomato and eat it right off the vine. We'd bring out a salt shaker, sit on the step of the front porch, and eat our tomato like an apple, with the juice running down our arms. One year, a little volunteer tomato plant started right by the porch, probably from some seeds that had slipped down my arm.

On most of those early summer mornings, Grandma would return while we kids were still in bed, light the stove, and mix up a pan of biscuits. We'd be called to a breakfast of fresh, hot biscuits, dripping with butter made with a churn, and crisp, hot bacon.

Oh, those were the days. No whole-grain cereal and yogurt, just good old country comfort food.

We kids had chores to do in addition to being spoiled by a loving grandma, but the chores were always made fun by our enjoyment of being together. Because we didn't have a well for drinking water, Carolyn and I had to walk down the hill to the neighbors' pump and fill a bucket. Together, we carried it back up the hill to Grandma's kitchen. Grandma's floors were all linoleum, and at least once during the summer, she'd take advantage of having some young and energetic helpers. She'd apply the wax, and then we'd rub it, first in circles, with our soft cloths. Next, we'd tie those rags to our feet and skate and slide around the room to make it look shiny and clean. Grandma would go out and sit on the porch and let us polish the floors to our hearts' content.

It was our duty to feed the chickens. That was sometimes fun and sometimes a little scary. We'd take a pie pan full of chicken feed out to the chicken coop and fling the contents over the fence. I remember hurrying with this job, because I thought that if I took too long, the rooster would flog me, but I'm thankful I never had that experience.

Another chore we were expected to help with was doing the laundry.

Each of us, even little Johnny, carried dirty clothes, soap, and clothespins down through the woods behind the house to a spring, where Grandma built a fire under a big iron kettle. When the water from the spring was hot, she'd throw in the soap and the clothes and scrub the daylights out of them on a washboard. Then we kids would rinse them in the cold spring water in another tub, wring them out by hand, carry them back up to the yard, and hang them on the line to dry.

The next day was ironing day, but we kids were not allowed to touch the irons. There were two in use, one heating on the stove while the other was run over the clothes. When the one being used cooled off, it was switched with the one on the stove.

Then Carolyn and I would hang up our little dresses and shirts from every available curtain rod or bookshelf. I loved the smell of the freshly ironed cotton, and when I was old enough to use an electric iron, my mother and I would spend Sunday afternoons together, sharing that job. While one would iron a piece or two, the other would sit nearby, drinking ginger ale and eating chips and dip. It was a pleasant way to get the job done while sharing stories, dreams, and plans for the future. I believe my love of ironing stemmed from watching my grandmother wield those heavy irons with ease and precision.

Grandma was known by people in the area as Doc Hagen. She only had an eighth-grade education, but she had taught school in a one-room schoolhouse, and later, she tended people who were sick.

One summer, she enlisted the help of us kids. Well, we really didn't help much, but it was an experience I will always keep in my box of most important memories.

Grandma had been called to bathe and put a clean nightgown on an ancient woman who was bedridden. It was a very long and hot walk on the gravel roads to that old lady's house. Keep in mind that in addition to no running water, there was no car. We walked for what seemed like hours, and when we reached the house out in the middle of nowhere, we were a little bit wary, but Grandma urged us on. The old woman was slumped in her bed, hair long and stringy, voice weak and quavery.

Grandma greeted her like a long–lost friend and set to work. She helped the woman to a chair and then changed the sheets. She washed the woman's hair, somehow without getting her into a tub, and then she washed her body.

As Carolyn and I sat stock still on the other side of the room on straight cane chairs, the old woman said we were welcome to have a drink from the bucket. It was well water and smelled of the earth it had come from, and the dipper was rusty. We said thanks but declined a drink despite our thirst. We were fascinated with how Grandma went about making that old woman feel better and more comfortable, and I believe that was when Carolyn decided to be a nurse.

In the evenings, after the dishes were done and we kids had wound down for the day, we'd sit on the front porch with Grandma for some peaceful and quiet times. That's when Grandma would undo the pins in her long, thick, shiny hair and let the braid fall over her back.

We'd count stars, or Grandma would tell us stories, but the best times were when we sang hymns together. Grandma would start with something like "Swing Low, Sweet Chariot" with the melody, and then when Carolyn and I would join in, Grandma would switch to the harmony. Then sometimes we'd sing the harmony, following Grandma's lead. We learned so many of those old hymns, and I often find myself humming those tunes, all these years later. My church doesn't use these really old–timey hymns, but they will be with me forever.

Now I must admit to you that Carolyn and I were not exactly angels. During the day, when we were out there on the swing, sometimes we'd change the words to more secular lyrics, lyrics that Grandma would never have approved of. Or maybe she would have giggled right along with us. My grandma had a twinkle in her eye that revealed her sense of humor as well as her good-natured love.

You probably can't imagine this about me—a city girl who can't stand heat and bugs, dirt and sweat, who depends on many electronic devices to get through the day, who would never enjoy watching a headless chicken flop around or go barefoot in the yard, climb a tree, or use a smelly old outhouse—but you just never know what's in someone's past. You can never know how that past can influence a person's life in later years.

You may have noticed that I never mentioned a grandpa. That's because he took off when my mother was a little girl, so I never met him. I did hear stories, though, of what a drunkard he was and a no-good husband or father, so it's just as well. Grandma did it all. She didn't need a man to get in her way of rearing her two daughters.

In fact, Grandma's own mother died when she was just eleven, and she took care of three younger siblings all by herself. Someone had to do it, and that someone had to be my grandmother.

Who knows what happened to her father? I know he came back to Grandma's to live out his last few years, because I have a picture of him in my memory. He's sitting in a rocking chair, dressed in bib overalls, chewing and spitting out tobacco under a tree, whittling and rocking most of the day.

I'm sure there were strong women before her, but in my lifetime, my grandma was the beginning of the line of women I respected and admired.

Cousin
Carolyn Kline O'Brien Stretcher Belew
1942–2010

If you were lucky enough to have a girl cousin who was like a sister to you, then you might bring this story up to your face, breathe in its meaningfulness, and make it your own. If you didn't have a sister, you will understand its importance to me.

Our relationship as nearly sisters began with our summers spent at Grandma's along with Carolyn's little brother, Johnny. I could fill a book with our adventures during those summer vacations, but for the purposes of this chapter, I'll only share one or two.

When the mail carrier stopped at our mailbox out by the road, we'd all run out to see if there was anything for us. Because Carolyn and I were older and therefore could run faster, Johnny was always last, which of course wasn't fair. So we decided to take turns going to the mailbox. Only we always told Johnny that it was his turn "yesterday," and he was young enough to believe us.

Each summer, our penultimate activity was to write and produce a play, to be performed on the front porch for my parents when they came to take us home. Carolyn and I were always the stars, but we made Johnny the king, which meant he sat on a throne—that is, a chair on top of a card table, with a bedspread wrapped around him like a royal robe. His role was to look kingly and not say a word.

You might think that Carolyn and I were mean to her little brother, and the truth is that we were. We weren't always, but when we were, we were unmercifully mean to him.

One afternoon, Grandma was at a neighbor's down the road

when she heard terrified screams coming from the direction of her house. She was sure one of us had fallen down the neighbors' well or had jumped off the roof of the shed and broken a leg. She ran all the way up the gravel road in her old-lady lace-up shoes, only to reach her front yard and see that all three kids were fine.

Carolyn, being the oldest, explained to Grandma with great indignation that Johnny had been bugging us, being a pest, so he deserved to be sprayed with insect repellent, which is why she chased him around and around the yard with a can of Raid, threatening to spray him. She could have easily caught him, but hearing him scream in terror was much more fun.

Carolyn and I shared a featherbed in the front bedroom, and after giggling and sharing secret aspirations, we'd settle down to sleep and dream the innocent dreams of children.

As Carolyn grew into her teenage years, while I was still in my pre-teen years, our age difference seemed to grow. Soon, she was married, divorced, married again, and then divorced again. She worked hard at being a single mom and struggled with alcoholism.

Eventually, she pulled herself out of that dark stage of her life, graduated from nursing school, and finally became the person she was meant to be. She worked in every field of nursing, from taking care of preemies to caring for end-of-life patients through hospice.

Writing this gives me a flashback to those summers with Grandma and how Carolyn loved to comb Grandma's hair and then braid it for her. I think it was as soothing for Carolyn as it was for Grandma.

Meanwhile, I lived my parallel life without the dark drama

of hers. But the next thing we knew, we were both nearing our retirement years and reaching toward each other once again as sisters.

We talked on the phone about once a month and occasionally spent a weekend together. She lived in Cincinnati, and I lived near Columbus.

One weekend, we were getting dressed to go out for the evening to hear my friend Bob Allen play at a very posh restaurant. We were dashing back and forth to the bathroom in our bras and panties, applying makeup, doing our hair, and selecting just the right jewelry—all the things you do when you're getting dolled up for a special occasion.

Carolyn suddenly stopped me in the hallway by putting her hand on my arm. "What's that dark spot?" she demanded.

"Oh, it probably just a bruise," I said. "I'm always bumping into things."

"That's not a bruise, Mary. You need to go see a dermatologist. I'm serious."

"Okay," I said, in the way that means maybe I will someday.

But Carolyn caught that tone. "I mean it, Mary. You need to call him on Monday morning."

I did call, and they gave me an appointment almost immediately. It seemed that everybody knew the seriousness of the spot except me. So I had the spot removed, like a mole that is too deep to freeze off.

Still, nobody said the M word. But the next day, the nurse called and said I needed to come in on Friday to have more tissue removed.

I told her that Friday wasn't good for me. Carolyn and I were planning a trip to go see my mother in Indiana.

"We need you in here this Friday," the nurse said sternly. "The doctor has rearranged all his patients so he can take care of this."

Now I was getting the idea that maybe Carolyn was right to be concerned. When I got to the doctor's office, they finally told me that the spot was melanoma, a cancer that spreads rapidly. They needed to take more tissue to see if it was spreading.

Since Carolyn had brought me, I asked her to go into the treatment room with me to hold onto my dog. Later, she could fill me in on what I might have missed.

Fortunately, they had caught it in time. It's not an overreaction to say that Carolyn saved my life. As a nurse, she knew what she had seen, but she didn't want to scare me.

Later that night at my mom's, when we were all settling down for bed, she tiptoed into my room and in a whisper asked if I was in pain and if I needed anything.

We had not told my mother. No need to alarm her, and my long sleeves hid the bandage covering the divot in my arm. I was never more proud of my cousin, the nurse.

As Carolyn and I aged, and as we had no significant men in our lives at that time, we decided that we should buy a twin single (or duplex) together: a dwelling that consisted of two separate living spaces that were attached. That way, we could be close enough to share dinners, play a game of Scrabble, watch a movie together, or sit out in the yard together, but we'd also have our own spaces, just in case we wanted to have some privacy for whatever reason. It was going to be the perfect setup for me.

But tragically, Carolyn developed brain cancer, and within a few months, she died.

Even near the end, she called to prepare her younger cousin. "No matter how things turn out," she said, "know that it's all right."

At the time, I thought it was a puzzling thing to say, but given her positive attitude and strong faith in a higher power, I understood that she was ready for whatever lay ahead for her.

At her memorial service, at the cemetery where our grandmother was buried, I was so grateful that Johnny had flown in from the state of Washington. He hated flying, but he knew I would need him. We clung together and wept aloud. I told him then that I needed him to be my brother, since my own brother had died, and now, so had our sister. We were sibling orphans, and we needed each other.

But two years later, cancer claimed Johnny, too. One by one, the people I loved most in the world were being snatched from me. First, it was Dick, my brother, whom I adored, then my Aunt Lynn, who lit the desire to write in me, and then my sister-cousin and her brother, John, who were the only people left in my generation who could share the precious memories of our grandmother.

Grandma and my dad had average lifespans, and my mother lived way beyond that, but they all had lessons to teach me, right up to the end.

Aunt Lynn
Bette Lorinda Hagen O'Brien Poling Dubreuil
1924–1980

My mother had only one sister. Her official name was Bette Lorinda, but I knew her as Aunt Lynn. She was eight years younger than my mother, and they were as different as day and night. My mother was as conservative as my Aunt Lynn was liberal. I loved my mother, but I adored my Aunt Lynn.

Mother was practical, tidy, and structured and lived by the rules. "Never put off until tomorrow what you can do today. A place for everything and everything in its place. Work first before you play." This is not to say that she wasn't loving, or that we never had fun together. But Aunt Lynn was wild in comparison, took risks, laughed uproariously, ate with gusto, and had her own sense of what was important in life.

When she was living in Las Vegas, I spent a summer with her. Just before my return to Cincinnati, Aunt Lynn took me to a fashionable beauty shop so I could come home with a new and sophisticated look. I was now a high school graduate, on my way to college. I needed to look the part. My hair was swept up from the back and over the top of my head and ended in bangs.

My name was Mary Wilson, about as plain a name as you can imagine. When my mother saw me, she said with icy disapproval, "You look like Wilson Mary," meaning that my hair was backward from the way it should be. But Aunt Lynn thought it looked fun and grown up.

My mother's towels always matched, were laundered regularly, and were always hung neatly, folded in thirds. Sheets were washed and put back on the beds on Saturday mornings. Dinner was put on the table as soon as my dad got home from work; it included a meat and two sides. On a saucer were slices of white bread, to be eaten with butter with the meal. The dishes were done immediately after the meal was over.

Mother taught me how to set a table properly and how to write a thank-you note. But Aunt Lynn taught me how to do cartwheels and a backbend, as well as how to walk on a rolling drum. She gave me tap dance lessons in her basement when we visited on Sunday afternoons, and she taught me fun songs like "John Jacob Jingleheimer Schmidt." She couldn't care less if her towels matched or not, and if we wanted a clean one, we'd just get one out of the closet.

My mother thought it was nice that her sister was teaching me to dance, but it was Aunt Lynn who saw my potential and gave me solos in her recitals. When I had learned everything she could teach me, she introduced me to the most prominent dance teacher in Cincinnati. Soon I was studying under Jack Louiso three or four times a week.

My mother was the one who had to drive me to my lessons and recitals, sew my costumes, and be a backstage dresser for me, but I have my Aunt Lynn to thank for lighting that particular spark.

I think it's fair to say that Aunt Lynn took the artistic tendencies in our family and ran with them. Her daughter, my cousin Carolyn, developed into a very good dancer herself, as well as a poet and an artist specializing in drawing.

As a child, Mom had the same artistic blood, starting with building her own first musical instrument by filling empty milk bottles with differing levels of water and then stringing them between two trees. She taught herself how to play tunes by striking each bottle with a stick. From there, she learned to play the piano, taught lessons, studied music in college, and accompanied hundreds of singers and musicians over the years of her youth. But as an adult, her time was spent on supporting herself, her mother, her sister, and her son by her first and very brief marriage.

Later, when she married the man who would become my

dad, she devoted her time to being a top–notch typist, wife, and mother of a visually impaired daughter. Still, whenever there was a need for a pianist for an event, she recalled the words of her mother, my grandmother, who said, "Now, Etta Regina, if anybody ever says, 'Who here can play the piano?' you get on up there and play."

Aunt Lynn did her share of hard work, too. During World War II, she worked in an airplane factory, climbing into the wings of planes to build the parts that fit into small spaces where only a small woman could fit. She held many jobs over the years, even when I knew her, everything from florist to photographer to TV repairwoman. But the job that brought her the most joy and the most success was that of author. She wrote some historical fiction, but mostly, she wrote paperback novels. As she once confessed to me, whenever she needed some extra money, she'd stay up all night and write a book.

One of the traits I loved most about Aunt Lynn was her love of people. Of course some of them became characters in her books, but she had many friends, and everyone in town knew her and loved her. She'd stop at the Post Office to buy stamps, and she'd come out a half hour later, because someone had seen her and wanted to tell her their life story. She listened, nodded in sympathy, and sometimes gave advice. She took people in who were down on their luck and nursed their psyches back to health, or at least until they got back on their feet. She even counseled my husband and me when we were in a rough spot. If someone needed her to stand on her head for a week, she'd do it if she knew it would help.

Mother taught me how to type, but Aunt Lynn taught me how to tell a story. One of our favorite games was "Who can tell the biggest lie?" It was Aunt Lynn who encouraged me to—no, insisted—that I write an article for the "Young Mother's Story" for *Redbook Magazine*. She promised to edit it for me and get it ready to send in. It was published in December of 1974. It was her faith in my ability that gave me the courage to roll up my sleeves, pull out the typewriter, and pound out my story, parts of which I have quoted in Chapter Nine of this book.

I have always wanted to be like my Aunt Lynn, and in some ways, I still strive for that. But I have too much of my mother in me to be just like my aunt. Like my mother, I like to hang my towels in thirds, and I like to have them match. I wash my sheets on Saturdays and go to church on Sundays. Just like my mother, I plan my days and make lists. But like my Aunt Lynn, I try to stop and listen to someone's story when they need to talk, befriend someone who has no friends, find the humor in my mistakes, and explore every artistic possibility that might come my way.

Aunt Lynn loved me as fiercely as she loved her own children, and that love spread even to my children. I am so thankful they were blessed with knowing her for a while. She died way too young, at about age 55, from having had rheumatic fever as a child. I was absolutely devastated. Aside from my children, she was the brightest star in my sky.

Recently, I had a dream that my Aunt Lynn told me about a book, a whole book of first lines for successful stories. Then she told me one, and when I woke up for a second, I thought, *That was a really good line. Now maybe I can write something significant and useful.* In the daylight, the line wasn't that great, but it was nice to see Aunt Lynn for a while. I adored her.

Mother
Etta Regina Hagen Oliver Wilson
1916–2014

And now we come to my mother, the most influential woman in my life. I've already written a book, called *The Bumpy Road to Assisted Living*, which is about the last two years of her life, and I've woven some of her personality traits into the section about my Aunt Lynn.

It's hard to talk about one without the other. Although there was a significant age difference, I have never known two sisters who complemented each other more. As much fun as I had with Aunt Lynn, I'm grateful for the education and lessons in life my mother gave me.

In her role as mother, Regina Wilson led a regimented life as an example to her children and as a model wife of the 1940s, '50s, and on until her widowhood and eventual death. She strove to be the perfect housekeeper and the most attentive parent in the universe. But I only knew her as my mother, a mother who expected excellence if not perfection. She only expected perfection from herself.

I suspect she was a bit of a flirt when she was young. My dad confessed on more than one occasion that he was attracted to this pretty little woman by the way she allowed her hips and her hair to swing as she walked. As a younger woman, before she met my dad, she played in a jazz band and enjoyed parties with young men as well as her girlfriends.

My mother was not an athlete by any means, but my dad was the manager of a bowling alley near the Chevrolet plant where my mother worked, so of course Mom joined the bowling league of "girls" from the office. My dad bought a boat and loved to fish. My mother was not a fan of fishing, nor did she enjoy sitting in a boat all day, but she did it because she loved her husband and thought it was her duty to please him. She hated playing cards, but I remember eternal Saturday nights when Mom and Dad played cards with friends. I went with them to entertain the other child who was dragged along, too, and we kids often went to sleep on the couch. I always thought she loved those card games, but the only thing she really liked was bringing some fabulous refreshment.

In short, she liked to please her husband and impress his friends.

My mother loved belonging to clubs and organizations, and in every one, she served as president or some other officer. I think she liked parliamentary procedure and being in charge. Since she worked full-time and didn't have the opportunity to have coffee with the neighbors, she did not have women friends, so her clubs provided them.

I often went with her to their Christmas parties and picnics, so I know she really did enjoy them and didn't attend them just because it was expected of her. She was happiest, though, when she had a part to play in the planning. One Christmas party featured a line of "the girls in the office" singing and dancing to "The Twelve Days of Christmas." There were rehearsals at our house, led by my mother, and as the evening progressed, so did the silliness. It was one of the few times I saw my mother truly letting go and having fun.

Mother loved me more than life itself, and she was willing to do without a night's sleep to sew a dance costume or type a term paper, to make my favorite foods and to have dinner on the table every night. When she wasn't able to be home for my birthday because of having to stay late to get the year-end statements done, she promised a party at the end of the week, although she had to be exhausted from working late every night, sometimes until 10:00.

One snowy afternoon when my school had been let out early, she was worried that I wouldn't be able to walk home by myself, so she walked all the way home in the freezing snow in her open-toed shoes. I was fine, but she was a professional worrier.

When she had to work on a Saturday, she took me with her, set me up on someone else's typewriter, and let me pretend that I was her assistant. She was always proud to introduce me to her co-workers, although as a little girl, I usually embarrassed her by hiding behind her skirt.

When I had a certain design in mind for the perfect dress to wear to my sixteenth birthday party, she created the pattern and made the dress exactly as I had imagined it. Mother made most of my clothes because of my small size, so I always thought she loved to sew. Never would she give me the impression that sewing was one of her least favorite tasks. I am so grateful to her for doing something that had to be very hard for her.

She allowed me and even encouraged me to be as independent as I wanted. She helped me assemble a wardrobe for college, helped me pack all my records and other essentials for college life, and then helped me move into my dorm at Ohio State, a hundred miles from home. When I think of how hard it must have been to send her visually impaired daughter off to college with a white cane and a little trepidation, I suspect she shed a few tears on the drive home while my dad held his tears back. I applaud their bravery and trust to let me go.

I always wanted to emulate Aunt Lynn, and in some ways, I still do. But the truth is, I am the next generation of my mother. I have a plaque that reads, "Mirror, mirror on the wall, I am my mother after all."

I don't pretend to have lived up to her standards, to have matched her IQ, or to have the strength and tenacity to endure the kind of hardships she had throughout her life, but I do recognize that I am my mother's daughter in many ways.

When my brother, Dick, my mother's son from her first marriage, was killed in a car crash, I was 19. He lived in Sarasota with his wife and her little girl. They were expecting a baby in about a month. I had come to spend the summer with them, but I quickly grew up in one night. When the adults in the room were discussing who was going to call our mother, I immediately spoke up and declared that I should be the one. It was without doubt the hardest thing I have ever had to do. But here again, it was what my mother would have done.

Without thinking about it, I have incorporated the philosophies and the legacies handed down to me from all the women in my life. I hope these legacies will be carried on through the branches of our family tree.

Legacies

1. Music is the breath of life. It brings joy and feeds my soul.
2. Dancing or any sort of movement, such as skiing, cycling, skating, jogging, or even just taking a walk, will always lift my spirits.
3. Keeping a journal is writing the history of my life. It helps to clarify my thoughts and reminds me of who I am.

4. The love of words and how to use them well makes me a better thinker as well as a better writer.

5. Planning ahead, making lists, and prioritizing my activities help me make the most of every day and the rest of my life.

6. Sometimes I just have to do something I don't enjoy, but it's best to do it first, so I have the freedom of knowing it's behind me.

7. If I want to join a group and it doesn't exist, I start one.

Advice to Myself and to You

1. Be spontaneous so you can be fun, but make a plan to get things done.

2. There is no need to prove you are right in a petty argument.

3. Care about everything you do.

4. Take risks. If you don't try it, you'll never know what you missed.

5. Take time to be kind.

And

You can do this. You can do it all.

Mary with Grandma Hagen

Grandma Hagen's house

Mary's cousin Carolyn, aunt Lynn, and mother

Mary's mother, Regina Wilson, at the piano in the 1940s

Mary as a little girl, with her mother and her doll

Acknowledgements

Many people have influenced my life, so to try to name them all would do a disservice to those I might not mention. But here are those who have etched their names in my memory and in the creation of this memoir.

Thanks to my late Aunt Lynn for awakening in me my love of writing and for fostering in me my love of dance.

Thanks to my daughter, Kara, for her meticulous proofreading of the next-to-last draft of this memoir. She prompted many changes, which made it a better book.

Thanks to my friend of 60 years, Lynda Satterfield Bragg, for proofreading the first drafts of every chapter.

My thanks also go to David and Leonore Dvorkin of DLD Books Editing and Self-Publishing Services for their meticulous editing, artful formatting, and cover design.

Thanks to my many friends and colleagues in The American Council of the Blind for shaping my ability to deal with blindness.

Thanks to Jack Louiso and to Mark Miller for strengthening my passion for the art of dance.

Thanks to The Singing Moms, later known as The Entertainers, for enhancing my joy of singing and performing.

Thanks to Toastmasters International for providing another platform for performing.

Thanks to Ski for Light for giving me the confidence to try something completely out of my comfort zone.

Thanks to my cycling friends who coached me and captained for me until I was able to ride with the "big boys."

Thanks to all the women who have hiked with me on the Hen Hikes. We are now a family.

Thanks to all the workers and members of the Gahanna YMCA who have shown me kindness and friendship.

Thanks to the pastors and members of Stonybrook United Methodist Church for their offers of help and for my faith in Christian fellowship.

Thanks to the writers' group in The Transition Network for your friendship and encouragement.

Thanks to The Seeing Eye, Inc. for the gifts of love and independence with five incredible Seeing Eye dogs.

Thanks to my former and late husband, Michael Hiland, for our two extraordinary children, Steve and Kara, and for their children, Meghan, McKenzie, Michaela, Brianna, and Bethany— all beautiful, charming, and talented, as my mother liked to say.

Thanks to my late mother for her undying support of every goal I set for myself.

＊ ＊ ＊ ＊ ＊

Note: The Seeing Eye and Seeing Eye are registered trademarks of The Seeing Eye, Inc.

About the Author

Mary Hiland, a native of Cincinnati, lives in Gahanna, Ohio, with her Seeing Eye® dog, Dora. She is a graduate of The Ohio State University with a B.S. degree in Social Work. She recently retired as Executive Director of The American Council of the Blind of Ohio. Before that, she served for over 21 years as Director of Volunteers for VOICEcorps Reading Service: *https://www.voicecorps.org/*

Ms. Hiland has been published in *Chicken Soup for the Parent's Soul, Redbook Magazine, Toastmaster Magazine,* and *The Columbus Dispatch.*

Visit her blog at *https://seeingitmyway.com/*

Ms. Hiland carried the Olympic torch, and in 2015, she received the Lifetime Achievement Award from her local Toastmasters Club.

Ms. Hiland has two adult children and five granddaughters. Her passions are reading, public speaking, cycling, cross-country skiing, swimming, hiking, and taking long walks with Dora. She writes for the pure pleasure of it.

Website and Contact Information

Website: *https://www.dldbooks.com/maryhiland/*
Email: *mary.hiland@wowway.com*

Mary Hiland, 2017

Mary at the Columbus Art Festival

Made in the USA
Monee, IL
08 June 2020